ROBIN DUNBAR

How Religion Evolved

A PELICAN BOOK

PELICAN
an imprint of
PENGUIN BOOKS

PELICAN BOOKS

UK | USA | Canada | Ireland | Australia
India | New Zealand | South Africa

Penguin Books is part of the Penguin Random
House group of companies whose addresses can
be found at global.penguinrandomhouse.com.

First published 2022
001

Text copyright © Robin Dunbar, 2022

The moral right of the author has been asserted

Book design by Matthew Young
Set in 11/16.13pt FreightText Pro
Typeset by Jouve (UK), Milton Keynes
Printed and bound in Great Britain by
Ashford Colour Press

The authorized representative in the EEA is
Penguin Random House Ireland, Morrison
Chambers, 32 Nassau Street, Dublin D02 YH68

A CIP catalogue record for this book is available
from the British Library

ISBN: 978-0-241-43178-8

Contents

List of Figures

Acknowledgments

This book is the result of a longstanding interest in the origins and evolution of religion and its role in community bonding. The opportunity to explore this topic in any detail, however, did not arise until 2015 when funding was obtained from the Templeton Religion Trust for a three-year research project (Religion and the Social Brain). The studies carried out under the auspices of this grant were largely intended to test specific hypotheses about the nature and evolution of religion, and they form the basis of this book. However, the book also builds on nearly two decades of research by my research group on the nature of sociality and the mechanisms of community bonding in primates and humans. Many of the ideas that underpin this story were developed in earlier projects funded by the British Academy (the Lucy to Language project) and the European Research Council (the RELNET project) that also involved a large number of collaborators, postdocs and graduate students, to all of whom I am grateful.

The Templeton project was a collaboration between researchers at the Universities of Oxford, Cambridge, Coventry and Lincoln, and the International Society for Science and Religion. In addition to myself, the members of the project were: Roger Bretherton, Sarah Charles, Miguel Farias,

Alastair Lockhart, Valerie van Mulukom, Ellie Pearce, Michael Reiss, Leon Turner, Beth Warman, Fraser Watts and Joseph Watts. Elise Hammerslag and Cassie Sprules were the project research assistants. Our external collaborators included Simon Dien (University College London) and Rich Sosis (University of Connecticut), and we greatly benefited from the wisdom of Armin Geertz (University of Åarhus), Jim Jones (Rutgers University) and Emma Cohen (University of Oxford) as members of the project's Advisory Board. None of them bear any responsibility for the views in this book, of course, but their individual and collective contributions proved invaluable to the development of the ideas that make up its central story.

Fraser Watts and Leon Turner kindly read the entire first draft of the book, and I am grateful for their comments. Roger Bretherton read Chapter 4, Miguel Farias and Sarah Charles read Chapters 7 and 8, and Alastair Lockhart Chapter 7. The drawings for Figures 7 and 8 are by Arran Dunbar.

Introduction

For as long as history has been with us, religion has been a feature of human life. There is no known culture for whom we have an ethnographic or an archaeological record that does not have some form of religion. Even in the secular societies that have become more common in the past few centuries, there are people who consider themselves religious and aspire to practise the rituals of their religion. These religions vary in form, style and size from small cults numbering a few hundred people centred around a charismatic leader to worldwide organizations numbering tens, or even hundreds, of millions of adherents with representations in every country. Some, like Buddhism, take an individualistic stance (your salvation is entirely in your own hands), some like the older Abrahamic religions[1] view salvation as more of a collective activity through the performance of appropriate rituals, and a few (Judaism is one) have no formal concept of an afterlife. Some like Christianity and Islam believe in a single all-powerful God,[2] others like Hinduism and Shinto have a veritable pantheon of greater and lesser gods; a few do not believe in any kind of god at all, as is, formally at least, the case with Buddhism (notwithstanding the fact that most schools of Buddhism make concessions to the frailty of mere mortals by allowing them to believe in semi-divine bodhisattvas).[3]

While many believe in living a moral life fully engaged with fellow citizens, others believe that salvation can only be achieved by abandoning even the trappings of everyday life, including the wearing of clothes – as is the case with some Hindu and Jain ascetics. In the Christian tradition, the Adamite sect in late Roman Egypt insisted on complete nakedness during their services.[4] Others, like the Russian Skoptsy (literally, 'castrates') sect,[5] took matters even further, advocating breast and genital mutilation in women and the removal of both penis and testes in men (all performed with red-hot irons) so as to restore their bodies to the original pre-Fall condition of Adam and Eve in the Garden of Eden. The variety is bewildering and seemingly incoherent, limited only by the inventiveness of the human imagination. To the outside observer, there seem to be few unifying themes.

Religion is not, of course, a modern phenomenon. Deeper into the past, there are clear hints that our ancestors believed in some form of afterlife. Burials accompanied by grave goods clearly intended for use after death become increasingly common from around 40,000 years ago. By far the most spectacular of these are at Sunghir on the upper reaches of the River Volga just east of Moscow. They date to around 34,000 years ago. A handful of graves lie clustered together near a small hill fort on the riverbank. Two of these were children aged about ten and twelve, buried head to head in a double grave. As with many burials from this period in both Europe and Africa, the burials are extraordinarily rich and elaborate in a way that only makes sense if those who buried them believed that they would continue to live in another world.

Like many burials of the time, the children's bones are heavily stained by red ochre which had been poured over their bodies. The ochre had been laboriously ground from haematite-bearing rocks – a task so arduous that no one would bother unless they thought it might play a seminal role in what happens to the body after death. In addition, they were each covered in around 5,000 pierced mammoth ivory beads, which would have required many thousands of hours of skilled work to shape and bore, never mind stitch on to the clothing in which the children had been buried. Each of the children had a circlet of about forty Arctic fox teeth around their foreheads that may have been part of a headband, as well as ivory arm bands, and a bone pin at the throat where it probably secured a cloak. The older one (thought to be male) has 250 pierced fox teeth forming a belt around his waist. Lying beside them are sixteen carved ivory spears varying in length from eighteen inches to eight foot, a human thigh bone whose shaft had been filled with ochre, several deer antlers whose ends had holes drilled through them, several carved ivory discs, a carved pendant of an animal and a carving of a mammoth. In short, it seems that the children had been so deeply mourned that they were buried in sumptuous clothing accompanied by a rich array of grave goods that had taken thousands of hours to manufacture. It was a level of generosity that seems absurd for a people with few possessions – unless they believed that these things would be used by the children in their afterlife.

Although it is very hard to imagine that such a burial

could reflect anything other than a belief in an afterlife, the evidence is, of course, indirect. And it doesn't tell us anything about the community's religious practices. Did they believe in gods, or even an all-encompassing God ruling over a spirit world as well as the Earth? Did they hold services with priests who intoned prayers and genuflected before altars? We can only speculate as to what their religious rituals were like, since behaviour doesn't fossilize.

These ancient burials raise some deep questions about how we recognize religions when we find them. One problem is that our view of religions is heavily influenced by the half dozen or so doctrinal, or revealed, religions that have come to dominate the world in the last few thousand years – Buddhism, Christianity, Islam, Hinduism, etc. These are characterized by sophisticated theological doctrines with beliefs about the afterlife, complex rituals that involve prayer and, sometimes, sacrifice, and ceremonials defined by very specific cultural traditions. These religions are latecomers onto the world stage. Even though they are now numerically dominant, they date back only a few thousand years at most. Of all the modern world religions, Zoroastrianism (the religion of contemporary Parsis) is considered to be the oldest, having been founded by the Persian prophet Zoroaster, or Zarathustra, some time in the first (possibly second) millennium BC. It is also the most influential, having, one way or another, influenced many of the others. The problem with these religions is that they are far from representative of the wide range of religions that our species has practised, and in some cases still practice.

The definition of religion is probably the single most

fiercely debated topic in the study of religion. Indeed, some scholars have even gone so far as to argue that the very concept of a religion is the product of the particular mindset that has characterized Western Europe since the Enlightenment. The Enlightenment, they argue, was dominated by a Christian dualist view that separates body and soul and draws a clear distinction between the earthly location where we humans live and the spiritual realm where God resides.[6] In many small-scale ethnographic (or tribal) societies, the spiritual world is a part of our world, not a separate world: spirits are embedded in every aspect of the environment. They share our world and are as corporeally real as we are, notwithstanding their ability to pass through walls or influence what happens to us. We can study a particular culture's beliefs or ritual practices, so the argument goes, but that's as far as we can go: we cannot really say how one culture's religion relates to another culture's because each culture views the world differently. We are reduced to being cultural tourists, who can observe and comment and, maybe, admire, but never get beyond the production of casual travelogues.

This seems to me an unnecessarily pessimistic view. It thwarts the very possibility of exploring the phenomenon even before we start. And it's a view that, ultimately, leads inexorably to unproductive solipsism.[7] Science, in contrast, enjoins us to take the world at face value. If we make mistakes of interpretation along the way, they will be corrected eventually by the acquisition of further knowledge – knowledge that can only be acquired by observation and the testing of our theories and beliefs against empirical facts. In short, it is one thing to say that many scholars have approached the subject from the perspective of their own Abrahamic religions and so overlooked much of the richness of human religious experience, and quite another to say it is impossible even to begin to discuss the nature of religious experience.

In fact, like many real-world phenomena, religion is just a rather blurry thing. Philosophers refer to definitions of this rather vague kind as being 'severally and jointly true'. In other words, some parts of the definition apply in all cases, but not necessarily the same parts in each case. It's a good model to follow, because it avoids us getting trapped into long, turgid arguments about the minutiae of definitional detail. It's as well to remember that we are trying to understand a real-world phenomenon, not a definition (something that exists only in our minds). So let's take a generously broad view of what constitutes religion, and see how far it gets us.

It's probably fair to say that there are two general views as to how religion has been defined. One, derived from Émile Durkheim, the great nineteenth-century founding father of sociology, asserts that a religion is a unified system of practices accepted by a moral community – a group of people who share a set of beliefs about the world. This takes an anthropological view and emphasizes the important practical role that rituals and other practices play in most religions: religion as something that people *do*. The other view takes a more philosophical or psychological approach: religion is a comprehensive worldview, a set of beliefs, that is accepted by a community as being true without need of evidence – religion as something that a group of people *believe*.

Although these seem like polar opposites, a more pragmatic view is to assume that both approaches are right and that beliefs and rituals represent separate dimensions of religion. An individual religion can be high on both dimensions, high on one but low on the other, or low on the both. It is not a matter of one definition being right and the other wrong: it is simply that the two definitions focus on different aspects of a multidimensional phenomenon.

In some respects, these two definitions reflect a distinction drawn by historians of religion between what were formerly referred to as 'animist' religions (the earliest, universal forms of religion whose origins disappear into the mists of deep time) and the doctrinal or world religions that emerged during the last few thousand years. In effect, it's the distinction between ritual and belief – between action and thought. William James, the great nineteenth-century American psychologist, referred to these as 'personal religion' and 'institutional religion'. What does unite both views, however, is the fact that most, if not all, religions have some conception of an unseen life force that influences the world we live in, and does so in a way that can affect our lives.

In the light of this, a minimalist definition of religion might be belief in some kind of transcendental world (that may or may not coincide with our observable physical world) inhabited by spirit beings or forces (that may or may not take an interest in and influence the physical world in which we live). That definition is wide enough to include all the world religions, including those like Buddhism that don't formally believe in gods. It suits equally well for pseudo-religions like New Age movements that believe in some mysterious power that lies at the unseen centre of the universe that influence our lives. If it includes a few obscure movements that we might decide later aren't actually religions, well that doesn't matter too much at this point. We'll figure that out once we've got to grips with the real thing.

Whatever else it may be, religion is a puzzle. And this raises two fundamental questions that are the focus of this book.

First, there is the issue of its seeming universality. There are very, very few cultures that do not have some recognizable form of religion, some sense of the transcendent. We live in an increasingly secular world, yet belief in religion persists. And it persists despite many attempts to suppress it. The French positivist philosophers of the nineteenth century (under the guidance of the polymath Pierre-Simon Laplace and the philosopher August Comte) argued that religion was largely superstition and the result of lack of education; so they advocated universal education, especially in the sciences, in the expectation that religion would eventually disappear. A more drastic attempt was made to suppress religion and replace it with state atheism in post-revolutionary Russia. Church property was confiscated, believers harassed and religion ridiculed. Later, in Communist China, religion was outlawed, the possession of religious texts criminalized, mosques and historic Buddhist monasteries bulldozed, religious minorities harassed or forced into 're-education' centres, and their clergy imprisoned. Yet, despite these determined onslaughts, religious belief and religious institutions survived, often underground. As soon as the restrictions were lifted, religion bounced back. Why are people so predisposed to be religious?

The second puzzle about religion concerns the fact that there are so many of them when we might expect there to be just one. This tendency for religions to fragment over time is especially evident in the rise of contemporary new religious movements, but all the established world religions have faced, and continue to face, the same process of fragmentation. Sometimes, the sects they spawn develop their own momentum and become established religions in their own right: Christianity and Islam as the offspring of Judaism are the two obvious examples, but Sikhism (a fifteenth-century development from the constellation of religions in north India) and the Bahá'í Faith (a nineteenth-century development out of Shia Islam) are two others. It is an odd fact that no one ever asks why religions should fragment so readily in this way; they merely observe that they do, and take this for granted. But if the true religion has been revealed to us, as many of the world religions believe, why do people keep disagreeing about just what has been revealed – disagreeing so fundamentally that the disagreements eventually give rise distinct religions?

These are the two principal questions I shall try to answer in this book. Although they may seem to be very different questions – one about beliefs, the other about history – I shall argue that they turn out, on closer inspection, to be closely related. They both relate to the role, or function, that religion served in prehistoric societies, and in many ways still serves in contemporary populations. So let me briefly outline the way I will approach these two big questions. For convenience, sources for particular studies or claims are given in the notes and Further Reading; in addition, Further Reading includes some general sources outwith the references that relate to specific issues.

The first chapter provides a more historical perspective on religion, both in terms of the broad historical development of religions and the approaches that have been used to study religion. The next two chapters will establish what I consider the essential groundwork: why humans seem predisposed to religious belief and why, in very practical terms, such belief might actually be beneficial. I will take a somewhat unorthodox stance on both of these. First, I will make a case for what I call the 'mystical stance' – that aspect of human psychology that predisposes us to believe in a transcendent world. My claim is that herein lies the origins of religion as we know it. Second, in contrast to most evolutionarily-minded commentators, I will argue that religious belief does have beneficial fitness consequences for the individual. My claim, however, is that although religion can, and does, give rise to direct health benefits to the individual, the really substantive benefit lies at the societal level in terms of the ability to bond communities so that they function more effectively for the benefit of their individual members.

This will lead us into a more detailed examination in Chapter 4 of the nature of human communities and the fact that these are in reality very small scale. There is a natural limit to the sizes of the social groups that we can maintain, and these limits have implications for the size of religious congregations and communities. Chapter 5 provides the psychological explanation for this, and introduces the neurobiological mechanisms that underpin social bonding. Chapter 6 will explore how these neuropsychological mechanisms underpin the role that religious rituals play in the processes of community bonding.

With this providing a framework within which to understand a religious predisposition and its function, Chapter 7 brings us back to the more historical question of when a religious predisposition evolved in our evolutionary history. Given what we have discovered about the neuropsychology of the mystical stance, I suggest that we can now be a great deal more precise about this than has hitherto been possible. While these essentially shamanic religions were around for many hundreds of thousands of years, Chapter 8 argues that the arrival of the Neolithic some 10,000 years ago created a series of demographic shocks that led to the development of the doctrinal religions. I shall argue that these forms of religion were essential for people to be able to live together in large, spatially concentrated communities. Chapter 9 explores the more general phenomenon of cults and sects, and the role that charismatic leaders have played in the history of religion and the origin of sects. Finally, Chapter 10 brings us back to the question of why there are so many religions. The answer, I shall argue, lies in what we have learned in the earlier chapters about the role of religion in the processes of social bonding and the nature of charismatic leaders.

The approach I adopt here will be very different from traditional approaches to the topic of religion in a number of important ways. The traditional approaches have typically adopted either a theological focus (what does a particular religion believe?) or a historical focus (how did a particular religion arise? which early religions influenced its views?), but more recently there has been an increasing interest in the cognitive science and the neuropsychology of religious behaviour. I will dip into these areas from time to time, but they will not be my major focus. I am conscious that I shall be ignoring whole fields that some might regard as central to any discussion of religion. My intention, as much as anything, is to explore issues that have largely been overlooked in the study of religion. I want to suggest that some of these dimensions might provide the basis for an overarching theory for why and how humans are religious, and so help to unify the myriad strands that currently populate this field.

How to Study Religion

Before we embark on a more detailed exploration of religion, it would be helpful to set the scene in two important respects. One is to summarize what we know of the history of religions, even if only briefly. This will allow us to see what it is we need to explain in terms of the grand sweep of how the religions we have came to be. The second is to summarize, again fairly briefly, the main approaches to the study of religion, and what they have to offer us. This is especially important because the perspective I shall be taking is very different from those adopted by most scholars of religion. My approach is an evolutionary one, and so will be firmly grounded in our current understanding of evolutionary theory. For this reason, I will end by providing a very short summary of what an evolutionary approach entails.

A Very Short History of Religion

There has been a longstanding view, dating back to the end of the nineteenth century, that the history of religion comprises two major phases: an early animist phase and a later doctrinal phase. The term 'animism' was coined in the mid-nineteenth century, but its use to describe the early phase of religion was really due to the British anthropologist Edward Tylor in his

1871 book *Primitive Culture*. The term derived from the recognition that many of the tribal peoples who had been encountered during the European explorations of the eighteenth and nineteenth centuries believed that other living organisms as well as springs, rivers, mountains and forests were all imbued with spirits (*anima* in Ancient Greek and Latin).

This conception of 'primitive religion' was much criticized in the twentieth century by anthropologists, many of whom came to see such labels as imperialist and racist. In fact, this criticism was a bit of a red herring for two reasons. First, what this claim confused was a distinction between folk psychology and the way university-educated scholars think. Folk psychology is the way people naturally think about the world, partly as a result of their everyday experience of the world (some of which is, of course, culturally inherited from their forebears) and partly because of the way the human mind is designed. Second, we are all susceptible to these kinds of 'primitive' beliefs because many of them seem to form the natural default in the way the human mind, or 'folk psychology', has evolved. This is not a matter of 'primitive' versus 'advanced'. Rather, it reflects the overlaying of education on an underlying platform of natural folk psychology.

In reality, the distinction is not between people who live in the West and those who live elsewhere, but rather simply between those who have been exposed to a heavy-duty science-based education and those who have not. Ironically, the nineteenth-century scholars may have been rather better informed about their subject matter than their later critics: they knew perfectly well from their own ethnographic research that these kinds of 'animist' views were not only prevalent in historical Europe among the Celts and Germanic tribes, but continued to be widely believed among their own contemporary countryfolk well into the twentieth century. Indeed, many seem to be still with us. Wishing wells are one familiar example of this.

In the northern European tradition, sacred springs and wells have a long history dating back to Celtic and Germanic tribal times. Some springs or wells were thought to have healing powers; others had the property of being able to fulfil any wish made at them. The habit of throwing coins or treasured objects into wells or pools (and making a wish while doing so) is still with us, even if – sometimes but not always – our belief in the efficacy of this practice is tempered with a degree of scepticism. Wishing trees are another example: the habit of attaching votive offerings or messages to the trunk or branches of a special tree were widespread throughout the British Isles and other parts of northern Europe. In India, the banyan tree (a member of the fig family) that sits at the centre of almost every village is also known as the *kalpavriksha* (wish-fulfilling tree). These kinds of phenomena attest to a belief in an occult world that is deeply engrained in all our psyches.

Another example of a country rite, common well into the twentieth century, is the old English country tradition of 'wassailling' whereby a Wassail Queen (usually a young prepubertal girl) was lifted up into the branches of apple trees to leave an alcoholic drink for the tree spirits so as to ensure a good harvest. Jennifer Westwood and Sophia Kingshill's *The Lore of Scotland* provides a lengthy summary of these kinds of country beliefs for just one small corner of the British Isles, most of it collected by enthusiastic folklorists during the nineteenth century. The belief that spirits or fairy folk occupy particular sites – hill tops, caves, springs, rivers, trees – is as near universal in northern Europe as it is possible for anything to be, and it has never entirely gone away – modern education notwithstanding.

In reality, the belief that the world we see is peopled by spirits has continued to exist happily alongside the more conventional religious practices and beliefs associated with later doctrinal religions. Many of these beliefs centre around the belief that spirits, and those who have access to the spirit world or have esoteric knowledge of such access (witches, sorcerers, witch doctors, shamans), are able to influence our world for both good and evil. The anthropologist John Dulin observed, during his field work in southern Ghana in the 2010s, that

> a traditionalist priest consulted his god on my behalf, [and] the god instructed me to avoid food offered by strangers lest I be poisoned, or suffer the dangers of magic that would force me to do things against my will, like give money away. When an elderly traditionalist priestess invited me to eat at her home, my charismatic Christian friends urged me to refuse her food for fear that I might fall in love with her. My mind would become so clouded, they told me, I would not recognize my wife. The prospect that I might eat the wrong thing, then forget my wife, and fall in love with an 80-year-old woman only has a hint of plausibility if you see your mind as potentially not your own, if you see it as vulnerable to hostile invasion by an outside force.[1]

Similar tales could be told from almost anywhere in the world. They are reminiscent of fears about the 'evil eye' (the ability that some people supposedly have to make you fall ill just by catching your eye) that were prevalent throughout much of Mediterranean Europe well into the twentieth century.

From our perspective, such beliefs might count as superstitions, but they are based on deeply held beliefs that influenced, and still surreptitiously influence, people's actions. A well-known one that has persisted into the twenty-first century is that of throwing a pinch of spilt salt over your shoulder (to ward off the Devil). Salt superstitions appear in many guises. One rather unusual one is the 'sin-eater', a custom that was common in Wales and the Welsh Border counties as late as the early 1900s.[2] After a death, the body would be laid out in the front room and a plate of salt with some bread placed on its lap. The belief was that the corpse's sins would be absorbed into the bread with the salt. Just before the corpse was removed for the funeral, the local sin-eater would come and eat the bread, thereby absorbing the dead person's sins so that they could go to Judgement with a 'clean' soul. The plate would then be buried with the corpse.[3] Sin-eaters were usually old, destitute men and women attracted to the role by the fact that they usually received beer and a fee in addition to the bread. They were often ostracized by the rest of the community because of a perceived association with witchcraft and the Devil. Similar practices occurred in other parts of Europe. Sometimes these practices lost their original purpose, but not their form and continued into the twentieth century as funeral rituals. In Bavaria, for example, a 'corpse cake' was traditionally placed on the breast of the dead and later eaten by the nearest relative. The Dutch traditionally prepared *doed-koecks* ('dead cakes') that were given to those attending the funeral. In the Balkans, a small bread image of the deceased was eaten by the assembled family.

The truth is that we may not fully believe in these superstitions, but at the same time we are not quite willing to let go of them completely – just in case they really are true. Witness the number of people that continue to consult their horoscopes. This tendency to continue to believe in folk myths occurs in many other areas of life. Despite the fact that physicists have developed complex mathematical descriptions of the universe, most of us actually operate with a much simpler version of 'folk physics' – the physics of everyday experience by which you and I live our lives, much of it derived from millennia-old folk beliefs and our own personal experience of the everyday world. Physics tells us that an object like a door really consists of a lot of empty space occupied by the occasional atom, but our everyday experience when we bump into one tells us that doors are very solid. The world of science and the world of everyday experience do not always connect especially well.[4]

The conventional view, then, was that the earliest forms of religion took the form of a rather generalized belief in spirits or a form of being that sometimes occupied a transcendental world parallel to the physical one in which we live, but also might occupy the same physical space as we do. In some cases, these spirits had no particular interest in our world; in other cases, they were responsible for causing—or curing— the illnesses that we fall prey to. These beliefs are often (but, of course, not always) associated with witchcraft, which in turn might be generalized into charms for luck, hunting, fertility or romance.

These older religions are religions of immersive experience, rather than religions of formal ritual with specialists who intercede on behalf of the laity. They are often (but not always) associated with trance states, usually induced by music and dance. In this, they share many underlying features with the mysticism that we find in all the doctrinal religions. By general consensus, mysticism involves direct ecstatic experience of the divine. It is a very personal form of 'religion of experience', a sense of immersion in the ineffable, the 'oneness of being' as the medieval Christian mystics described it. In its modern forms, these features tend to reflect the particular beliefs of the religion to which the mystic belongs. Mystics from the Christian, Sufi Islam and Sikh traditions will experience this as immersion in the oneness of God, whereas Buddhists experience it as immersion in the luminous universal mind (the *tathāgatagarbha*, or 'womb of the Buddha'). Sometimes these trance states (often described as 'visions') are spontaneous (as seems to have been the case with many historical Christian mystics like St Teresa of Ávila or the German Dominican friar Meister Eckhart); in other cases, trance may be brought on by group rituals, usually involving music (as in the trance dances of the San Bushmen) and sometimes assisted by plant-based psychotropic (or mind-altering) drugs (many South American tribes), or individually by meditative practices (as in the yogic tradition).

In some animistic religions, this phenomenon is associated with shamans as specialists who have the ability to enter into trance. The term shaman derives from eastern Mongolian cultures, where it is associated with individuals who serve a long apprenticeship to acquire the necessary knowledge and skills to intervene on our behalf with the spirits that influence our world. In traditional Mongolian and Siberian cultures, their major function was a combination of divination, curing diseases, and ensuring the success of hunts and the avoidance of disaster. In healing ceremonies, the shaman acts as an intermediary between the patient and the spirit(s) that cause the disease. We might think of this definition as 'shamanism *sensu stricto*' (meaning in the strict, or narrow, sense). However, a looser sense of the term refers to a more general phenomenon whereby individuals enter trance to engage in travels in the spirit world, with no particular medical or divination purpose; this often requires no special training, and may be part of group rituals that are learned by observation and practice. This form is widespread, and we might think of it as 'shamanism *sensu lato*' (meaning in the broad sense). Because the use of trance in one form or another is so widespread in these animist forms of religions, I refer to them collectively as 'shamanic religions', or 'immersive religions'.

At some point, there was a transition to a more formal kind of religion marked by regular places of worship, gods (who sometimes actively intervene in human affairs), religious specialists or priests (who intervene between the community and the gods, in some cases via trance-based rituals), more formal theologies, and moral codes that have divine origins – Moses receiving the tablets with the Ten Commandments directly from God on Mount Sinai, the Prophet Muhammed receiving the dictation of the Koran from God, John Smith receiving the golden plates of the Book of Mormon. Most of these doctrinal religions also have origin stories, often associated with the revelatory experiences of a specific individual as founder – Zoroaster in the case of the Zoroastrians of ancient Persia; Siddhārtha Gautama for the Buddhists; Jesus Christ for Christians; the Prophet Muhammed for Islam; Guru Narnak for Sikhism. Because these religions typically have quite explicit theological doctrines, they are often known as doctrinal religions. They are also known as world religions because most of them now have very large followings spread over most of the planet (notwithstanding the fact that this is actually a very recent phenomenon).

Most doctrinal religions are organized in a formal way, with priesthoods or committees (for example, a court of elders) responsible for overseeing the activities of the mosque or parish. In some cases, they have a hierarchical structure beyond the local level that is responsible for maintaining theological integrity or at least providing a pathway of theological justification descending from some authority figure (the bishops and archbishops of the Catholic, Lutheran and Anglican branches of Christianity). Sometimes these involve only informal allegiances (as in the case of Islam and Buddhism).

This partition into shamanic (or 'primitive') and doctrinal religions is not, of course, hard and fast. There are many tribal religions and even some contemporary cults that do not fit entirely comfortably into either slot. That, however, is what we might expect of any evolutionary process: evolutionary transitions are rarely absolute, even in the biological world. The problem is that humans are not especially good at handling complexity, so we often divide phenomena into simple dichotomies for our convenience even when they are not strictly binary – short versus tall, black versus white, East versus West. However, simple dichotomies have the advantage of simplifying the phenomenon we want to explain, and so help to sharpen the contrast between, what in this case at least, is the beginning and the end of a long historical process.

The important point to emphasize is that this sequence is not necessarily a process of replacement of one kind of religion by another. It is, rather, one of accretion – one form of religion (a doctrinal phase) being bolted onto the earlier (shamanic or animist) form. Evidence for this is present in many of the great feasts that form so central a part of modern Christianity. The word Easter as used in the Roman (as opposed to Greek Orthodox) tradition, for example, derives from the Old English *Eostre*, the month dedicated to the Germanic goddess of that name – herself an ancient Indo-European goddess of dawn who, given the spring date associated with her, may well have been a fertility goddess. The date chosen for Christmas (25 December) conveniently coincided with the date of the winter solstice and the rather drunken Roman festivities of Saturnalia that celebrated the god Saturn at this point in the year.[5] It seems that the early Christian Church adopted a number of existing pagan festivals for their major celebrations, perhaps to distract their new converts from their previous religious adherences. The point is – and this is something I shall come back to later – new forms of religion don't usually sweep away older forms, but rather are grafted onto them precisely because the older forms are so deeply engrained into people's psyche that they are difficult to erase.

In other words, beneath the surface veneer of doctrinal rectitude lurks an ancient foundation of pagan mystical religion. This is the core message of this book, and in the following chapters I shall argue that appreciating this has important consequences for our understanding of religions and their evolution.

Some Approaches to the Study of Religion

At least for the first century of its existence as a discipline, anthropology had an enduring interest in religion, especially its social functions. Indeed, it might even be said that religion was its single most important focus after kinship. This, as we saw earlier, had its origins during the nineteenth century in a growing interest in both European folklore and the ethnography of traditional small-scale societies. Seminal among the early influences were James Frazer's *The Golden Bough: A Study in Comparative Religion* (1890) and Edward Tylor's 1871 book on *Primitive Culture*. Frazer's approach was to try to piece together the common principles and concepts of primitive religion from a study of (mainly European) folklore and traditional beliefs. Tylor's approach was based on comparative ethnography from tribal societies round the world, and explicitly sought to apply the new ideas of Darwin's theory of evolution to culture. He saw the human mind as universal (all humans have the same mind and mental abilities) and that religion had evolved historically in small-scale traditional societies as an attempt to explain and control the world within the context of local beliefs – beliefs adapted in a Darwinian sense to local conditions and experience.

Two later formative influences were William James's 1902

book *The Varieties of Religious Experience* and Émile Durkheim's *Elementary Forms of Religious Life* (1912). Neither had ever studied tribal societies. James took a firmly psychological stance, whereas Durkheim's perspective was sociological. James drew an important distinction between the origin and value of religion, reminding us that the answer to either of these questions does not necessarily determine the answer to the other. (We'll see how crucial this point is in the next section.) He drew an important distinction between 'healthy-minded' and 'sick soul' religion – the one characteristic of those whose religion provides them with contentment and happiness, the other characteristic of those who are deeply troubled and experience religion in the form of what we would now call 'crisis conversion'. He viewed mysticism as being central to religious experience. At the heart of Durkheim's view was what he termed 'collective effervescence', the sense of emotional excitement and awe created by religious rituals. Although Durkheim saw religion as the basis on which society was constructed, later anthropologists reversed his causal logic to argue that the rituals and beliefs of traditional religions merely replicated or reinforced a society's social and political structures—in effect, the marriage of Church and state for political ends. Up to a point this is true, but it misses the central insight of Durkheim's view.

Later still, developments in the 1980s associated with the rise of cognitive anthropology (an attempt to understand the psychology underlying the way humans think about their world) gave rise to what has since become known as the cognitive science of religion, some (but not all) of whose advocates are strongly grounded in evolutionary psychology.[6] By and large, this has been dominated by the view that there are no fitness benefits to religion. This view stems from the assumption that religion is a society-level phenomenon that often obliges individuals to sacrifice their personal interests. Since group-level benefits are viewed with suspicion by evolutionary biologists (more on this in the next section), they argue that religion must be a maladaptive by-product of mechanisms designed for other more explicitly useful purposes. The focus of the cognitive science of religion has thus been on natural psychological mechanisms and the way these have accidently predisposed humans to behave in religious ways.

An example of this approach is the concept of the HADD (the 'hyperactive agency detection device'), a concept associated in different ways with the anthropologist Pascal Boyer and the psychologist Justin Barrett. Essentially, this proposes that the animal mind is furnished with sensitivities to cues that allow it to detect salient phenomena that have direct effects on biological fitness (the ability to survive and reproduce successfully). For example, being able to infer that there is a predator approaching when hearing the snap of a twig in the forest is beneficial if you want to avoid falling prey to a predator or an enemy. Such mechanisms, they argue, are likely to be risk-averse because it is always better to mistakenly assume that there is a predator approaching than to mistakenly ignore the significance of such a cue when there really is a predator approaching (an example of Pascal's Wager).[7] As a result, we humans are predisposed to attribute any phenomenon that we cannot readily explain to some mysterious being that we cannot see. There is no question that this effect is widely prevalent in humans: it is redolent in the way we attribute motivations to physical phenomena. We speak of the sea being angry or the sky lowering. On this view, then, religion is an inbuilt error in the biological system.

Another classic example of this approach is the suggestion that gods are typically 'minimally counterintuitive', meaning that they have to be able to break the normal laws of everyday physics – but not by too much, otherwise they just become implausible. In essence, gods have to be able to do something that the rest of us cannot do – walk on water, pass through walls, levitate, fly through the air, foretell the future, cure the sick. If they cannot do such things, it means they are merely human and there would be no point seeking their help in preventing disasters or changing the future. And, of course, that would mean, equally, that they cannot harm us – an important issue given that many spirits seem to be genuinely malevolent.

In general, evolutionary cognitive science of religion has adopted one of two views to explain how and why religion evolved. One is that religion is an unavoidable, and hence evolutionarily largely uninteresting, consequence of the way the human mind happens (or had) to be designed to support other evolutionarily more important functions. Religion is simply the cost that had to be paid in order to maximize evolutionary fitness. Alternatively, it might be an example of cultural evolution exploiting the way the human mind is designed so as to maximize *cultural* fitness despite the negative effect this might have on the fitness of the individuals whose minds are being parasitized. Both are, as we shall see in the next section, perfectly plausible explanations from a conventional Darwinian point of view.

Cognitive science of religion provides convincing explanations as to how human cognition underpins many aspects of religiosity and how these might have been exploited for these purposes. However, its focus is mainly on beliefs and so it overlooks some important features of human religious experience that in many ways constitute the core fabric of religion – in particular, ritual and the role that religion plays in creating communities. In part, this is because it is based on a rather narrow understanding of what constitutes biological fitness. I'll explain why this is so in the next section.

However, this does highlight an important issue. It has been suggested that rituals may be explicitly designed to inculcate a mental state that is conducive to a particular religious experience by transforming how we experience the world.[8] Taking such a view is desirable because it steers us away from seeing religion as 'just' a set of beliefs (the view that has come to dominate the study of religion in the past half century) and refocuses attention on the older view of religion as a set of practices. This is an important point, and one I shall return to in later chapters.

Unpacking the Evolutionary Background

Before we proceed to explore religion and its evolution in more detail, I need to summarize very briefly what is involved in an evolutionary approach.[9] One reason for doing this is to dispel some old *bêtes noires* that will otherwise get in the way of a proper understanding of what follows. Many of these arise from misunderstandings as to exactly what a Darwinian approach entails.

Darwin's theory of evolution by natural selection is widely

regarded as the second most successful theory in the history of science (after quantum theory in physics) in terms of its ability both to explain the natural world as we find it and to predict novel, unexpected features of that world. Its fundamental premise is that, because of the way biological (that is, genetic) inheritance works, species evolve toward those forms that are most successful at solving the problem of surviving and reproducing (a property known as *fitness*), with the trait or character that evolves under selection being said to be adapted to, or an adaptation for, solving that particular problem. A peacock's fancy tail is an adaptation for attracting mates; long legs are an adaptation for running fast.

It is important to appreciate that, technically, fitness is a property of a trait or gene (or sometimes, in a loose but perfectly acceptable sense, an individual). It is not a property of a group or a species, and hence evolution cannot, and does not, occur for the benefit of the group (or species). Group selection, as the latter is known, requires the differential survival of whole groups and was often viewed as the explanation for altruism or population regulation: some animals don't breed in order to ensure that the population or species does not exhaust its food supply and go extinct. The problem is that there is no known genetic mechanism that would allow this: any species that behaved in this way would quickly find its altruism undermined by individuals that reproduced selfishly as fast as they could. This is not to say that group selection cannot work. It can, but it requires very high rates of group extinction and very low rates of migration between groups, and so far no study has found rates of group (or even culture) extinction that are anything like high enough to allow it to work. For this reason, biologists look with deep suspicion on any suggestion that benefits might accrue solely for the benefit of the group and against the interests of the individual.

Maladaptive traits are perfectly possible, and common, under Darwinian evolution, providing the costs they incur for the individual do not exceed the overall fitness that the individual gains from all its other traits. This is a natural consequence of the fact that an individual has to solve many conflicting demands in order to contribute genes to the next generation. These include such things as eating enough to fuel the demands of survival, avoiding becoming someone else's dinner, finding an appropriate mate, siring or gestating offspring, and, once you've managed all this successfully, ensuring that these offspring make it through to adulthood so that they reproduce in their turn. You can produce as many children as you like, but if that overtaxes your ability to rear them such that none survive, then, from an evolutionary point of view, you might just as well not have bothered. Evolution, as the evolutionary biologist John Maynard Smith once quipped, is not interested in children; it is only interested in grandchildren. The problem is that most of the steps in this sequence are mutually incompatible: they cannot all be solved to perfection at the same time. So individuals have to find suitable compromises in how they satisfy these various components, severally and jointly, and that usually involves trading one off against another. In other words, most organisms are less than perfectly adapted in a Darwinian world because the real world is full of unavoidable compromises.

The fact that religion can incur serious costs in terms of self-imposed pain, celibacy and even self-sacrifice has led some evolutionary psychologists and cognitive science of religion scholars to conclude that religion and religiosity cannot be adaptive, but must instead be the maladaptive by-product of traits or cognitive processes that evolved for other perfectly respectable biological purposes. Such cases are far from rare in everyday biology. The example we might all be most familiar with is lower back pain – the unfortunate, but unintended, by-product of our ancestors' decision to switch from walking on all fours to a bipedal stance, which had the effect of creating an unstable joint in the lumbar spine. It might well have been possible to find a solution to that problem by evolving a larger, more solid spine, but that would have meant sacrificing spinal flexibility – such that running and spear-throwing would have been impossible. The end result is a trade-off that works fine most of the time, but now and again breaks down. This is because natural selection, the motor of evolution, is not far-sighted: it deals with the problems of the here-and-now and cannot anticipate the future.

For social species like monkeys and apes, however, there is a sense in which benefits can accrue at the level of the group. When individuals gain greater benefits by cooperating with each other than they could if they acted alone, those benefits accrue at group level. Group-living is an example of this. Animals do not live in groups because they like each other. They live in groups for the specific purpose of solving one or more of the components of fitness. Some species live in groups to forage more efficiently (as lions and hyaenas do), some to rear offspring more effectively (as many monogamous birds and mammals do), while others live in groups to reduce the risk of predation (as is the case for most primates and herd-forming antelope and deer). In all these cases, the benefit arises only because the group exists, but its impact on fitness always accrues at the level of the individual, or even the gene. If the group does not provide a benefit for the individual, individuals will not put up with the inevitable costs of living in a group. Evolutionary biologists refer to this process as group-*level* (or group augmentation) selection, or more simply as mutualism.

This is essentially the same process as that involved in symbioses, where two species live in close harmony with each other, thereby enhancing each other's survival chances. Lichens, for example, are actually not a single plant but an algae living in such intimate association with a fungus that it is impossible to distinguish between them simply by looking at them. In fact, even we are composites in just this sense. The vast majority of our genes are actually viruses and other single-celled organisms that, over the course of evolutionary time, have inserted themselves into our genome, where they make use of our procreative abilities to piggyback their way through evolution. Some of these, such as the mitochondria that now provide every living cell with the energy it needs, are so crucial to life that multicellular life would be impossible without them. In a word, cooperation allows *individuals* to succeed (that is, have higher fitness), not groups to succeed against the interests of the individual.

Another important point to appreciate is that the function of a trait and its mode of inheritance are two separate, unrelated things. Any mechanism that allows a trait to be passed on from one individual to another, whether or not they are biologically related and share any genes, acts in a Darwinian fashion. Learning or cultural transmission is such a mechanism, and hence can be analysed using the same mathematics as is used to explore the evolution of genetically inherited traits. Culture is a Darwinian process, and cultural traits (or even entire cultures) evolve under selection, much as individuals and species do. Culture, however, can evolve both in ways that influence an individual's biological fitness and in ways that influence the fitness of a given cultural element[10] within a purely cultural world. In theory, there is nothing evolutionarily implausible about a cultural phenomenon driving the genes of the bodies (or minds) that they parasitize to extinction – providing they can jump from one mind to the next (by cultural transmission) faster than they cause each body they inhabit to die. After all, this is all that viruses do. Of course, in the long run, it doesn't really pay a cultural element, any more than a virus, to drive its host to extinction. In most cases, they will come to some evolutionary compromise with their hosts.[11] This is why viruses always lose their virulence after a while. If they didn't, they would soon go extinct because they would be left with no hosts left to parasitize.

One last, but very important point. Darwinian biological evolution is not a linear process in which all species proceed through the same stages on their way to some final state of perfection. Linear theories of evolution do exist, and certainly imply successive steps towards some higher end-state. But these are not Darwinian theories, and most have long since been discredited. The most famous such theory was formulated by the great French zoologist Jean Baptiste de Lamarck in the early nineteenth century. It was based on the concept of the Great Chain of Being that has its origins in the biology of the philosopher Aristotle, gifted to us via the sieve of the medieval Christian theologian-philosophers who adapted it to their own theological ends by adding God and his angels as the final stages of the chain. In this view, all species start as microscopic forms of life and are constantly being created spontaneously, even this very minute. They all pass through the same series of stages from simple to more advanced, until eventually they become humans and in due course, at least in the medieval Christian version, angels – before, presumably, finally being united in the Godhead.[12]

This sequence is completely fixed and inevitable. Each of the species we see today is caught momentarily at a different stage along this universal trajectory, depending only on how long ago it was created. Humans differ from simple organisms only in that their complexity implies that they were created long ago and so have had more time to work their way up the Great Chain. Eventually, all species will reach the same pinnacle of evolution. In 1857, Darwin's radical theory completely overturned Lamarck's theory. In a Darwinian world, there is a single origin for all of life,[13] and not multiple origins; and there is no inevitability about the direction or speed of evolution, since this is entirely contingent on the challenges that animals happen to encounter and the serendipitous ways they find to circumvent these challenges. Rather than being linear, evolution is a branching process in which species are progressively modified as they adapt to unique new circumstances.

I won't go into any more detail here. Suffice it to say that religion is as much subject to the processes of Darwinian evolution as any other biological or cultural phenomenon. The bottom line is that a Darwinian approach is not restricted to phenomena that involve genetic modes of transmission. So long as there is some mechanism that ensures that ancestors and descendants (or teacher and pupil) resemble each other on the trait of interest, it doesn't matter from a Darwinian point of view whether the mechanism of inheritance is genetic (as in conventional biological evolution) or learning (as in both simple learning and cultural evolution). The rules of the Darwinian evolutionary process apply in all these cases.

There is, perhaps, one last point I should make. I have, in fact, already alluded to it several times in the preceding paragraphs, but I really need to spell it out before we move on. Biologists commonly differentiate between four different kinds of questions that we can ask. These are known as Tinbergen's Four Why's in reference to the fact that the ethologist Niko Tinbergen spelled them out in a seminal paper in 1963. Though they were originally formulated as four different 'Why' questions (just as a child keeps asking '. . . but why?'), they are perhaps better thought of as questions about *why*, *what*, *how*, and *when*: what is the function or purpose of a trait (the 'why' question), what mechanism allows it to produce that effect, how does the trait develop in the organism during the process of ontogeny (the process whereby the fertilized egg develops eventually into an adult – a combination of inherited genes, learning and the environment it develops in), and when in its history did a species acquire the trait?

The important point that Tinbergen emphasized is that these questions, and the answers they produce, are logically and biologically independent of each other. We can answer each one without having to worry about, or even prejudice the answer to, the others. Of course, eventually, we want to be able to tick all four boxes. But in the meantime, we can deal with the questions piecemeal. We can examine the function (*why*) of a trait without having to worry about its mode of transmission (*how*). We just need to know that there is *some* mechanism of inheritance that is reasonably reliable. It is this separation of function that allows us to discuss the evolution of biological traits and the evolution of cultural phenomena in the same breath without self-contradiction.

I won't have much to say about the third Why (*how* does religion develop in children, or to put it another way: to what extent is religiosity hardwired in our genes versus learned during childhood). This topic has been studied in some detail by others.[14] Instead, my main focus will be on the *why, what* and *when* questions: the functions that religion has served (and to a large extent still serves) for us, the psychological and neurobiological mechanisms that make this possible, and the timing of the origins of religion.

CHAPTER 2

The Mystical Stance

Mysticism has been a major component of all the major religions. By mysticism, I mean a feeling of divine transcendence that comes over an individual from time to time, sometimes spontaneously, sometimes as a result of deliberately engaging in ritualized activities. It is variously referred to as ecstasy or enthusiasm (from the Ancient Greek word *enthousiasmós*, meaning 'possessed by god'). In its most developed forms, it usually involves a sense of drifting into a different plane of consciousness, of becoming so detached from the world of everyday experience as to no longer notice the sights and sounds of the physical world, a sense of losing track of time, of peacefulness – sometimes described in the mystical literature as the 'stillness of the mind'. It is not something everyone feels to the same extent, of course. In that respect, it is a bit like falling in love. Falling in love is also a human universal, and almost every culture has something like it. But within cultures, not everybody experiences it in equal measure. Some of us fall in love at the drop of a hat; others are more reserved and need some persuasion – or perhaps don't experience it at all. The same seems to be true of trance.

Although the mystical stance, as I shall call it, focuses on the capacity to enter trance states, in practice in a religious context it involves three distinct features. These are a susceptibility to enter trance-like states, a belief in the existence of a transcendental (or spirit) world, and a belief that we can call on hidden power(s) to help us. The mystical stance is the belief that that we can experience this hidden essence directly only through our minds.

The three elements that make up the mystical stance are not necessarily closely related, and belief in them is not always in equal measure. Exactly how they are experienced depends to some extent on the culture within which the individual is embedded. Nonetheless, the mystical stance is broadly true of all religions and is of very ancient origin. It is part of what it is to be human. In the best traditions of evolutionary psychology, the capacity to enter trance may well be an exaptation,[1] a by-product of the way the human mind is designed. In this chapter, I want to sketch out what is involved in the mystical stance and why it is so important to our story.

Into the Mystic's Mind

Pretty much every religion either has a mystical component of this kind or has a branch or sect that is explicitly mystical in nature. Hinduism and Jainism share the yogic tradition with its concept of *samadhi* (literally 'the stilling of the mind'); Buddhism obviously bases much of its practice on formal meditation; Sikhism has a mystical tradition based around the practice of *simran* (literally 'remembrance (of God through the recitation of his name)'); Judaism has the Merkabah and Kabbalah traditions; Islam has the Sufi tradition; Christianity has a long mix of individual mystics and mystical sects.

The Christian mystical tradition was established right

from the outset. As the New Testament Acts of the Apostles relates it, the Holy Ghost descended as tongues of fire on the disciples gathered to celebrate the Jewish Pentecost shortly after the Crucifixion, as a result of which they began 'speaking in tongues'. Glossolalia, as it is technically known, is a phenomenon often associated with mystical experiences, then and ever since. The real impetus, however, came just a century after the death of Jesus when Montanus, a recent convert in what is now western Turkey (where he may have been a priest of Apollo) experienced a seizure and became convinced that the Holy Ghost spoke through him. With his two female companions Prisca and Maximilla, he promulgated an ecstatic form of Christian mysticism known at the time as the 'New Prophecy'. Ecstasy, he believed, gave humans direct access to God. During ecstasy, he famously said, we become the lyre that God strums. In the three centuries that followed, Montanism developed a popular momentum and prospered throughout Asia Minor and North Africa. A string of mystical writings emerged over the following centuries, culminating during the late fifth century AD in the writings of Pseudo-Dionysius the Areopagite,[2] whose ideas were promoted widely throughout the eastern Mediterranean and had an important influence on the later medieval Christian mystics.

Many of these Christian mystical movements were gnostic in character. Directly or indirectly, they were associated with a series of Gnostic 'gospels', most of which were written in the first century after Christ. These include the apocryphal Gospels of St Thomas, St Philip, Mary Magdalene, St John and St James and the respective Apochrypha of St John and St James, most of which only came to light when the Nag

Hammadi cache of papyri was discovered in Upper Eygpt in 1945. The word 'gnostic' derives from the Ancient Greek meaning 'knowledge', by which was meant secret knowledge of the meaning of life or of God himself – knowledge that was gained directly through ritual practices that induced trance states of one kind or another.[3]

These early mystical movements spawned a long tradition of mysticism within the Catholic Church in particular. Among the many who became household names were Meister Eckhart, the ever-iconic St Francis of Assisi, the eleventh-century Hildegard of Bingen (she of 'I am but a feather on the breath of God' fame, as well as the composer of much beautiful sacred music), the fifteenth-century Englishwoman Marjery Kemp, the Dutch friar Blessed[4] Jan van Ruusbroec (sometimes known as the Ecstatic Doctor), and, perhaps the greatest of all of them, the sixteenth-century Spanish noblewoman, Carmelite nun, reformer, theologian and Doctor of the Church[5] St Teresa of Ávila. The tradition continued in the late nineteenth century with St Gemma Galgani and St Thérèse of Lisieux and, into the twentieth century, with the Capuchin friar Padre Pio (canonized in 2002). All of them were famous for becoming lost in trance as they contemplated God or Jesus Christ or the Virgin Mary; all had miracles attributed to them, and many of them were said to levitate while entranced, in some cases even to appear in two places at once. They attracted large, often adoring, followings even in their lifetimes, and were frequently sought out for advice, healing and spiritual direction. Some, like Meister Eckhart and Teresa of Ávila, became hugely influential both theologically and spiritually; others are now remembered only by the cognoscenti. Many, like Padre Pio, exhibited stigmata – open wounds on the hands, feet and (less often) side that were interpreted as the wounds of Christ's Crucifixion, and widely viewed as a sign that the person had been touched or blessed by Christ, hence confirming their status as a very special person.[6]

Despite its pretensions to being a more rigorous, muscular form of Christianity free of the superstitions and laxity of the old Roman Church, the Protestant tradition in Christianity has not escaped a mystical dimension. The Pentecostal churches are the obvious examples, with swooning and speaking in tongues still forming a regular part of some of their services. Many of the more familiar, established Protestant churches, including the Methodists, Baptists and Quakers, had their origins in the ecstatic sects that abounded in seventeenth- and eighteenth-century Europe. Other sects from the same period, including the English Ranters, the Brethren of the Free Spirit, the Mulhausen *Chriesterung* (or 'Bloodfriends') and the Munster Anabaptists, initially had considerable local popularity but disappeared within a generation or two of their first appearance. Most of this latter group made the mistake of allowing their enthusiasm to spill over into promiscuous free love, which, added to their often rather exotic theologies, did not endear them to the local religious or secular authorities. Those sects that survived invariably did so because eventually someone was able to impose discipline and suppress their more irregular beliefs and practices. John Wesley, the founder of the Methodists, for example, expressed considerable anxiety in his diaries about the activities of some of his chapel congregations, and fretted a great deal over how to control their more excessive exuberances.

While on the extreme end of the continuum, the Munster Anabaptists offer a classic example of the type, in terms of both the fanatical zeal with which they pursued their millenarian objectives and the vigorous response of the mainstream religious authorities. The Anabaptists achieved a particular infamy when, in 1534, they took over the city of Munster and declared a millenarian kingdom, enforcing re-baptism on the citizens and imposing draconian religious discipline. After their leader had been killed, his successor, the Dutchman Jan Bockelson (also known as John of Leiden), declared himself to be the successor to King David. He adopted the title King of the New Jerusalem, and lived in regal style – even while the citizens of the town starved during the siege by the evicted Prince Bishop of Munster's very secular forces. Among the more unusual edicts he promulgated was one forbidding any woman from rejecting a proposal of marriage, which had the inevitable (perhaps intended) consequence of encouraging the men to collect wives as fast as they could. Jan is said to have availed himself of sixteen (one of whom he later had publicly beheaded for refusing to obey him). When the rebellion was eventually suppressed, Bockelson and the ringleaders were executed and their bodies hung in cages from the tower of a local church.[7]

Islam has its own mystical tradition in the form of the Sufis, whose name derives from the white wool garment (*suf*) worn as the sign of an ascetic in early Islam. Islam's expansion eastwards into Persia and beyond into India during the Mughal period resulted in Sufism becoming especially associated with Shia Islam. There it gave rise to a remarkable form of religious singing known as *qawwali* that is designed to lift both performers and audience into a state of ecstatic religious consciousness. In Turkey, the Sufi tradition is associated with the so-called 'whirling dervishes' of the Mevlevi order who use a twirling dance (*semazen*) while engaging in *dhikr* (remembering Allah through the recitation of Islamic prayers) to lift the dancer into a state of trance. In classical Persia, Sufis were associated with an extraordinary upwelling of romantic and semi-religious poetry that included household names like Omar Khayyam and Jalāl ad-Dīn Muḥammad Balkhī (better known in the West as the poet Rumi).

The idea that there is a transcendental sphere that we can access directly through our minds is neither confined to the major world religions nor simply a reflection of an uneducated past. There has been a long tradition in the West of interest in eastern beliefs and religious practices, especially those claiming to offer occult insights. Spiritualism and Theosophy are among the foremost examples from the late nineteenth century. The hippy movement of the 1960s was heavily influenced by eastern religions, with many people joining Indian communes and ashrams in a search for meaning and enlightenment. Most of these movements were based on the claim that there is some form of hidden knowledge known only to a small group of adepts. Theosophy referred to these as the 'Masters', a mysterious coterie of individuals who were said to have achieved a level of moral and intellectual development that conferred on them supernatural powers including clairvoyance, the ability to travel outside the body, and extra-long lifespans.

The mystical stance seems to emerge out of two separate, but related psychological components. One is a need to believe in a spiritual dimension to human life. This may well derive from a deep-seated reluctance to believe that death really is death, the end of life and being. The other has to do with altered states of consciousness, both those induced by trance and those that arise from accidents of experience (such as epileptic fits) or the use of mind-altering drugs.

While perhaps not universal, belief in some kind of life force or spirit that lives on beyond physical death is extremely widespread. Since this life force obviously doesn't exist in the physical world – we cannot touch it or interact directly with it – it must exist somewhere and that somewhere can only be in some kind of parallel spirit world. One reason why this belief might have come about is the grieving process: humans develop such deep personal attachments to close family and friends that the death of these individuals inevitably causes intense grief. Believing that the dead live on somewhere gives comfort and hope that one day we will meet up with them again. How else might we explain the fact that so many people hold conversations with their dead relatives? Or the fact that, on the Day of the Dead (31 October, or All Hallows' Eve), members of the Pomuch community in Mexico visit their local cemetery, lovingly remove the bones of grandparents and great-grandparents from their niches, carefully clean them, dress them in new clothes and replace them until next year. As the Pomuch observe, 'This is how we stay in touch with our ancestors.' Rather similar practices exist in some parts of Italy.

The capacity to enter into trance states also seems to be extremely widespread scross human cultures. One survey of 488 ethnographic societies drawn from all continents concluded that no less than 90 per cent incorporated altered states of consciousness into their belief systems.[8] Trance takes you into a mental world that seems very real, but at the same time is obviously not the same as the physical world in which you clearly still exist. Here, seemingly, is unassailable evidence that there is another world that we can occasionally have access to. This is a conundrum that requires explanation – especially if, when in that trance world, we meet both the kinds of people we know and love who are no longer with us (our ancestors) and the kinds of beings we fear in the everyday world (ogres and malign spirits).

The Experience of Trance

Trance is a recurring motif in most of the phenomena that we would count as religious. By trance, I mean the voluntary or involuntary ability to enter into an abnormal psychological state wherein the practitioner, though fully awake, is unresponsive to external stimuli and does not engage with the conventional physical world. It is a state of mind that bears a close similarity to reverie and to the distracted state of mind of someone who is deeply infatuated with a romantic partner. Their normal senses seem to be switched off, or at least heavily attenuated.[9] In trance, this can sometimes be associated with violent limb and body movements, but need not be; some trance states (notably those produced by yogic mediation practices) can be extremely calming (the 'stillness of the mind').

The experience of trance also bears a close similarity to those that occur during near-death experiences. Indeed, near-death experiences often lead to 'born again' religious conversions. An analysis of over two hundred cases of near-death experience found that these were often associated with a suite of psychological states of mind, including a sense of invulnerability, a feeling of special importance or destiny, a belief in having received a special favour from God or fate, and a strengthened belief in a continued existence after death.[10] Raymond Prince referred to this as the 'omnipotence maneuver'.[11] We feel empowered to take on the world, undaunted by the worst it can throw at us. Invariably, this is accompanied by a desperate need to persuade others of this extraordinary new knowledge we have acquired.

In some cases, the form of trance and the methods used to achieve it are very sophisticated (as in the yogic and Buddhist traditions); in many shamanic forms, on the other hand, it involves brute force methods that use privations, vigorous movement (dance) or even psychoactive drugs to trigger a trance state; in yet other cases, it might be completely spontaneous (as was often the case for many of the better-known medieval Catholic mystics). The variety is so great that it is too easy to get lost in the detail. Rather than falling into that trap, we need to step back and see the broad picture. This was the approach adopted by the celebrated Romanian historian of religion Mircea Eliade in his seminal overview of the ethnographic evidence on trance.[12]

In many ways, the archetypal form of trance is the kind found among hunter-gatherers like the San peoples of Botswana and Namibia. San use dance to trigger trance. Conventionally, it is the men who dance and the women who provide the musical accompaniment by clapping and singing. In most cases, the men dance in a circle until exhaustion sets in, triggering trance. The use of music to trigger trance is widespread, being a common feature of shamanic practices in Siberia and eastern Asia as well as among African hunter-gatherers and Native Americans. Without necessarily involving an explicit trance element (other than for healing rituals by medicine men or women), music and dance have been, and still very much are, a central feature of many of the social and religious rituals of tribal cultures in West Africa.

Music and dance are not, of course, the only way to achieve trance-like states. In South Asia a long history of experimentation with ritual practices associated with meditation has yielded a variety of alternative techniques for inducing trance. Most of these place great emphasis on breathing control, the adoption of sometimes physically stressful postures (such as the well-known lotus position) and an ability to focus the attention inside the mind so as to cut out intrusive auditory and visual distractions. Most of these require discipline and practice, but once achieved are extremely effective at inducing trance. Another common feature of trance induction is some form of privation. Fasting is common before taking part in shamanic ceremonies, as is exposure to intense heat or cold. Fasting, pain and overheating were associated with the sweat lodges of the Native American tribes of the Great Plains and Midwest.

Why, and how, trance should be induced by these behaviours will be considered in more detail in Chapter 5. Here I simply want to explore trance as experienced by the adept. In most ethnographic societies, the moment of going into trance commonly involves a sense of entering a hole or tunnel, sometimes associated with a sacred tree (identified in many traditions as the 'cosmic tree').[13] Entering into trance is often associated with a burst of intense bright light. The San observe that entering trance (a process they refer to as *!kia*) feels like an explosion in which the dancer is physically thrown up into the air. Others describe it as a feeling of 'bursting open, like a ripe pod', of the emotions being intensified. It often involves feelings of intense heat, during which your *n/um* (or psychic energy) 'boils', a process that is often experienced, even by trance masters, as painful and frightening. The San consider that a long training under the tutelage of an experienced master is needed to cope with the psychological and physical pressures involved – a view endorsed by many of the cultures that have shamans.

Once in the spirit world, the traveller is usually free to roam at will. However, the spirit world is peopled with ogres and therianthropes (animal-headed humans) or ancestors whom the adept has offended in some way in the past, all of whom may be intent on waylaying the adept's spirit and preventing it getting back to its own world. The way back out to the real world is through the same tunnel, and failing to find the entrance is one of the greatest fears of trance dancers. Failure to find the exit is tantamount to a death warrant because the soul, or spirit, is separated from the physical body left behind inert in the real world; if the two cannot rejoin, the physical body will die. There may well be some reality behind this belief: trance dance is exhausting, and it may be that from time to time a dancer does collapse and die. To the onlooker, it seems that they have gone into the spirit world and not found the way back. This makes it all the more important to have a friendly spirit-guide who can ensure that your spirit returns to the exit again after its travels in the other world. In most cases, these benign spirit-guides are good ancestors, who no doubt have a vested evolutionary interest in ensuring that their relative gets back to the real world where they can continue with the business of producing descendants for them.

In all cultures, adepts emerge from trance with a sense of calmness, a sense that the cares of the world have fallen away from their shoulders. This is not simply the effect of exhaustion from the physical exertion required to bring on a trance state. The San describe the experience (known as //hxabe) as exhilarating and intensely pleasurable. It is said 'to make the heart sweet', a feeling that can last for a whole day. Those who practise yogic-style meditation-induced trance describe the same feeling of calmness and contentment.

To what extent the actual *experience* of trance is universal has been much debated. Some contemporary authorities on trance think it probably is, and argue that the *interpretation* of the experiences one has during trance are culture-specific even though the experiences themselves are universal because they are based on the same underlying neural processes. Others, however, have argued that different ways of eliciting trance give rise to different experiences. The differences are surely interesting, but in the grand scheme of things they don't really alter the broad facts of the case. Trance is trance, but you, as an individual, make of it what you will.

Trance features in many modern sects of Christianity. The anthropologist John Dulin describes the possession experiences of Fante charismatics in the Pentecostal churches of coastal Ghana in West Africa. '[Speaking in] tongues, boisterous prayers, and collapsed shaking bodies overcome with the Holy Spirit are standard fare,' he observes. In this, they mirror the descriptions of many eighteenth-century Protestant sects in Europe. It was not for sitting quietly as they do now that the Quakers gained their popular name. In many ways, this simply reflects the ease with which trance and other forms of mystical experience float up into the religious consciousness.

Syncretic religions involving trance have appeared frequently in the New World, where echoes of the traditional African religions brought in via the slave trade have collided with the more formal religions of Western Europe. In Brazil, for example, the Umbanda (literally 'white magic') religion appeared around a century ago. It is a blend of traditional West African spirit religions with aspects of conventional Catholicism and French Spiritualism. It is pantheistic, recognizing a large number of deities of West African (mainly Yoruba) tribal origin, each usually equated with the Christian God or one of the saints. Services centre around trance dancing in which priests and priestesses act as mediums who function as the mouthpieces of the individual gods. Since the spirit beings intervene in the followers' daily lives, the principal function of these services, which can sometimes last all night, is to appease the various deities; as part of this, offerings of food and drink are usually made to them in the course of the ceremony.

The Shaman's World

The great majority of small-scale and hunter-gatherer societies have shamans, who serve a specialist role as diviners and healers. In contrast to San trance dances, which are public rituals that the entire community is involved in, shamans are usually specialists whose skills are sought, often at a price, for particular purposes. Trance is invariably involved in all these cases, as are music, dance, smoky vapours, exotic noisy behaviour and, probably, a good deal of showmanship. So much so, in fact, that many observers have concluded that shamans are either frauds or suffer from some kind of psychopathology – or are just the lucky practitioners of a placebo effect whereby suggestion effectively engineers a cure even though no active ingredients are involved. Though there are no doubt genuine examples of all of these, none of these explanations really hold water in all cases.[14] There are too many exceptions, not least the fact that shamans really do believe in their abilities. Moreover, some of their practices are simply too painful to be worth undergoing just to fake trance or deceive their clientele. In any case, what shamans do, how they do it, and what they experience when doing it, is remarkably consistent the world over, despite enormous differences in culture, language and tribal origins.[15] The characteristics that define shamans must arise out of a common psychological substrate. Whatever it is, shamanism is clearly a coherent phenomenon.

Most shamans undergo a long and arduous training, and only those with an aptitude acquire the knowledge and skills to become fully accredited healers or diviners. It has been estimated that, among the San, only around half of the adult men and 10 per cent of the women successfully complete the training to become healers. This is rarely a formal process: individuals simply attach themselves to an adept and learn on the job. They succeed if they can stand the pace, otherwise they give up and drop out. Like apprentices of old, they start to practise on their own once they feel confident in their abilities.

Although shamans probably focus mainly on divination and healing, their advice or intervention can be called on for a wide variety of social functions, including the provision of hunting magic, influencing the weather (for example, as rainmakers), conducting rituals associated with births, marriages and deaths, providing advice or magic related to economic, military or other socio-political events, and sometimes even acting as charismatic leaders (as did many of the famous 'medicine men' of the American Plains Indians, such as Sitting Bull of the Lakota Sioux).

We can group the functions that shamans perform in small-scale societies into three main types: those related to the uncertainties of life (divination, healing, foraging success), those related to rites of passage and other social phenomena (births, deaths, marriages, warfare,[16] settling disputes and rainmaking) and those related to managing communal matters (legal and political issues, acting as a charismatic leader). Figure 1 shows that the first of these (mitigating the uncertainties of life) is by far the most important. Shamans were involved in the rituals of life in about half the societies, but they were much less frequently involved in socio-political matters. Those tasks tended to be associated with village headmen or political chiefs – or, in some cases, democratic discussion.

Divination (predicting the future) has been a perennial concern of humans as far back as written history goes. We still worry about it – otherwise we wouldn't continue to show such an interest in horoscopes, and we certainly wouldn't bother with weather forecasts. Given that the future often seems random and capricious, it is not hard to see how valuable the services of someone who claims to be able to foretell the

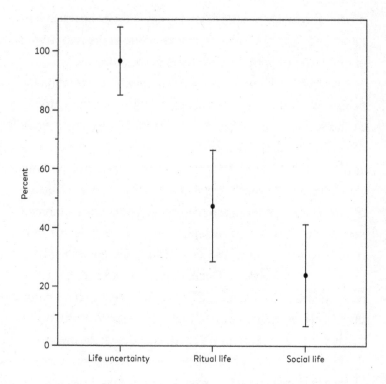

Figure 1
Mean (±2 standard deviations) of the percentage of small-scale hunter-gatherer societies in which shamans were responsible for performing magic or rituals associated with different aspects of life. The data are sourced from Manvir Singh (2018).

future might be, especially in the context of a small-scale tribal society where a single disaster can easily wipe out an entire community. In reality, whether or not the shaman really can predict the future or cure diseases may actually be much less important than being able to put someone in the right frame of mind to cope with the exigencies of the moment.

Successful diviners, or at least diviners with a reputation for being successful, often attract considerable followings. Among the most celebrated of these was the Oracle from the Temple of Apollo at Delphi. Once a month, the Oracle (always a priestess)[17] would go into public trance to provide cryptic prophecies for those who sought her advice. The trances were induced by sitting above a fissure in the ground from which emerged fumes from the river that flowed beneath the temple. It seems that these sessions were so exhausting that, combined with the probably poisonous effect of the fumes, most of the priestesses died relatively young. The Oracle seems to have come into existence around 1400 BC and to have lasted until AD 390 when the Roman Emperor Theodosius the Great destroyed the temple as part of a campaign to eradicate paganism within his newly Christianized empire. In her heyday, however, the Oracle was so famous for the wisdom of her frankly impenetrable prophecies that she attracted supplicants from all over the eastern Mediterranean.

Impenetrability seems to be an important requirement for diviners, since it allows each person to read into the prophecy whatever suits their individual circumstances, thus allowing the diviner to blame the supplicant for misreading the prophecy if things do not turn out as expected. Witness the enduring reputation of the sixteenth-century physician and astrologer Nostradamus (Michel de Nostradame), whose famously obscure prophecies continue to excite interest five centuries after his death.

The second most important role that shamans play is undoubtedly healing. It seems that whenever humans cannot see an obvious cause for something, they have a near-universal tendency to blame accidents, sickness and death on the actions of evil spirits or malicious witches (usually but not always female) within their own community. This is due to a ubiquitous and very human tendency to blame anyone or anything other than ourselves for the disasters that befall us (a psychological phenomenon known as *externalization*). Even now, bewitching continues to be an important explanation for illness among both the indigenous and Hispanic populations of Central and South America, including the southern USA, as well as throughout much of Africa – and probably a great deal more widely. We need only remind ourselves of the epidemic of witch-hunting that blighted much of northern Europe in the seventeenth century. Between 1590 and 1706, some 5,000 people were tried for witchcraft in Scotland alone, of whom around 1,500 (three-quarters of them women) were executed – at a time when the total population of Scotland was only about 400,000 adults. That's one in every forty of the adult population put on trial.

Healing rituals are particularly widespread in traditional societies. Shamanic healing typically involves the shaman using trance to 'see' the spirit that's causing the disease, and then to engage in appropriate rituals to remove the cause, usually by transferring it into their own body, into another animal or back into the spirit world, as appropriate. Among the San Bushmen, for example, the trance master draws the sickness out of the victim's body into their own, often through violent shaking and a characteristic loud shriek or wail (the *kowhedili* shriek) that ejects the evil spirit from the body of the sufferer.

Shamans as healers are by no means confined to traditional societies, of course. Faith healers are common in the Christian Pentecostal and charismatic evangelical traditions. More generally, 'living saints' and holy men and women have been sought out for good luck, fertility and cures since time immemorial in the Mediterranean and the Near East. Jesus himself, of course, famously cast several devils out of the much-tormented Gadarene into a nearby herd of swine, thereby restoring the man to full health – and condemning the pigs to drown themselves in the nearby Sea of Galilee. Exorcism remains a formal, sometimes troubling, part of the armoury of many Christian sects, including the mainstream churches.

Even within the otherwise austerely esoteric confines of Buddhism, shamanic tendencies can be found in the Tibetan lama schools. Tibetan Buddhism has its origins in the wandering medieval *mahasiddhas* (great adepts, or yogis) of northern India, who promoted a mixture of Buddhist and tantric beliefs and rituals that included the use of singing, dancing, sex rites and the ingestion of a variety of psychoactive substances including alcohol. In Tibet, the Vajrayana Buddhism that this gave rise to mingled with the native Bon religion that had its own origins in Siberian shamanism.

The Doors of Heaven and Hell

In 1954, the author Aldous Huxley published two short accounts (*The Doors of Perception* and *Heaven and Hell*) of his experiments with mescaline in California. The psychedelic experiences he had led him to view mescaline as a means of achieving higher levels of consciousness, and in doing so provided the launchpad for the 1960s counterculture that developed in California shortly afterwards. Mescaline is an alkaloid extracted from the peyote cactus that has been used for well over 5,500 years by the Indian tribes in western Mexico to induce visions, effect healings and enhance 'inner strength'. Mescaline acts on the serotonin receptors in the brain, making them more active, which results in altered thought processes, a distorted sense of time and self-awareness, and visual illusions.

Mescaline is, of course, by no means the only drug that produces these effects. Very similar effects are produced by LSD (a derivative of the ergot fungus) and by psilocybin (produced by upwards of 200 species of mushrooms), as well as by the natural plant derivative DMT that has been widely used in the shamanic rituals of Amazonian tribes since pre-Colombian times. DMT can be inhaled by smoking the dried leaves of certain plants, but is more often ingested in liquid form in the beverage known as *ayahuasca*.

In 1962, the famous Marsh Chapel Experiment gave either psilocybin or a placebo (in this case, a harmless vitamin compound) to a group of theology students taking part in a Good Friday Easter service in the chapel.[18] Those who took the psilocybin reported having profound religious experiences during the service that some of them later described as some of the most intense they ever had. This study has since been replicated at least twice. The main benefits of all these natural drugs seems to be that the effects come on quite quickly and last some considerable time. Although adverse effects like toxic delirium can occur, providing the substances are used under the supervision of experienced guides they seem to produce relatively few harmful long-term side effects.

The use of psychoactive substances in shamanic practices or to induce visions has a very long history. Smoky fires onto which handfuls of 'sacred herbs' are thrown are a regular feature of shamanic rituals, and, of course, incense has been widely used in Christian and biblical Judaic services[19] since time immemorial. Tobacco was used in religious as well as civil ceremonies by Native Americans, who viewed the smoke as a vehicle for carrying prayers to the spirits in the sky. The smoking (or eating) of marijuana (an extract of the hemp or cannabis plant) is documented in the Hindu religious text the *Veda* as early as 1500 BC, where it is described as one of five plants that free us from anxiety. It still plays a role in some Hindu religious ceremonies, and is often given as a gift to passing *sadhus* (ascetics) and yogis, who use it to enhance meditation. Despite the prohibition on the use of intoxicants in the Buddhist scriptures, marijuana was also used to heighten the experience of meditation by some of the tantric sects in the Himalayan region. And, of course, it plays a seminal role in the religious services of contemporary Rastafarians.

Cannabis was also used by diviners and necromancers (magicians) in ancient China (where it was cultivated in Neolithic times and appears among the grave goods in Tarim burials from as early as 1800 BC). We find it in burials in Central Asia from as early as the fifth century BC and even in the grave goods associated with some of the Egyptian pharaohs (notably Rameses II), as well as in archaeological remains from all over the eastern Mediterranean. Cannabis was burned in the temples of Babylon during Assyrian times (its aroma was said to be pleasing to the gods) and by the Old Testament Hebrews. The Roman historian Herodotus records it as being used for both social and religious purposes by the Scythian and Thracian tribes of the Eurasian steppes on the eastern edge of Europe. It was used by the nearby Dacians during the first millennium BC in a shamanic cult known to the Greeks as the *Kapnobatai* (literally 'those who walk in the smoke'). Historically, it was used by the Norse in the erotic religious ceremonies associated with Freya, the goddess of love. Some Islamic Sufi sects (notably the Melamis) used it in their services.

Many of these psychoactive drugs have medically beneficial properties and were also widely used for medicinal purposes. Cannabis elevates mood and reduces anxiety, and was used in ancient China as an anaesthetic during surgery as well as to treat constipation. In the Middle East it was used from ancient times right through the Islamic period to treat epilepsy, inflammation and fever. Opium was also used for medicinal purposes in the Middle East, from where it was introduced to both China[20] and India by Islamic traders during the first millennium AD. Opium is mentioned both as an anaesthetic and as a treatment in many ancient medical texts, and it continued to be recommended as a treatment for nervous complaints in Europe until the early decades of the twentieth century. The medicinal properties of many of these psychoactive drugs may have been instrumental in earning shamans their reputations as healers, especially for those psychological conditions that resist all other conventional forms of treatment. However, their original function was probably to induce altered states of consciousness in which practitioners experienced direct communion with the gods.

It has not been my intention in this chapter to justify the activities of shamans, or to test the validity of their claims. My point has simply been to establish that there is an undercurrent of belief in a spirit world (the mystical stance) that not only has a very long history but is still widely identifiable in the contemporary world. It seems to induce a 'raw feels' component to human psychology that can be overpowering in its influence on us, but which we find great difficulty in describing in words. I suggest that, with or without the help of psychoactive drugs, this mystical component, with its strong emotional overtones, underpins all religious behaviour, no matter how sophisticated the religion. It is the motor of religiosity and consequently colours everything that emerges from this experience in the form of religion. This claim provides the foundation for the argument that I will develop in the chapters that follow.

CHAPTER 3
Why Believing Can
Be Good for You

As I noted in Chapter 1, most evolutionarily-minded research-ers have argued that religious beliefs, and hence religions, are a maladaptive by-product of psychological mechanisms that exist for other perfectly good evolutionary reasons. This is not entirely unjustified.[1] Many aspects of our biology and psych-ology are serendipitous by-products of something that evolved for perfectly good reasons, but left some highly maladapted features in their wake. However, it seems to me that nothing which is so costly of time, emotion and money as religion can possibly be entirely maladapted or functionless. Evolution is simply not that inefficient. Religion must have *some* benefits.

So what does religion do for us?

Over the last century or so, a number of scholars have made suggestions. Broadly speaking, these boil down to five general themes: religion as a form of primitive science, reli-gion as a form of medical intervention, religion as an enforcer of cooperation, religion as a mechanism of political oppres-sion (in the words of Karl Marx, the opium of the people), and religion as a mechanism for community bonding. Each has its ardent defenders and each looks plausible on the grounds ar-ticulated by their respective protagonists.

I will argue that, while all the benefits listed above may well be at least partially true (hence the evidence in their support), we completely miss the fundamental biological point if, as almost everyone does, we focus exclusively on immediate individual-level benefits as the motor of evolution. First, however, let me begin by outlining these five classic explanations and some of the evidence in their support. I will do so by considering them in three separate sets: those that have individual-level benefits (religion as a means of explaining the world and religion as medical intervention), those that provide societal-level benefits (religion as an enforcer of good behaviour or for the oppression of the masses for the benefit of an elite), and those that view religion as a mechanism for bonding communities.

Individual-level Benefits

One widely articulated view is that religion provides a unifying framework for the world in which we live: it allows us to make sense of our world in a way that enables us to function effectively because we can control its more erratic behaviour. The natural world is notoriously unpredictable. Terrestrial environments are particularly susceptible to the vagaries of climate, and climatic instability has been the single most important motor for the evolution of life since the beginning of time. Climatic variability causes famines, the collapse of ecosystems, and the disappearance of the plants and animals we eat, not to mention floods, droughts, tidal surges and lightning strikes. On top of that, we never know when we are likely to encounter any of the many more immediate threats to life – predators, plagues and pathogens, poisonous plants, and other humans (raiders). Or for that matter, the malevolent spirits that inhabit (or more correctly *are*) various natural features.

Traditional religions play an important role in this respect through divination and the production of charms against natural disasters. It is notable that people are more likely to resort to shamans, religious institutions or even pure superstitions if the benefit of some event is particularly large (for example, a life-or-death issue) or uncertain (for example, the coming of rain or the birth of a child of a particular sex) compared to when the benefit is minimal. When he was studying the Trobriand Islanders in Melanesia during the First World War, the anthropologist Bronislaw Malinowski noted that fisherman always used magic when going out deep-sea fishing, but never when fishing inshore in the lagoons. Deep-sea expeditions are fraught with life-threatening dangers and great uncertainty, whereas inshore fishing rarely carries any risks.

Many of the churches in Europe owe their existence to vows made by a medieval knight to found a chapel or religious community if he returned safe from a crusade or was successful in some other great adventure. On the eve of the battle of Winwead in 655, Oswiu, the Christian Anglo-Saxon king of Bernicea in the northeast of England, prayed for victory in a forthcoming battle with King Penda of the Mercians, the last pagan king of England, promising to make his daughter a nun and donate twelve of his estates to found monasteries if he won. Apparently it worked: he triumphed over his opponent, paving the way for the final conversion of England.

Religion has not always been successful in this respect, however. During the 1340s, for example, many people in Europe viewed the Black Death as divine punishment for society's failure to live the good Christian life. To bring an end to the plague, bands of penitents known as Flagellants wandered from town to town, singing hymns and scourging themselves in an orchestrated effort to beg God's forgiveness. In fact, all they did was to carry the plague from one village or town to the next – so much so, in fact, that eventually many towns bolted their gates and refused to allow them entry.

In more recent times, tribal societies have resorted to magic to defeat invaders or natural disasters. By far the best known case is the infamous massacre of Lakota Sioux at Wounded Knee in 1890. The Lakota had been persuaded by a visionary named Wovoka that the white settlers would be driven from their lands if the tribes performed a traditional Ghost Dance. The ghost shirts worn by Lakota dancers were believed to confer spiritual powers, and in this instance the powers were extended to making the wearer invulnerable to bullets, guaranteeing victory. In the confrontation with the US cavalry at Wounded Knee, the strategy inevitably failed tragically, resulting in the massacre of up to 300 men, women and children.[2]

An almost identical case occurred in southern Tanganyika (the mainland part of modern Tanzania) in 1905–7 when the tribes in the region launched a rather bloody rebellion against their German colonial masters. It became known as the Maji Maji Rebellion because they were persuaded by the witch doctor Kinjikitile Ngwale that he had specially powerful medicine that would turn the Germans' bullets into water (*maji* in Kiswahili).[3] All they had to do was to take his medicine (actually a mixture of water, castor oil and millet seeds) and shout '*Maji maji!*' as they went into battle. Needless to say, it was no defence against modern weapons handled by the well-trained native troops of the German administration.

An even more desperate case occurred in 1856 in South Africa's Eastern Cape. Under the combined pressure of encroaching Europeans and an epidemic of cattle lung disease that was decimating their herds, the Xhosa were persuaded by a 16-year-old visionary named Nongqawuse to kill all their animals and destroy their crops.[4] She claimed that two of her ancestors had appeared to her in a vision and told her that the tribe's troubles would come to an end if they did this. A mass slaughter of the cattle might well have solved the lung disease problem with only a limited temporary impact on the Xhosa (it is, after all, exactly how we now control epidemics of foot-and-mouth in cattle), but destroying the crops left the population without any form of subsistence. As a result, three-quarters of the Xhosa died of self-inflicted starvation, effectively destroying an entire culture forever.

The second explanation for religion is that it provides direct benefits in terms of health. Many modern religions take the view that God will look after us – *inshallah* (God willing), as the common expression has it in Islam. In the Christian world, not to mention the other world religions, people continue to this day to pray to saints, leave messages asking for prayers to be said for them by strangers, or make offerings for everything from curing their disease to success in a business venture.

Belief that invisible forces are responsible for what happens in the world, and especially injurious things, is widespread in all cultures and times, and remains prevalent even today. Many religious rituals do provide cures for certain diseases or conditions, either through placebo effects or because the herbs and plants provided by witch doctors really do have medicinal value. We should not be overly surprised by this last point. Humans are exceedingly good at recognizing correlations in the world. Indeed, even wild chimpanzees have learned to consume certain medicinal plants that are effective treatments for intestinal parasites.[5] You don't need to know the scientific explanation for a cure to know that it works, and that leaves the way open for religious explanations.

Nonetheless, the cures effected by shamans, medicine men and wise women must work at least sometimes, otherwise people wouldn't continue to believe in their efficacy. The issue, however, is: how often is enough? At least one study found that traditional Quichua healers in the Andes correctly identified individuals with a diagnosed psychiatric disorder with a success rate of around 65 per cent of cases.[6] Psychopathologies make up the great majority of cases dealt with by shamans worldwide.[7] This may be because these are easier to diagnose (they are very familiar to us, after all) and, in some ways, easier to deal with than most physical diseases, which often require more technical skill. To the extent that they may be psychosomatic in origin, placebo effects may be very successful.

On a more general note, there is evidence that religious people are happier and more contented with their lives. William James first made this observation more than a century ago, and I will provide further evidence on this point later. There is also evidence that actively religious people may be healthier than non-religious people. A study of 21,000 American adults found that those who never attended religious services had a risk of dying during the eight-year follow-up period that was nineteen times higher than those who went to services at least once a week.[8] Another meta-analysis of forty-two studies, totalling nearly 126,000 subjects, found that active religious involvement increased the chances of being alive at follow-up by 26 per cent compared to those who never went to church, even when controlling for socio-demographic variables and existing health.[9]

So far, then, contrary to the claims often made, at least in the evolutionary literature, there is clear evidence that being actively religious does provide benefits at the personal level that are likely to have a direct effect on individuals' evolutionary fitness. The evidence is probably stronger for the direct effects of religion on health than for indirect effects that come through interventions by a shaman healer or saint. Whether or not it works in the way religion claims it does is, of course, neither here nor there. The only question is whether it works, even if this is via a placebo effect.

Societal-level Benefits

Human societies are, essentially, social contracts in which individuals agree to live together in order to share the costs of survival and reproduction. By doing so, they are able to benefit from the whole-is-greater-than-the-sum-of-the-parts effect that group living provides: I help you harvest your fields, and you do the same for me on some future occasion. So long as you pay me back by returning the favour, the evolutionary equation will balance and the behaviour will be selected for.

The problem is that, in a Darwinian world, altruistic behaviour is always at risk of being taken advantage of: I pay a cost to help you out, but you don't pay me back. That way you benefit twice over: you gain from my altruism *and* you don't have to pay the cost of reciprocating, while I lose out twice over (by helping you *and* by not receiving any help from you later). All else being equal, whatever genes underpin altruism will inexorably be selected against, and those for selfishness favoured. The population will quickly consist entirely of selfish individuals. Freeriding of this kind is a perennial problem for all social species since it is very destructive of social cohesion, and hence undermines the benefits that the community was created to provide. The only way to protect yourself from it is confine your generosity to the half dozen people you can really trust. In other words, a community that is invaded by even a small number of freeriders will very quickly either become dominated by selfish individuals or will fragment into small inward-looking subgroups.

Part of the problem is that we are not naturally prosocial – something that is surely evident from the fact that both secular and religious authorities, not to mention family, constantly have to enjoin us to fulfil our obligations in this respect. We are forever reminding children to share their toys, and adults to stick to the socially agreed rules of behaviour. In reality, in the absence of social and religious admonitions, prosocial behaviour (altruism, offers of a helping hand, etc.) is largely confined to close family and friends.[10] Many ethnographic studies demonstrate that aid is usually freely given to family and friends without expectation of return, but is given to those outside this magic circle of a few hundred people only on the explicit agreement to reciprocate or repay the favour.[11] The demands of living in super-large communities have made it necessary to impose demands of generosity – or at least neutrality – in our interactions with those with whom we live, lest crime and delinquency burst the fragile bonds that hold our communities together.

This problem has been studied in some detail using an experimental design known as the Public Good Dilemma.[12] Players are offered a chance to invest some of their money in a common pot, which at the end of the game increases in value and is then shared out equally among all the investors. The optimal solution is for everyone to put all their money in the pot, since that maximizes their return. Yet, in scores of experiments run by behavioural economists and evolutionary biologists, players invariably reduce their investment to the minimum over successive rounds. It seems that, after the first few rounds, people always end up being risk averse for fear of being exploited.

Yet we are, nonetheless, willing to cooperate with, and be casually generous to, strangers. Neither economists nor evolutionary biologists have managed to find a convincing explanation for this, despite several decades of intensive experimental study. The best they have been able to do is suggest one of two possible mechanisms that seem to work: reputation and punishment. We all monitor each other's behaviour and keep a note of how often others fail to provide support for us, and then choose to give our support in the future only to those who are reliable. It works, but it is by no means a perfect solution, not least because all I ever have to go on is what I actually see of your behaviour. Of course, humans use gossip to overcome this constraint: those who see what you are up to out of my sight tell me later how badly you behaved.

What does seem to work better, at least in the context of

economic experiments, is allowing people to punish backsliders. Even if they have to pay a fee to punish freeriders, some people are willing to do so – and it really does keep freeriders in check. This does, however, raise the problem of altruistic punishment: if I am the only one willing to pay to punish selfish individuals, then everyone else benefits from their improved behaviour without having to pay for it, and I bear the entire cost. Why should I be willing to do that? We very quickly get into a vicious circle that has no exit other than a retreat back to a situation where no one is willing to cooperate.

One suggestion as to how we might have solved that dilemma is by having a Moralizing High God[13] who acts as an all-seeing policeman-in-the-sky. God is a particularly effective threat precisely because He sees everything even when the rest of us might not. This is one obvious suggestion for the switch from having no gods (or, perhaps, having many little gods only interested in receiving offerings at their shrines) to having a single omniscient, all-powerful Moralizing High God who takes an active interest in human affairs and punishes those who step out of line.

One study used a standard cross-cultural sample of ethnographic and historical societies that contained over a thousand variables to test whether this suggestion really worked. It seemed that having a Moralizing High God did make it more likely that the members of a society would be socially compliant in terms of willingness to pay taxes, lend money to each other and accept the presence of a police force and other secular means of sanctioning backsliders. There was, however, no evidence that a belief in a Moralizing High God was associated with the size of the tribe as a whole or the size of the community in which individuals typically lived (that is, the village or hunting camp), or with the level of conflict either with external neighbours or within the community itself – something that others have suggested might be the case.[14]

There is, however, plenty of evidence that being actively religious increases people's willingness to behave altruistically. One recent study used a standard experimental economics game known as the Trust Game to see if religious people were more generous and trusted others more than non-religious people do. In the Trust Game, there are two roles: a Proposer or Trustor who is given a pot of money and allowed to decide how much money they would be willing to share with the other person, the Trustee. The amount donated is trebled by the experimenter, and the Trustee is then asked how much they would now give back to the Proposer. The optimal strategy would be for the Proposer to hand over all their available capital and for the Trustee then to split the money-plus-interest equally between them: that way they would both maximize their take-home earnings. However, since this is a one-time game, the Trustee would always do best to keep all the money or just offer a token amount back. Therein lies the issue of trust in the game. In fact, Proposers who self-identified as religious typically offered more than non-religious Proposers, and especially so if the Trustee was also religious. Religiousness did seem to act as a guarantee of trustworthiness.[15]

In another experiment, two anonymous members of the same Israeli kibbutz were independently asked to say how much money they would take from a sealed envelope, subject to the proviso that if their combined sums exceeded the amount of money in the envelope neither would get anything.[16]

Members of a religious kibbutz (who were, therefore, presumably religious) took less money from the envelope than members of a secular kibbutz, although this was largely due to the behaviour of the men. The men in this sample were more religious than the women (at least, as indexed by the frequency of their attendance at synagogue), and men who were more religious took less money from the envelope. In contrast, religiousness had no effect on how much money the women took. Attending secular events, such as communal meals, had only a very slight effect on either male or female members. This study seems to suggest that regular involvement in religious rituals makes men (who are usually significantly less generous than women in real life as well as in these kinds of economic games) more prosocial. That's better than nothing, you might say, but it's a lot less than ideal.

In another experimental study of fifteen ethnographic and urban societies, pairs of people were asked to take part in one of three kinds of economic games: a dictator game (in which player-1 decides how to split a sum of money with player-2, a measure of baseline generosity or prosociality), an ultimatum game (in which player-1 decides how to split the money, but player-2 has the option of rejecting the offer if they think it too low – a measure of relationship-level fairness regulation) and an ultimatum game with punishment (in which a third party, player-3, can pay to punish player-1 if they think player-1 has been too mean – a measure of the societal-level regulation of fairness). The results revealed that the more integrated into a market economy the society was, the more likely the players were to split the money equally. At the same time, the larger the size of the community the players lived in, the more likely they were to reject a low offer in the ultimatum game and the more likely the third party was to impose punishment. More interesting for us, however, was the fact that, except in the punishment version, offers were more likely to be closer to a fair 50:50 split if player-1 belonged to a doctrinal religion (in this case, always Christianity or Buddhism) than if they belonged to no religion or to a tribal shamanic-type religion.[17]

We need, however, to exercise some caution in how enthusiastically we interpret these results. Many expriments of this kind have used a priming design: this is a technique used by psychologists to put the subject subconsciously into a particular frame of mind. The subject might be asked to write a paragraph on either a religious or a secular theme, or asked to recite either a prayer or a nursery rhyme, so as to induce a feeling of religious or secular sentiment. Analysis of data from twenty-five experimental studies (totalling nearly 5,000 subjects) that had used religious versus non-religious priming yielded rather ambivalent results.[18] Although a religious prime did elicit more altruistic behaviour overall, in only nine of the twenty-five studies was the effect significant. Five studies actually yielded a negative effect (religious primes resulted in *less* altruism). It is not at all clear that the kinds of religious primes used in these studies really do make a religious person more likely to be altruistic. Moreover, even when it does, the effect is very modest. This conclusion has since been borne out by a number of other recent experimental studies and reviews.[19]

Nonetheless, the benefits of cooperation might still be the reason why religion became necessary: enforcing social rectitude may help to preserve the fabric of society for the other benefits that society confers. One analysis of cross-cultural data for eighty-seven countries looked at the extent to which believing in God, or in the possibility of reward or punishment in the afterlife, influenced attitudes towards moral transgressions in this life.[20] In this context, moral transgressions included things like failing to report damaging someone else's vehicle, self-interested lying, having an affair while married, and driving under the influence of alcohol. Individuals who professed a belief in God were more likely to view moral transgressions as reprehensible, even when holding culture, religious denomination and education constant. The same was true for those who expressed a belief in Heaven and Hell, and for those who believed in a personal God compared to those who believed in a more generalized spiritual Life Force. Apparently, a personalized deity is perceived as being more likely to be watching your behaviour than some more nebulous supernatural force.

However, in another analysis of data from a large cross-cultural ethnographic sample, no correlation was found between fear of supernatural punishment and the prevalence of belief in supernatural agents or the prevalence of belief in witches and sorcerers (as the living agents of supernatural forces). Nor was there any consistent relationship between fear of supernatural punishment and the size of the community characteristic of the society – something that had previously been suggested might be the case.[21] This suggests that the phenomenon may be more complicated than the original hypothesis presupposed.

It has been suggested that accusations of witchcraft serve a similar policing function. In most cases, those accused of witchcraft were old, with few relatives to defend them, but their fate may have served to terrorize the rest of us into remaining on the right side of the moral code. The Salem Witch Trials of 1692–3 are a stark reminder of just how susceptible communities can be to suspicions of witchcraft.[22] In this iconic episode in the early history of the United States, 200 members of a small, rural community in Massachusetts were hauled up before the investigating magistrates on the say-so of a group of teenage girls. Thirty of them were convicted, of whom twenty-five were executed or died in jail before the sentence could be carried out (the remaining five were lucky enough to be tried last, and had their convictions quashed the following year). Many were elderly women, confused by the legal process and unable to effectively defend themselves. They had the bad luck to be caught in the middle of fractious disputes within the village at the same time that the Puritan colony of Massachusetts was much exercised by the need to maintain religious discipline among its settlers in the face of external threats both from local Indians (in the aftermath of the Metacom War – said to have been the most destructive war in terms of loss of life per head of population in the history of North America) and from half a century of conflict with the French in Canada (most recently culminating in King William's War of 1689).

Similar examples can be cited from almost every part of the world. In a study of homicides among the New Guinea Gebusi, for example, 80 per cent of the victims had been accused of being a sorcerer.[23] Sorcerers were much feared and frequently blamed for otherwise inexplicable deaths, injuries, illnesses or accidents. In this context, accusations of witchcraft were often ways of dealing with disruptive individuals or settling old scores.

The second possibility under this heading is Marx's famous claim that religion is the opium of the people – the invention of an elite anxious to subdue an unruly populace. In other words, religion prevails on the populace to behave in ways that suit the elite. 'Thou shalt not steal', so the argument goes, is not an injunction to be obeyed with respect to everybody, but rather one to be obeyed by the peasantry with special respect to the property of the elite. If this is true, we might expect religion to be associated with ostentatious threats of the fate that await those who fail to adhere to the social rules. In fact, the more fire-and-brimstone in sermons the better.

This suggestion might explain particular cases where religion and the secular power are hand-in-glove. Examples would include Pharaonic Egypt, the attempts by several Roman emperors to promote themselves as gods, the Aztecs, the Islamic empires of the later medieval period, perhaps even the Holy Roman and Spanish Empires. But many large political powers (including the Ottoman and British Empires) were content to allow their citizens free choice of religion – in the latter case even encouraging it in the interests of preserving the cultures of their subject peoples. More importantly, religion – and especially the growth of new religions – appears to be a bottom-up phenomenon: it is the poor and downtrodden, not the elite, that initiate this process.

In short, as a general explanation for the evolution of religion, this suggestion seems implausible: it will only work providing people are already religiously predisposed. You cannot *make* people religious so as to force them to obey your rules. They may superficially acquiesce, but their good behaviour is more likely to be dependent on your police force than their religious convictions. Sooner or later, they are likely to revolt. In other words, since religiosity must precede the establishment of the state for the state to be able to exploit it, the interests of the state (or its elite) cannot be the cause of the evolution of a religious predisposition.

Nonetheless, the rituals of religion might be coopted later by the state to reinforce its interests or those of the elite. Dire warnings of what might befall those who don't toe the communal line might send a message that encourages compliance. Human sacrifice might be a case in point. Many of the societies that engaged in ritual human sacrifice were stratified, with an elite ruling over a populace, and a middle class who provided the enforcement muscle. The Aztecs are the archetypal example. The historical records claim that at the re-consecration of the Great Pyramid of Tenochtitlan in AD 1487 as many as 80,000 prisoners were sacrificed. Even if that particular claim is aggrandizing licence, the Aztec historical record clearly indicates that very large numbers were sacrificed on a regular basis in ceremonies large and small. The victims were often war captives, but could be criminals, slaves, concubines (especially when a great leader was buried) or even random members of society, including children. Ostensibly, human sacrifice was intended to placate the gods, but there can be no doubt that the drama would have impressed the masses and perhaps dissuaded them from stepping out of political or social line.

Ritualized sacrifice of humans to propitiate gods is widely reported in historical sources from the Canadian Arctic, Central and South America, Austronesia, Arabia, Africa, India, China and Japan. We know that in Austronesian cultures, at least, sacrifice was explicitly used as a punishment for taboo violations. A study of ninety-three historical Austronesian cultures revealed that the presence of sacrifice was strongly associated with stratified, and especially highly stratified, societies (examples include Hawaii and Tahiti in the Pacific, the Ngaju people of Borneo, the Kayan of Burma), whereas it rarely occurred in egalitarian societies (such as the Onlong of Java or the Mekeo of Papua New Guinea).[24] These results point to two important conclusions: once a society has adopted sacrifice it is very likely to become stratified, and once it has stratification-with-sacrifice it is unlikely to lose stratification.

In sum, terrorizing the populace probably does work to the advantage of the ruling classes, even though it likely stores up trouble for the future in the form of revolt if it is seen to be too unfair. However, it seems likely that a pre-existing predisposition to be religious is being exploited for these purposes rather than being invented to justify the existence of an elite. In other words, these kinds of social benefits are more likely to constitute windows of evolutionary opportunity (additional ways to exploit religious sentiments after the fact) rather than being the evolutionary causes of religion.

There is one other possibility that falls into this category of explanations, and that is religion as a way of absorbing excess members of the population, in particular young males. The Tibetans provide an unusual example. Traditionally, they were polyandrous: all the sons of one family married the same woman, taking over the running of the family farm as they did so.[25] The main reason for this was to avoid having to divide the family farm when it passed from one generation to the next, an issue of some economic concern in a high-altitude location where the fertility of the land was poor and the area that could be cultivated was very limited. With all the sons forming a single family unit with just one shared wife, the family farm remained intact as it passed down the generations. This worked because the boys typically ranged in age from their early twenties down to a 5-year-old. The age disparities between the brothers helped to minimize the sexual conflict between them: in effect, they took it in turns to be the sexually active husband. However, the two older sons were often already at that stage when the brothers married their wife. To avoid unnecessary sexual conflict between them, the second-born son was usually hived off into the local monastery – often when he was only eight or nine, so that he was well settled into monastic life by the time of the marriage.[26] The cultural justification would, presumably, be that he could look after the family's spiritual interests. The economic reality was very different.

An analogous solution was adopted by late nineteenth-century farming families in Ireland: to avoid having to partition the family farm, families with more than the average number of sons prevailed on their younger sons to go into the local seminary to become Catholic priests.[27] In this case, the parents seem to have been trying to minimize the risk of within-family conflict over the inheritance of the farm since these boys would remain celibate for life.[28] In eighteenth- and nineteenth-century England, the nobility and wealthy middle classes adopted a similar strategy: the eldest son inherited the family estate, the second joined the military and the third trained for the Church (whether or not he had a vocation). It's one of the reasons so many of the vicarages of this period are so substantial: being from the same class, their wives expected a domestic establishment commensurate with their social station.

The converse case occurred among the Portuguese nobility in the fifteenth and sixteenth centuries: if they had too many daughters, they risked ending up with excess girls they couldn't find husbands for, especially as the girls were not allowed to marry beneath their social class. To solve the problem, they placed their younger daughters in the local nunnery. To sweeten the pill, the girls were provided with a dowry, and were given the title 'Brides of Christ'. The deal was that if the older sister died, the younger one could be relieved of her religious vows and take her dead sister's marital place.[29]

These examples provide an interesting light on the social value that religion might provide. However, once again, it only works if religion already exists: it is unlikely to be a cause for the development of religion. And it only applies in a small number of cases where there is a clear economic or social advantage to be gained and the local religion offers appropriate arrangements (for example, monastic celibacy). In short, it looks more like an example of how society (or individual families) might exploit religion after the fact.

Communitas and Commitment

Top-down coercion certainly forces people to behave better (or, at least, in ways that suit the elite), but in these cases the oppressed lower classes will always seek to bypass the constraints imposed on them whenever they can. This inevitably makes the strategy unstable in the long run. In contrast, bottom-up commitment whereby the individual *voluntarily* signs up to the community ethos will always be a more successful strategy simply because the motivation comes from the individuals themselves rather than being imposed on them by others.

A number of recent studies have viewed the rituals of religion as a declaration of commitment in just this sense. An analysis of nineteenth-century American utopian communities found that the more commitments a new member had to make when joining one of these communities (for example, giving up swearing, tobacco, alcohol, meat and, in extreme cases, even sex), the longer the community survived, but only for religious communities.[30] This seemed to reflect the cost the aspirant was prepared to make, and hence their personal commitment to sticking with it despite all the ups and downs of communal life. However, there was no such effect in the case of secular communities. As a result, secular communities had much shorter lifespans (on average, a mere ten years) compared to religious communities (whose typical lifespan was nearer seventy years). It seemed that a religious ethos added a significant factor to the mix.

Émile Durkheim was much impressed by the fact that religious rituals produced a sense of elation and arousal that he referred to as *effervescence*. He considered that this played an important role in creating a sense of belonging to a community. This idea was elaborated in the 1970s by Victor and Edith Turner in their concept of *communitas* as a form of collective bonding created during rituals such as rites of passage – or for that matter religious services, though they were not especially concerned with these. In recent decades, this suggestion has been lost sight of by anthropologists as well as psychologists.

The key to group-living is cohesion. Maintaining group cohesion, however, is not a trivial task. Living in close physical proximity to others incurs considerable costs, in terms of both the ecological costs and the social stresses. In addition to disadvantages such as longer day journeys and competition for food resources, the psychological stresses of living in groups have a dramatic effect on the fertility of female mammals: stress shuts down the brain/ovarian endocrine system that regulates the menstrual cycle, resulting in reduced fertility.[31] These costs, and especially the infertility costs, need to be mitigated, otherwise the group will fragment and disperse.

In any community, what begins as a petty frustration can rapidly escalate into jealousy, anger, quarrels, a failure to share the rewards of hunting and, eventually, armed conflict. Among hunter-gatherers like the San Bushmen, these frictions, if left unresolved, inexorably lead to the fragmentation of the group and a loss of the communal solidarity on which everyone's survival depends. Trance dances are part of their solution for this: whenever relationships within the community or camp start to become overly fractious, someone calls for a trance dance. Trance seems to reboot the system, restoring relationships among the members of the community back to their pristine state. As time passes, the stresses and niggles of everyday relationships slowly build up again, until once more someone calls for a trance dance.

In a recent online survey that focused explicitly on people's religious activities, I found that both the frequency of attendance at religious services (of whatever denomination) and the degree of personal religiosity significantly influenced the degree to which people engaged with their local community, as well as their sense of life satisfaction and the number of close friends they had. More importantly, the more often someone attended religious services, the more bonded they felt to their personal group of friends and family *and* to the congregation of which they were a member.

In the wider population, most people will list around fifteen people as the number they feel they can depend on, but this rises to include virtually the whole congregation of several hundred people for those who attend religious services on a daily basis. In effect, people who are regular worshippers come to feel closely bonded to most of the people who attend the same services, in part because they see them so regularly and so get to know them well (I'll have a lot more to say about this in Chapter 5), but also because of the rituals that they jointly take part in (more on that in Chapter 6).

It seems that being actively religious (as opposed to just turning up for services) makes you feel bonded to a larger group of people who are more likely to provide you with support. As a result, you also feel happier and are more contented with your life. While the latter observation might seem to give direct support to the religion-as-the-opium-of-the-people claim, in fact one can put a much more positive spin on this. Irrespective of whether an elite is involved, active involvement in religion both makes you feel happier and provides you with a level of support that helps you cope with the many economic and social ups and downs of everyday life that are as much a part of hunter-gatherer life as they are a part of the lives of downtrodden peasants or anyone else.

Making Sense of Complexity

Two things should strike us about the findings in this chapter. One is that there is some evidence to support all five of the hypotheses for the function of religion. This should alert us to the fact that there is something wrong when someone uses confirmatory evidence for one hypothesis to claim that it is *the* only function of religion. Given the evidence in support of all the other hypotheses, it simply cannot be that only one of them is correct and all the others wrong. The second observation is that the evidence is by no means overwhelming. In almost every case, there is some evidence for, and some against. Why would that be? The answer was, in fact, given at the end of Chapter 1: Tinbergen's Four Why's. Everyone seems to be treating these different hypotheses as though they are logically equivalent and hence mutually exclusive: if one is right, all the others must be wrong. But if they are in fact answers to different *why* questions, then they are not mutually exclusive: they can all be right at the same time. We need to look at the hypotheses more carefully and ask what questions, exactly, they are answers to.

Perhaps the easiest way to do this is to set out the five hypotheses in a path, or flow, diagram that specifies the causal relationships between the different components. Normally, one would consider all possible combinations and permutations of these relationships and ask which best explains the observed data. However, with five hypotheses there are 120 different ways of rearranging the reationships between them. So let me simply cut to the chase and offer my suggestion for the pattern that seems to me to make most sense of the evidence. This is summarized in Figure 2, which plots the five hypotheses (identified by the five grey boxes) in relation to two other key variables that have to be part of the story, namely group (or community) size and external threats.

External threats are the primary reason for group living in all birds and mammals, and especially primates. This acts as the fulcrum on which the rest of the edifice is supported. For most species, these threats mainly take the form of predation risk, but in some monkeys and apes, and especially in humans, they can also include the threat posed by raiding or attack by neighbouring groups. The arrow between the 'External threat' and 'Group size' boxes in Figure 2 is to be interpreted as stating that when external threats such as predation risk increase, group size will have to increase proportionately to counteract the threat. However, as group size increases the stresses imposed on the members – in terms of ecological competition, social frustrations and infertility – unavoidably increase. Bonding provides the solution to this problem (the bigger the group, the better the bonding has to be). The arrow down from the 'Religion' box indicates that religion allows the group to be better bonded. These three arrows are larger to indicate that they form the core set of causal relationships. In effect, this explicitly identifies the primary function of religion as being community bonding. The smaller arrows then indicate secondary benefits that arise once religion is in place. Once religion has evolved, it provides direct health benefits and an improved understanding of the world such that the vagaries of lived experience can be better predicted and managed (the box labelled 'Science'). An improved understanding of the world reduces some of the intrusiveness of external threats (indicated by the double-dashed arrow with a negative sign by its head). This sets up a self-limiting circuit that keeps the costs of the external threats and the size of social communities in dynamic balance with each other.

In addition, there are two loops that add further benefits, one in which religion plays no part (indicated by the dotted arrows) and one in which religion plays a part through its influence on group bonding (the thinner solid arrows). In the latter case, better bonded groups allow more cooperation, which in turn feeds back to reinforce the size of the bonded group by ensuring that failure to cooperate doesn't result in groups fragmenting because of fractiousness. The other loop arises directly as a consequence of an independent effect of increasing group size. Ethnographic, archaeological and computer modelling evidence suggests that when communities get above a certain size they have a natural tendency to give rise to an elite that manages the community (more on this in the next chapter).[32] One consequence of stratification is to allow a leadership (whether secular or religious) to emerge that can both exhort members to behave well and punish those who fail to obey the rules, thereby enforcing cooperation. Of course, once you have a stratified society of this kind, it inevitably provides the elite with the opportunity to exploit the masses.

There are, of course, many other ways to construe the causal relationships between these key variables. Figure 2 is simply my best guess based on what we know so far. The merit of this approach, however, is that it allows us to specify how the components might relate to each other and so to set up alternative models based on different causal relations so that

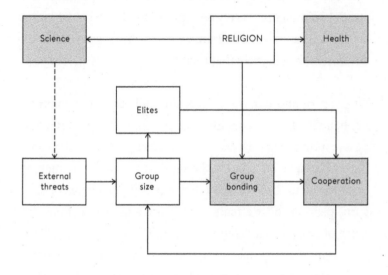

Figure 2
A flow diagram showing the most likely causal relationships between the five hypotheses for the function of religion (grey boxes). The thick solid arrows identify the main set of positive causal relationships that are fundamental to the existence of the whole system: without them, the benefits would not be strong enough to enable the other benefits of religion. The thinner solid arrows indicate positive relationships that arise as by-products of religion once it has evolved. The dotted lines indicate subsidiary positive causal links that emerge naturally when groups reach a particular size. The double dashed line indicates a negative causal relationship, as indicated by the negative sign by the arrow: improved knowledge about the world reduces environmental risk.

we can test between them to see which best explains what we see. This way we are led by the evidence rather than ideology. However, this is a major undertaking, so I won't do it now. Instead, I offer Figure 2 as my best guess based on what we know so that we can use it as a framework for the argument that I develop in the chapters that follow.

One way or another, then, there are individual and communal benefits associated with religion. They fit together like a jigsaw, interacting with each other and amplifying or dampening each others' effects. This being so, it raises a fundamental question as to the role that faith (belief in the claims of religion) plays in these effects. This is not a question about the truth of a particular religion, or of religions in general. That is a completely separate issue that need not concern us here. Rather, the issue is whether you *need* to believe in the tenets of the religion to get these benefits, or whether it is the rituals and actions associated with the religion that are the important component. I will come back to this question in Chapter 6. First, we need to explore in more detail the constraints that limit group size, and the relevance of these to religion.

CHAPTER 4
Communities and Congregations

Half a century ago, Allen Wicker, one of the founding fathers of organizational psychology, wanted to test some predictions about how size affected the functional efficiency of organizations. He lit upon church congregations as an ideal example. In a comparison of two Methodist churches, one with around 340 members and the other around 1,600, he found that people from the smaller church were more actively involved with their church's activities, approved more highly of what it did, attended Sunday services more often, donated a larger share of their income to the church and generally felt more engaged with their church community. Significantly, new members assimilated more easily into the smaller congregation.[1]

Subsequently, in a larger sample of all the churches in two Wisconsin church districts (ranging in size from 47 to 2,400 members), he confirmed that weekly attendance at services and individual donations to the church declined significantly as church size increased.[2] Since then, other studies have reported a similar negative relationship between church size, member satisfaction and how long individuals remain a member. One reason for this might be, as one study of 300 Lutheran churches found, that larger churches (those with about

800 members) become increasingly focused on external projects such as missionary activity to the detriment of investment in their own members.[3]

In this chapter, I want explore this size issue in more detail in order to establish both the size of community that religions were adapted to historically and the contexts involved at the time they originally evolved. I then want to ask whether this still holds true in the modern post-industrial world. Or, to put that question in a way more directly relevant to our concerns here: is there an ideal size for congregations?

Community Size and the Social Brain Hypothesis

Monkeys and apes – the zoological family to which we humans belong – live in groups that are very different to those found in almost all other mammals and birds. In effect, they are implicit social contracts: the groups exist to protect members against external threats such as predators and neighbouring groups. In most cases, this group defence is passive rather than active: living in a group deters predators without the need for collective defence simply because most predators (including humans) are reluctant to attack prey when these are in a large group. While most birds and mammals also cluster together when predators threaten, the groups they form when doing so are temporary: once the threat has passed, the herd disperses until the next time a predator hoves into view. Their herds are anonymous and animals do not often care who joins them so long as there is *somebody* to form a group with.

In contrast, primate groups have a characteristic bonded quality. It is the identity of the other group members that is important. This is reflected in the fact that group members make great efforts to ensure that they do not lose sight of each other; they are usually suspicious of strangers joining their group, and will act together in defence of the group when faced with external threats. This bondedness is a consequence of the fact that they invest a great deal of time in creating and maintaining close bonds with each other through social grooming. We will see in the next chapter that this process of bonding is a crucial part of the explanation for why religion might have evolved. These bonded groups are *very* different in character to the more casual groups of other mammals and birds. The only groups of these species that have the same social intensity as primate groups are the monogamous pair-bonds that characterize many birds and smaller mammals. The difference is that monkeys and apes scale these relationships up to groups of fifty or more individuals.

These bonded groups do not depend just on the glue provided by social grooming, however. Part of the mix that makes them work as protective coalitions is that individuals know and understand each other intimately as individuals. It is this cognitive component of primate social life that marks primate sociality out as unique in the animal kingdom. This cognitive component is reflected in what has become known as the social brain hypothesis.[4] The brains of all vertebrates evolved to allow them to engage more effectively with the world in which they live so as to maximize their chances of survival and successful reproduction in a world that is not always conducive to this end. Primates, however, have brains that are significantly larger for their body size than all other groups of animals, including the elephants and whales. This reflects the additional computing power needed to manage the dynamic complexity of their bonded social groups.

One reason why primate social groups are so demanding computationally is that interactions with other group members are not simple dyadic relationships in the way they are in anonymous herds. When I threaten you to make you move out of my way, it is no longer just an argument between the two of us; in bonded groups, you have friends and family, so my attack on you has repercussions for them. They are likely to come to your aid to defend their own status on future occasions, sometimes even to exercise a policing function to prevent disputes getting out of hand and causing others to leave the group in search of a quieter life. Since this complexity increases exponentially with the number of individuals in the group, brain size increases in proportion to a species' typical group size, giving rise to the social brain hypothesis.

The core of the social brain hypothesis is a simple linear relationship between the typical social group size of a species and the size of its brain – or, more strictly, the size of its neocortex. The neocortex (literally, 'new cortex') is the part of the cortex that supports all the clever thinking that we do. It has evolved out of all proportion to the size of the rest of the brain in the primate lineage. In mammals as a whole, it occupies 10–40 per cent of brain volume, but in primates it begins at 50 per cent and rises to 80 per cent in humans. This relationship between neocortex size and group size in primates allows us to estimate the equivalent 'natural' group size for humans: it is simply a matter of plugging human neocortex size into the equation for the monkeys and apes, and then reading off the corresponding group size. The group size for humans predicted by this equation is 150, to the nearest round number.

That this is the natural group size for humans has been confirmed by some two dozen studies that have measured either the size of natural human communities or the size of personal social networks (the number of friends and family you have).[5] Community size has been determined for hunter-gatherer societies, and for village size in small-scale agricultural societies (including the size of villages in Norman England as recorded in the Domesday Book and the size of medieval Alpine grazing associations), as well the sizes of military units in modern armies, academic research specialities and Twitter networks. Personal social networks have been measured from Christmas card distribution lists, egocentric social networks (for which people list all the friends and family they make an effort to keep in contact with), phone calling patterns (in both Europe and China), wedding guest lists, email networks, the number of friends listed on Facebook (one study sampled the number of friends listed by a million Facebook users) and science co-author networks (who co-authored papers with whom). All of these give averages that range between 100 and 200, with an overall average of almost exactly 150 individuals. Considering the wide range of sources and time periods involved, these data are remarkably consistent. The key point for us, perhaps, is that this is the typical size of hunter-gatherer communities, the form of society in which we have spent more than 95 per cent of our existence as a species.

That the size of our social groups is determined by the size of our brains is given added support by around a dozen neuroimaging studies of humans which show that the number of friends and family that individuals have (indexed by soliciting lists of names or counting friends listed on Facebook) correlates with the volume of particular regions in the brain.[6] This set of highly interconnected brain regions is known as the default mode neural network and involves a set of brain units in the prefrontal cortex, the temporal cortex, the temporo-parietal junction (TPJ) and the limbic system. This network makes up a significant proportion of the neocortex outside of those parts whose sole function is processing sensory inputs (such as the visual system, which occupies most of the back of our brain). These regions are responsible for recognizing animate beings, for processing and making sense of others' beliefs and mental states, and for managing our relationships.

To this general point, we should add a further refinement. Casual observation tells us that our circle of friends and family are not all equally valued by us. We distinguish fairly clearly between those whom we would consider intimates, good friends and, well, just friends. In fact, analyses both of the frequencies with which people contact or phone the members of their social networks and of their own ratings of how emotionally close they feel towards them indicate that this group of 150 people actually consists of a series of circles of very explicit size. These circles, when counted cumulatively, include 5 (close friends), 15 (best friends), 50 (good friends) and 150 ('just friends'), and then the layers continue out beyond through a layer of acquaintances (typically 500 people), 1,500 (faces you can put names to) and 5,000 (people whose faces you recognize), as illustrated in Figure 3.[7] We find the same structure in the patterns of interaction in online multi-player games and even in Twitter

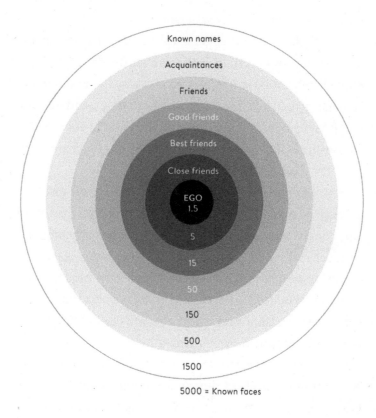

Known names

Acquaintances

Friends

Good friends

Best friends

Close friends

EGO
1.5

5

15

50

150

500

1500

5000 = Known faces

Figure 3
The fractal structure of personal social networks. The layers count cumulatively: the size of each layer includes the layer immediately inside it.[9]

conversations. Many of the people in the two outermost layers (1,500 and 5,000) will be faces we are familiar with from the media, or that we have seen regularly around town, rather than people we know personally.

Notice that the layers have a scaling ratio of almost exactly three: each layer is roughly three times the size of the layer immediately inside it. We have no idea why this scaling ratio is so consistent, but it turns up in every dataset, and we even find it in the layered structure of the societies of animals like chimpanzees, baboons, dolphins and elephants that live in complex societies.[8]

An important feature to note about these layers is that they correspond to rather specific frequencies of contact, perceived emotional closeness and willingness to give help. Not only are we much more willing to help (without expectation of reciprocation) those who are within our 150 circle compared to those in the layers outside it, but we also ration our altruism according to the friendship layer that the person lies in.[10] Conversely, we expect those in the innermost layers to leap to our help at the drop of a hat when we are in need, whereas we make no such presumption about those in the outer circles. To ensure this, we invest our social effort more heavily in the members of our innermost circles. So much so, in fact, that, of the three and a half hours we spend in social interaction with friends and family each day on average, about 40 per cent is invested in the five members of the innermost circle of close friends, and 60 per cent is invested in the fifteen people that make up the circle of best friends.[11] The rest of our time is distributed increasingly thinly among the remaining 135 members of our social network – an average of barely 30 seconds a day each.[12]

These effects reflect two important issues. One is that friendships, in particular, are very prone to decay if we do not invest time and effort in them. In a longitudinal study of 18-year-olds heading off to university, we found that if they made no effort to continue seeing their old school friends the emotional closeness ratings to these friends started to decline within a matter of months. Over the course of twelve months, average emotional closeness fell by about 15 per cent.[13] This means that within about three years, someone who had once been a close friend would end up as a mere acquaintance – someone you had once known but now probably wouldn't make the effort to contact. Within five years, they would have dropped off the edge of your social world altogether. Friendships are fragile and need continuous reinforcement. The second issue is that people's willingness to help us out, or provide us with emotional or other kinds of support, depends critically on how much time we invest in them. This, in turn, reflects the functions that the layers serve for us. Those in the innermost layers are the ones who will most willingly give us the emotional and other support we need when our life falls apart, and will do so without expecting anything in return – our 'shoulders to cry on' friends. Those in the outermost layers will certainly be willing to do small favours for us, but, unlike the shoulders-to-cry-on friends, they won't be willing to put their own lives on hold for months on end to help us to sort ourselves out.

How Small is a Small-scale Society?

Throughout our long evolutionary history, humans have lived in small-scale societies similar to those still found among contemporary hunter-gatherers. In these societies, families live in small, mobile bands or camp groups of five to ten families (30–50 men, women and children). Several of these camp groups form a distinct community (known as a clan in some societies) that usually has its own territory. Families can, and do, move between camp groups, but almost always within the same community. And when they do transfer between communities, it usually involves neighbouring communities that belong to the same tribe (the group of people who speak the same language or dialect).

The tribe seems to function as an ecological buffer: when famine or some disaster like a flood or a raid by another tribe hits your community territory, you can seek shelter with another of your tribe's communities who are far enough away to have avoided the catastrophe. Among Australian Aboriginals, for example, each band, or living group, 'owns' a portion of its tribe's ancestral myth – an origin story that is said to unfold across the tribal landscape like a giant snake, holding it all together as a coherent whole. In times of stress, a band will abandon its foraging territory and seek shelter with another band that shares the same myth. Fitting the two segments of the myth together like a key in a lock is the guarantee that these people are *your* people.

What defines all these groupings is that their members are related. The community itself seems to be delimited by the fact that it is, in effect, an extended family: all its members (aside from spouses, who usually come from a neighbouring community) will be the descendants of a single couple who are the great-great-grandparents of the current generation of children. These are the set of people who are related to us at no further remove than third cousins – the offspring of our grandparents' cousins. In fact, no culture in the world has a term to identify people who are more distantly related than this.[14] It essentially demarcates the limits of the extended family.

The tribe is, of course, an extended kinship group too, but one that is much larger: no member can hope to have personal knowledge of all the individuals involved. Instead, the tribe relies on tokens that identify membership, one of which, of course, is language. Ethnographically, a tribe is a group that shares a common language (or dialect, if the language has become especially widespread). The 'shibboleth effect' – how you pronounce particular words, or whether you know the meanings of certain obscure terms – is enough to identify whether or not you are a member of my tribe the moment you open your mouth. In the 1960s, social linguists estimated that you could identify a native English speaker's birthplace to within twenty-five miles from their dialect alone.

So how large are these groupings?

Analyses of data from contemporary hunter-gatherers suggest that these groupings of hierarchically organized social layers have pretty much the same sizes across all cultures. Bands, or camp groups, are, as I mentioned earlier, typically 30–50 individuals in size. Communities, or clans, typically number around 100–200, with an average very close to 150. And tribes typically number around 1,500 individuals. In between, there is usually another layer (sometimes referred to as a mega-band) at around 500, forming a very distinct series 50–150–500–1,500 (see Figure 4), with each layer once again including everyone in the layer inside it. In effect, a community of 150 consists of three bands of 50; a mega-band consists of three communities, and so on.[15]

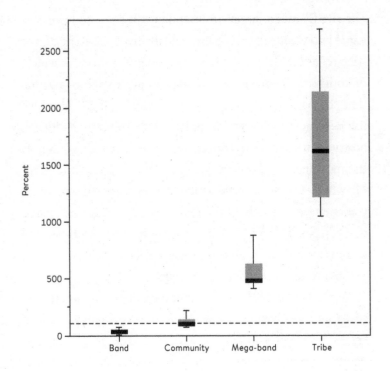

Figure 4
Mean (and 95% range) sizes of different groupings in a
sample of contemporary hunter-gatherer societies. The
horizontal line is at 150, the mean size for communities.[16]

In other words, prior to the Industrial Revolution, there seems to have been a characteristic community size that applied throughout most of the world that remained astonishingly stable over a very, very long period of time. To be sure, here and there we find larger communities that rank as towns and cities, but these were very rare and were invariably associated with seats of political power (petty kings, local overlords). However, these urban centres didn't appear until around 8,000 years ago during the Neolithic. But even after this, small communities seem to have been – and still are in terms of our personal social networks – the norm. There seems to be something that is psychologically very fundamental about the size and stability of a community size of around 150.

Is There an Optimal Congregation Size?

The fact that natural human communities have a size of about 150 people raises an obvious question: is this a natural size for religious congregations? In a widely cited study published in 1974, David Wasdell analysed data on congregation sizes at regular Sunday services for over 10,000 English parishes, and concluded that the number of attendees plateaued at around 175 people irrespective of the size of the local population – even when the local population was as large as 20,000 people. He referred to this effect as the 'self-limiting church'.[17] Other studies have reported that congregations with more than 150 regular attendees are more likely to lose members than gain them.

The expanding literature on church growth has also identified a distinct barrier at around 200, at which congregation sizes will stabilize because numbers leaving balance numbers joining.[18] Congregations will tend to oscillate around this size as members leave and join in increasing numbers unless steps are taken to mitigate the factors that cause people to leave. Some interest has also been expressed in what have been termed the 'Circles of Christ'. There were the three 'beloved disciples' (Peter, James and John), the twelve (originally thirteen) apostles, the approximately seventy disciples, and the 120 who gathered in the upper room on the first Pentecost, not to mention the feeding of the 5,000.[19] I am not entirely sure what to make of these kinds of numbers, but they do bear an uncanny resemblance to the values in Figure 3.

Many commentators have, on these grounds, recommended that 120 is the ideal congregation size. The theologian Gerhard Lohfink has argued that 'Only at that size can . . . each member . . . be aware of the sorrows and happiness, the cares and the joys of the others . . . [It] is the upper limit if a community is not to become an anonymous cultic society.'[20] Howard Snyder, who has been much concerned with evangelism programmes and establishing new churches, has suggested on the basis of his experience that '150–200 generally provides a good basis for spinning off daughter or sister congregations'.[21]

The Amish and Hutterites bear out this recommendation. These two Anabaptist sects moved from their respective homelands in Central Europe to North America in the early eighteenth and late nineteenth centuries, respectively. Both are fundamentalist, communalistic Christian sects that endeavour to live by the Bible, including, in the case of the Amish, refusing to use any form of modern technology (they use only horse-drawn transport, for example). Both have agricultural economies based on communally owned and managed farms run on a strictly democratic basis. The average size of eight Amish communities surveyed by one study was 113, roughly the average number of people that can be comfortably accommodated in their places of worship. The average size of fifty-one Hutterite communities was 109. These values reflect a strategy of splitting communities once they exceed 150 in size. This is done deliberately, so the Hutterites say, because it becomes impossible to manage the community by peer pressure alone once it exceeds about 150 in size. For community size to increase beyond this without collapsing in chaos, it would be necessary to have a formal system of laws and law enforcers. Since this would be against their entire ethos, they prefer to split the community and find a new farm for the daughter group. The average size at which communities split in one hundred community fissions over the last century was 165. Of particular interest is the fact that daughter communities of around 50 and 150 at foundation seemed to last longer without having to undergo fission again than communities at intermediate sizes.[22] It seems that there is something especially stable about these two numbers, with some suggestion that communities might try and delay fission until their size is large enough to allow daughter communities of about these magic numbers.

During the eighteenth and nineteenth centuries, a large number of millenarian communities established themselves in the USA, in part because of its more relaxed attitude towards freedom of religion and in part because there was the space to avoid getting into conflict with neighbours who held different views. Many of these communities eschewed the evils of the secular world, and deliberately secluded themselves on self-contained farms. In many cases, they were influenced by the ideas of the Welsh social reformer Robert Owen and sought to establish a new, more equitable and humane society.[23]

Some of these communities were based on strictly secular philosophies, while others had a strongly religious ethos, and there were a number of illuminating differences between these two types. When they were founded, communes averaged about 150 if they had a religious basis and about 50 if they were secular. More importantly, longevity was maximized at exactly these values, with the average lifetime of a community being just fifteen years for secular communities compared to 100 years for the religious ones.[24] Somewhat similar findings were found for Israeli *kibbutzim*. The 240 *kibbutzim* sampled averaged about 470 members at the time they were surveyed in 2000, very close to the 500-layer in Figure 3. The economy of these communities is mainly commercial agriculture, so it is understandable that their size might be larger since they need a larger workforce than the self-sufficient Hutterite and Amish family-based farms. Even so, religious *kibbutzim* were able to cope with larger numbers of people: on average, they were approximately 168 people larger than secular kibbutzim, controlling for their age.[25]

The differences in size and longevity between religious and secular communities suggest that a religious ethos somehow enables the members to keep a lid on the fractiousness and squabbles that inevitably arise in small communities, thereby preventing the community from tearing itself apart. Whether this is because of a Moralizing High God effect, or because having to make costly commitments in order to join makes it more difficult to leave (and so you had better make the best of it), or because the religious rituals they practise together engender a sense of belonging and commitment is not clear. Notably, one of the longest lasting of the American religious communities (the Shakers) made extensive use of simple, highly synchronized dances in their religious services, and this would undoubtedly have enhanced the sense of community bonding (see Chapter 5). In the absence of a religious *esprit de corps*, communities probably have to resort to a more vigorous enforcement policy to prevent things getting out of hand. This was, in fact, evident in the Israeli *kibbutzim*: as their size increased (and the stresses of communal living presumably escalated), secular *kibbutzim* responded by instituting a variety of surveillance mechanisms to monitor members' behaviour, whereas religious communities seemingly found this unnecessary.[26]

Even the Shakers were not immune to the problems created by living in large communities. In an analysis of the covenants (when joining) and wills and discharges (when leaving voluntarily)[27] of eighteenth- and nineteenth-century Shaker communities, John Murray concluded that there was an increasing tendency over time for the less literate to join the communities but the more literate to leave.[28] Assuming that literacy corresponded roughly to wealth, he attributed the first to a tendency for the less well-off to join the communities in search of a more stable income, and the latter to the wealthier members becoming increasingly disillusioned with the number of freeriders and shirkers exploiting their goodwill and the generosity of the community. That the latter might have been a problem is indicated by the fact that many of the later meeting-house bell towers had balconies or windows that allowed the activities of those working in the fields to be monitored. In addition, meeting-room walls often had spyholes though which the diligence of the congregation could be checked.

Taken together, these various findings suggest that there is an optimal congregation size of about 150 people. At this size, both the priest and the congregation members know each other personally. This discussion has obviously been limited to data from a variety of Christian denominations, mainly because I have not been able to locate any information on the size of congregations for other world religions. However, the effect seems to be robust, so I would be surprised if other religions exhibited a vastly different pattern. Certainly, most synagogues, mosques and Sikh *gurdwara* seem to be about the same physical size as churches, suggesting that their congregations are unlikely to be any larger.

Dynamics of Congregations

A recent analysis of data from 250 congregations (representing over 50,000 church attenders) identified four distinct size clusters: small congregations (around 40 members), average (around 150), large (500) and mega-churches (2,000+). Those in larger churches were less likely to be socially embedded in their congregations, even though larger churches might have more capacity for engaging in outreach within the wider community – mainly, of course, because they receive more in gross donations and because they have relatively more individuals with the capacity to undertake these additional activities. There was some suggestion that there might be a phase transition at a size of about 150 where a congregation switches from being a community that is focused in on itself to one that, while more fragmented internally, is more open to broader civic involvement.[29]

These numbers map quite closely onto the layers in Figures 3 and 4. The principal issues faced by congregations larger than about 200 are the pastor's inability to cope singlehandedly with the demands of the congregation (both in terms of knowing individual members well enough and in terms of pure time demands) and a loss of focus by the members themselves. Complaints among the parishioners often centre around the fact that they no longer know everyone and they lack a sense of belonging. If churches become much larger than this, they can usually do so only if they evolve a range of small, intimate groups with very specific foci, such as bible-reading groups, discussion groups, prayer groups, volunteer groups, and so on. Such groups will usually need to meet regularly (for example, weekly) and their optimal size appears to be around fifteen people. Joining these can restore the sense of belonging and commitment.

A recent survey of over 300 church members found that members' satisfaction was determined mainly by their religious commitment, their life satisfaction and their emotional closeness to the rest of their congregation. In other words, religious commitment seemed to drive both a greater sense of satisfaction with one's church and with the trajectory of one's life. These effects declined as congregation size increased, thus adding to the earlier findings that large congregations lead to an increasing sense of dissatisfaction. From a survey of satisfied and dissatisfied church members, the study concluded that there were three dimensions to

satisfaction with one's congregation: an affective component (feeling comfortable in the congregation and being willing to give to the church), a purposive component (the ethos
and vision of the congregation) and a social component (how
well embedded within the congregation the person is). As
before, these were significantly correlated with religiosity.[30]

Another study identified a 'pastoral-to-program plateau
zone' between 150 and 250 at which congregations become
quite unsettled. It seems to involve a kind of in-between
zone where the congregation is too large for the pastor to
engage with church members at a personal level, yet too
small to provide the financial and other advantages of the
next size up. Three stable phases in church size were identified, with upper limits at 50, 150 and 350 members – 'Family
size', 'Pastor size' and 'Program size', respectively. These
limits seemed to correspond to a series of switches between
diffused and centralized forms of leadership. Family-sized
churches of up to 50 can effectively work as leaderless de-
mocracies, whereas pastor-sized churches of 50–150 require
someone to act as the leader and symbolic anchor for two or
three sub-groups within the congregation. Once congregation size enters the third phase, however, it is too large for a
single pastor to manage, and a team approach is required.[31]

These results mirror quite closely the switch from democratic to formal management organization in the business
world. Emily Webber, who advises organizations on person-
nel management, sampled informal Communities of Practice (CoPs) in the business world.[32] When we analysed her
data, we found that there was a transition at a community
size of about forty from communities managed without any

formal leadership to ones with some kind leadership team structure.[33] As with congregations, larger CoPs experienced increasing levels of dissatisfaction, failure to attend meetings regularly, and complaints about others' unwillingness to help with organizing meetings. Mirroring the contrast we found in the nineteenth-century American millenarian communities, the limiting size for secular CoPs before needing management structures was about forty, in contrast to church congregations where the equivalent seems to be around 150. Once again, it seems that a religious ethos has added value in creating stability.

These results suggest that what limits congregation size is the balance between the forces of belonging (which are higher in smaller groups) and the forces of fragmentation (which increase with group size). Large congregations result in an increasing sense of dysphoria and alienation for those members of the congregation that are not part of the central core responsible for running the parish and an increasing sense of lack of control (your activities are at the behest of a small elite cohort over which you have no control). To grow larger than 150, new structural arrangements are necessary. These might involve formal management systems (and discipline imposed from above), or they might involve the sub-structuring of the congregation in ways that allow members to focus on special interests that they can share with like-minded individuals.[34]

At the outset of this chapter, I stressed the remarkable sociality of primates for two reasons. One is that the equation for the primate social brain hypothesis allows us to predict, with surprising accuracy, the natural size of human social groups. This, it turns out, also seems to be the optimal size of church congregations. The second, as we shall see in later chapters, is that our origin in this remarkable group of animals provides a very coherent explanation for how and why religions evolved – and why they evolved only in the human lineage. To set the scene for this, let me summarize the main points so far. These are: (1) primates live in bonded social groups in order to protect themselves from external threats, (2) a species' brain size limits the size of its groups (which in turn is adapted to the level of threat a species typically experiences, given its preferred habitats and foraging patterns), (3) natural human social groups and personal social networks fit rather neatly into this pattern, (4) there is a distinct limit at about 150 on the size of natural human communities, personal social networks *and* church congregations, and (5) this limit seems to be set by the effect of group size on the members' sense of belonging, personal knowledge of the other members and general satisfaction with the benefits of membership.

In the next two chapters, I explore in more detail the psychological and behavioural bases of the bonding processes that create this sense of belonging, and the way these relate to the role of rituals in religion. I shall then use these findings in the chapters that follow to explore the role that religion has played historically in the bonding of small-scale communities, and the reasons for the transition from shamanic to doctrinal religions.

CHAPTER 5

Social Brain, Religious Mind

The central problem faced by all mammal societies is how to overcome the naturally centrifugal forces that threaten to fragment social communities. These stresses arise out of the fact that every individual has their own objectives and life schedules. Disagreements, even about such trivial matters as which direction to forage in, quickly lead to the fragmentation of groups. Monkeys and apes solve this problem by creating networks of bonded relationships through social grooming. Grooming provides the glue that maintains social cohesion, and it does this mainly through a sense of commitment and obligation that regular grooming partners have for each other. But precisely because grooming is an intensely intimate activity, it ultimately sets an upper limit on the number of individuals an animal can groom with, and hence on the size of the bonded social group. In monkeys and apes, this limit is at around fifty individuals.

Hunter-gatherers typically live in camp groups or bands of fewer than fifty individuals, but these, unlike most primate groups, are embedded in higher-level groupings – several camp groups make up a community, several communities a mega-band, several mega-bands a tribe (Figure 4). The community of about 150 represents the social and cognitive equivalent of the primate group, so our ancestors had to find ways to break through the grooming glass ceiling at fifty in order to be able to evolve the large, bonded groups of 150 that we now live within. And, having done so, they then had to find ways to create the higher-level groupings beyond the community that they subsequently developed. How we managed this is the subject of this chapter.

The Bonds That Bind

Social grooming occurs in a number of mammal lineages, but nowhere is it used to quite the same extent as among primates. Some of the more intensely social monkeys and apes can devote up to a fifth of their entire day to this seemingly frivolous activity. During grooming, one animal leafs through the fur of another, removing burrs and bits of vegetation, scabs and other blemishes. While a useful function, the real importance of social grooming actually lies in the hand movement itself, and the way the hands brush across the fur and surface of the skin. In doing so, they trigger a highly specialized set of neurons in the skin that respond only to light, slow stroking. These neurons, known as the afferent C-tactile (or CT) neurons, connect directly to the brain and their sole purpose is to trigger the release of endorphins deep within it.

Endorphins are the brain's own painkillers and their effects are exactly those created by more conventional opiates to which they are chemically closely related: a sense of calmness, warmth, happiness and 'all is well with the world'.[1] Activation of the endorphin system is reflected in elevated pain thresholds: the opiate-like effects of endorphins allow us tolerate higher levels of pain. They also have two important downstream effects. One is that they stimulate the production of NK ('natural killer') cells by the immune system. These cells are an important part of the body's armoury for detecting and destroying viruses and other pathogens that have found their way into our bodies, as well as some cancer cells, which may partly explain the health benefits of religion that we remarked on in Chapter 2. The other major role of endorphins, however, lies in creating bonded relationships. The warmth we feel from the release of endorphins during grooming seems to create a sense of belonging and trust with the individual who is grooming us. Thus, not only do endorphins lighten our mood and make us feel more engaged socially, they also 'tune' the immune system and help to keep us healthy.

Although we lost most of our fur around two million years ago, we still 'groom' – though this now mostly takes the form of stroking, hugging and cuddling.[2] Using PET neuroimaging technology, we have been able to confirm that lightly stroking the skin surface floods the brain with endorphins.[3] There is, however, a problem with grooming as a bonding mechanism. Touching someone is a very intimate action. So much so that neither monkeys nor humans ever groom two individuals simultaneously. Combined with the fact that we have to keep investing a great deal of grooming time into each friendship to make it work as a relationship, this limits the number of individuals with whom we can form bonded relationships.[4] In monkeys and apes, this sets the upper limit on the size of bonded social groups at around fifty individuals. The problem that our ancestors faced when they needed to increase the size of their social groups was, in effect, how to groom with two or more people simultaneously. The only realistic solution was to find ways of triggering the endorphin system that did nor require direct physical touch.

The solution they found was a series of behaviours that all trigger the endorphin system and which now form the core of our social interactions with each other. These are, in the order in which they were probably acquired: laughter, singing, dancing, emotional storytelling, feasting (communal eating and the social drinking of alcohol) and, last but not least, the rituals of religion. For obvious reasons, these are all unique to humans, necessarily so for those behaviours that depend on language. The only partial exception is the earliest, laughter. Laughter derives from the monkey and ape play vocalization – a distinctive panting vocalization that they use both to invite play and to comment on play ('What I am about to do is to be interpreted as play and not as aggression'). The only difference is that we have adjusted the structure of laughter from a series of simple, low-key pants to heavy-duty exhalations in which the chest wall muscles vigorously pump air out of the lungs with great force, thereby emptying the lungs and leaving us gasping for air. The physiological stresses involved in doing this trigger the endorphin system in a very effective way.

These novel forms of grooming-at-a-distance now form the toolkit that underpins the way we interact socially, especially in the context of community building. As we have shown in a series of experimental studies over the last deacde, all these activities trigger an endorphin response in the brain, and in doing so they create a sense of bonhomie and bonding. Of particular interest in the present context is the fact that emotional storytelling elevates pain thresholds and enhances bonding – mainly because psychological pain is experienced in exactly the same part of the brain where we experience physical pain. To show this, we asked people to watch either the emotionally charged film *Stuart – A Life Backwards* or some fairly dull factual TV documentaries in groups that varied in size between five and fifty.[5] Even though the people in any given group were strangers to each other, those who responded to the emotional charge of the film had significantly elevated pain thresholds after watching it (indicating endorphin activation) *and* at the same time felt more bonded to the strangers with whom they had watched the film.

The big advantage of all these activities is that we can do them at a distance without having to touch anyone. Consequently, we can 'groom' simultaneously with more than one person without also triggering the intimacy problem that physical touch causes. There is a limit, of course, on the number of people that can take part and feel the effect, but that limit is much greater than the one person possible with social grooming. The most restricted seems to be laughter: there seems to be a limit on the size of natural laughter groups at around three people (effectively the size of a natural conversation group).[6] That's still three times more efficient than grooming, of course, where only the recipient of grooming gets the hit. Singing, in contrast, seems to scale up almost infinitely: in one of our studies, the endorphin hit and heightened sense of bonding was significantly higher in an amateur choir of 200 than in sub-choirs of 20 from the same group.[7]

The mechanism involved in all these activities is the same as that which makes social grooming work as a bonding process. Given how easily emotionally arousing stories like *Stuart* activate the endorphin system, should we be surprised that the

stories that form the bedrock of most religions invariably involve trials that were surmounted only with difficulty or end
in martyrdom, or that sermons are often emotionally arousing
(even when they are not of the fire-and-brimstone variety)?

There is one aspect of bonding, however, that seems to
be particularly relevant to religion. This is the fact that the
feelings aroused in certain religious contexts are surprisingly
similar to those associated with an intense romantic relationship.[8] So much so, in fact, that it is not unusual for religious people to declare that they are 'in love with God'. The
writings of many of the Christian mystics (Teresa of Ávila,
Thérèse of Lisieux, Julian of Norwich, John van Ruysbroeck)
give an unambiguous impression to this effect. No one illustrates this better than Thérèse of Lisieux.

In 1888, aged just fifteen, Marie-Françoise Thérèse Martin
followed her two oldest sisters into the cloistered Carmelite
community at Lisieux in Normandy.[9] Nine years later, aged
twenty-four, she died of tuberculosis following a long strug-
gle with both the disease and self-doubt. After her death, her
autobiographical *The Story of a Soul*, written to encourage the
young postulants she mentored at the convent, was published
by her sister (by then Mother Superior). It captured the public
imagination through its combination of simplicity, humility, intense exhilaration and emotional warmth. She quickly acquired
a large posthumous international following. In 1925, she was
canonized as a saint of the Catholic Church, quickly becoming the second most popular of all its saints after St Francis
of Assisi. In 1997, she was declared the thirty-third Doctor of
the Church, the youngest ever to be elevated to this very select
group of theologians and educators.

Here, from her *Story of a Soul*, is just a flavour of this sense of the intensity of religious emotional attachment:

How lovely it was, that first kiss of Jesus in my heart – it was truly a kiss of love. I knew that I was loved, and said 'I love You, and I give myself to You for ever . . .' 'Ah! Love, my radiant beacon light, I know the way to reach You now, and I have found the hidden secret of making all Your flames my own!'

We find similar sentiments in other religions. In the Sufi tradition of Islam, the mystical songs known as *qawwali* arouse the performers and listeners to the edge of religious trance. Many are based on Arabic or Persian *ghazal* (poems of unrequited love) and are deeply infused with an ambiguous sexuality. These lines are from one of the most beautiful, the Urdu poem 'Kali kali zulphon ke phande (You with such long beautiful hair)':

The glance that pierces me
calms my heart;
beneath the shade of your tresses
the darkness is pleasing.

This is the same sense of unrequited love as we find in the Old Testament *Song of Solomon*:

I opened to my beloved,
. . . But my beloved had turned and gone.

These poems are all invariably interpreted as referring to God, but there is no mistaking the underlying psychology. This is romantic attachment of the kind that is directed at both conventional romantic partners and platonic friend-ships (the 'best friend forever' phenomenon that is particu-larly characteristic of women).[10]

When we fall in love, we do not fall in love with a real person 'out there' but with what is, in effect, an avatar – an idealized mental construction in our heads. Of course, in real life, periodic face-to-face engagement with the object of our desires provides an important degree of ground-truthing that gradually imposes some discipline on our runaway thoughts. But when that ground-truthing is thwarted, our minds are liable to run away with us. We see this most conspicuously in the context of romantic scams on the internet, where the fact that scammers carefully avoid meeting their victim allows a level of immersion in the relationship to build up to the point where the victim is simply unable to back out or think ra-tionally about it. At this point, they are willing to give and give and give. Unrequited love seems to ramp up this effect dramatically.[11]

In part, this seems to be due to the fact that immersion in the relationship causes the faculty for critical thinking to be inhibited. There is evidence from brain scan studies that, when this happens, it is the ventral prefrontal cortex that seems to be involved.[12] This brain region is not only heavily involved in processing emotions and the emotional side of social relationships, it also dampens down the limbic sys-tem's more automated panic 'fight-or-flight' messages when it thinks these are inappropriate or would prevent us achiev-ing our desired objective.

Trust and the Seven Pillars of Friendship

Primate social bonding is the outcome of a dual-process mechanism. The endorphin system, and the sense of bondedness this produces, creates a pharmacological environment of trust that allows a second, more directly cognitive, mechanism to kick in. In monkeys and apes, this takes the form of understanding another animal's actions and responses. In humans, this pulls into play a set of cultural criteria that function mainly as cues of community membership, and hence trustworthiness. When we looked at the traits people share with their friends and family, we found that these distilled down to seven key dimensions, the Seven Pillars of Friendship.[13] They are: sharing the same language, place of origin, educational trajectory, hobbies and interests, worldview (religious, moral and political views), musical tastes and sense of humour. The more of these that you and I have in common, the stronger the relationship between us will be and the more willing we will be to act altruistically towards each other. This is as true for family members as it is for friends.

Each layer in Figure 3 corresponds to a particular number of 'pillars' (six or seven for the innermost circle of five, no more than one or two by the time you get to 150). When we meet someone who seems potentially interesting as a friend, we devote a great deal of time to them, meeting them as often as we can and engaging them in conversation. What we are doing, in fact, is assessing where they stand on the Seven Pillars, gauging their similarity to us. Once we have determined this, we reduce the frequency of contact to the level appropriate for the layer that their similarity on the Seven

Pillars would put them in. It is this that gives rise to the striking homophily – the tendency for 'birds of a feather to flock
together' – that is a defining characteristic of human friendships and even, it seems, family relationships.

We think that the reason the Pillars work is that they all
point to the small community in which we grew up – the
community where we learned who we are, why and how we
belong to a particular confraternity. We know the same folk
tales, the same songs, the same dances, the same places; we
believe in the same things, share the same attitudes, the
same morality . . . we think about the world in the same way.
It is this sense of belonging that allows us to develop a strong
sense of trust. I know exactly how far I can trust you because
I know intuitively how you think.

An important feature of these communities in small-scale
ethnographic societies, and until relatively recently in our
own village societies, is that these cues identify a group of
100–200 people who are related by descent or marriage. They
are an extended kinship group. In addition, these small communities were bound together as much as anything by the
moral persuasion of great-grandmother sitting by her fireside,
wagging her finger at the behaviour of miscreants who dare
to step out of line or behave badly towards one of her many
descendants. Such communities are interconnected networks
of relationships round which gossip flows, and within which
relationships of obligation reverberate through many routes.

Although the primary function of the Seven Pillars is to
identify those whom we are likely to feel emotionally close
to, they also provide a useful first-pass basis for assessing
the trustworthiness of strangers. For this, simply satisfying

one of the Pillars is enough to establish the basis for a casual, working relationship – not a relationship of great intimacy, but one that is at least based on some commonly held interests or principles.

In one of our experiments, we asked the subjects how they might view a stranger with a particular set of values on the various Pillars. When it comes to evaluating complete strangers, the most important traits for predicting both likeability and emotional closeness are having the same religious views, the same moral views, the same political views and the same musical tastes (Figure 5). The first three of these, of course, belong to the same Pillar (your worldview). We were, however, struck by how often musical tastes kept cropping up. We wondered if this might reflect the important role that singing and dancing play in triggering the endorphin system and promoting social bonding. If you like the same music, you know how to dance in synchrony with the rest of us. Notice, by the way, that, even in the context of meeting a complete stranger, ethnicity plays a very marginal role, and is much less significant than shared culture.[14]

That religion exerts such a strong hold on friendships may perhaps explain the fact that members of the same religion often seem to gravitate towards each other and to be unusually willing to go to each other's aid even in contexts of considerable personal risk – despite the fact that they have nothing else in common. It might also account for the fact that religions frequently use the language of kinship, and especially close family relationships, when referring to their members. The terms 'father' (as a term of respect for priests, as well as for God), 'mother' (as a term of respect for senior nuns and

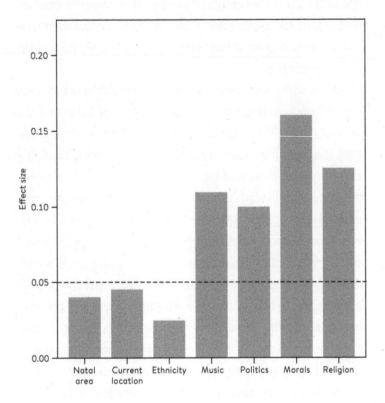

Figure 5
Weightings of different traits on ratings of likely emotional closeness (indexed by the Inclusion of Other in Self, IOS, rating scale) to a stranger – in other words, how likely they are to make a good friend. The factors are the similarity in a stranger's profile on a trait to that of the subject. The horizontal dashed line indicates statistical significance. Note that traits like musical tastes, moral views and religion are much more important than ethnicity or where you happen to live now (current location, as opposed to where you grew up).

for the Virgin Mary), 'sisters' and 'brothers' (both as terms of address for monastic religious and as a general term referring to co-religionists) are widely used, especially among the Abrahamic religions. Indeed, the term 'family' is often used for the religious community itself – the 'family of the church', the Bruderhof (or Society of Brothers), the Family Federation for World Peace (otherwise known as the Rev. Moon's Unification Church), the Plymouth Brethren, and so on. It seems suspiciously like an attempt to use a priming effect to exploit the emotional pull of family. Family has very powerful appeal.

The significance of the Seven Pillars is that they allow us to form large groups based solely on shared cultural icons. For this, even a single Pillar is enough to create a community. It is this that has allowed us to evolve our super-large communities – weakly bonded because they may rest on just one Pillar, but good enough to present a common front to whatever external threat demands a super-large coalition. This is made possible by the fact that, while we form small groups as a result of our bonds with specific individuals just as monkeys and apes do, the Seven Pillars also allow us to be bonded to the wider group as an abstract concept, irrespective of its actual membership. In other words, we can form clubs whose membership can be quite anonymous, but by virtue of being attached to the concept of the club, however tenuous, we *feel* that we are 'brothers in arms'. This seems to be a uniquely human capacity, but it seems to explain why membership of a religion can create this sense of belonging and a willingness to go to the aid of a fellow member of the club.

CHAPTER 5

Minding Your Ps and Qs

Of all the things that go on inside our heads on the average day, the most important for our present concerns is the capacity to mentalize. Also known variously as theory of mind or mindreading, mentalizing is the ability to understand someone else's intentions. The concept was originally proposed by the English philosopher of language Paul Grice, who in the 1950s suggested that much of the work in conversational exchanges was done by the listener rather than the speaker: the listener has to work out what the speaker is *intending* to mean, not least because the actual words uttered by the speaker are often ambiguous – we often find it difficult to express in words our inner feelings and emotions. This capacity is exemplified by the ability to use words like *knowing, thinking, supposing, wondering, imagining, intending* – known collectively to philosophers of language as intentional terms.

In the 1980s, these ideas were developed by the philosopher Daniel Dennett in his concept of the *intentional stance*, the suggestion that evolution has designed the human mind to interpret the world in intentional terms – mainly, of course, because both the core to that world and our interface with it is through interactions with other people. He pointed out that this phenomenon of mindreading is recursive, with a potentially infinite series of recursions: I *think* that you *suppose* that I am *wondering* why you *believe* . . . (with the successive mindstates being identified by the italicized verbs). Each mindstate is characterized by an 'intentional' word – that is, an active verb that describes someone's thought process. In this case, there are four embedded mindstates, making this a fourth-order intentional statement. The sequence must always begin with your mental state (you have to be thinking of something), but the mindstates that you are reflecting on can be a mix of your own and any number of other people's.

Being able to reflect on your own mindstate is defined as having first order intentionality (I *know* the contents of my own mind). Formal theory of mind is defined as the capacity to reflect on someone else's mindstate. Doing so enables us to realize that others have minds of their own and hence might have a view about the world that is different from the one we believe to be true (a so-called false belief). It is the equivalent, in the philosopher's schema, of having second-order intentionality ('I *know* that you *know* . . .'). Children acquire this capacity at around the age of four to five, having previously assumed that other people believe exactly the same as whatever they happen to believe (they are first-order intentional). Acquiring theory of mind has a dramatic impact on what children can do, since once they have crossed this particular Rubicon they can engage in imaginary play (knowing that it is only pretence), construct fictional stories and lie convincingly (because they understand how you will interpret what they say and so how to manipulate that).

Psychologists tend to stop at this point because most of the those who study theory of mind are developmental psychologists interested in children's early years or clinical psychologists interested in psycho-pathologies such as autism where lack of theory of mind is a defining characteristic. However, as Dennett pointed out, intentionality is a naturally recursive phenomenon and normal adults can manage much higher orders of mentalizing. What he did not know the answer for was how many orders of intentionality a normal adult could cope with.

Over the years, we have run a number of studies to explore this question, and they all agree that the upper limit on intentionality is typically around fifth order, meaning I can manage four other people's mindstates at any given time in addition to my own. In other words, we can manage to keep track of a sentence as complicated as 'I *think* that Bill *supposes* that Jennifer *wants to know* wheter Peter *intends* to ask Susan whether she *believes* that the meeting was arranged for two o'clock', where the italicized verbs identify the successive mindstates, but that's the upper limit for most of us. There is, inevitably perhaps, considerable individual variation in this capacity, with normal (or 'neurotypical') adults ranging between third and sixth order. Only about 20 per cent of the adult population can do better than fifth order, however. We have also shown that our mindreading capacity (how many mindstates we can handle at any given moment) determines a number of crucial aspects of our social behaviour. These include the complexity of the language we can use (in terms of the grammatical structure of its sentences), the complexity of the fictional stories we enjoy most, the typical size of conversation groups and the number of close friends we have.[15]

We and others have shown, in a number of neuroimaging studies, that the size of the network of neurons in the brain known as the default mode network correlates with both your mentalizing competences *and* the number of friends you have. It seems that the causal pathway here is that the size of these brain units determines your mentalizing competences, and your mentalizing competences then determine how many relationships you can manage to maintain at any one time.[16] The default mode network (also known as the theory of mind network) is a group of brain regions that interconnect directly with each other through major fibre tracts (the bundles of neurons that provide the wiring of the brain). It involves four main brain units. The prefrontal cortex right at the front of the brain (an area broadly associated with both rational thought and the interpretation of emotional cues), the temporo-parietal junction (a small region just behind and above the ear where the parietal and temporal lobes meet that is strongly associated with responses to living beings), parts of the temporal lobe (the brain's sausage-like extension along the side just inside the ear, associated mainly with memory storage) and the limbic system, especially the amygdala (which is responsible for processing emotional cues). This large neural network is heavily involved in interpreting social and emotional cues, and in managing our relationships.

Mentalizing and the Religious Mind

Psychologists and philosophers have always viewed mentalizing as the ability to reflect on mindstates, whether your own or someone else's. But if you think about it in terms of the brain's computational demands (its ability to process information), what it actually involves is the ability to step back from the world as we directly experience it and *imagine* that there is another parallel world (your mind). I have to be able to model that other world in my mind and predict its behaviour while at the same time managing the behaviour of the physical world right in front of me. The important distinction here is between your *behaviour* (which is part of that physical world that I perceive directly) and your *intentions* (or mental states) that I cannot perceive directly but have to imagine (usually by inferring your inner thoughts from some aspect of your visible behaviour – what you say, how you say it, the grimaces and handwaving movements you make). In effect, I have to be able to run two versions of reality simultaneously in my mind. It seems to be this extra level of mental work – simultaneously running two versions of reality (your mind and my mind) that might be at odds with each other – that is computationally so expensive for the brain. This explains why, as we showed in one of our experiments, many more neurons are recuited when we are thinking about someone's mental state than when we simply think about their behaviour, and why this recruitment increases with every additional mindstate added into our thought process.[17]

Mentalizing is so natural a skill, and we are so well practised at it by the time we are adult, that most of us don't give it a second thought, never mind appreciate just how sophisticated it is in information-processing terms. Yet it was fundamental for the appearance of religion for at least four reasons. First, without the capacity to imagine that there is another, transcendental, parallel universe inhabited by spirit beings, it is not possible to have a religion of any kind. To do that, I have to be able to step back from the world in which we live and ask whether such a world could even exist. Mentalizing is what makes this possible. Second, without the ability to understand that other organisms have mental states, it is impossible to imagine that there might be intentional beings that live in that alternative spirit world. With second-order intentionality, I might be able to imagine that such a spirit world exists just as I can imagine that the world of your mind exists. But at the moment, it is still only a belief I think you have; I haven't yet agreed with you. Nonetheless, for me even to begin to imagine that you hold such a belief requires, at an absolute minimum, third-order intentionality. Third, our ability to unpack the grammatical structure of sentences, or propositions, turns out to be directly related to our mentalizing competencies.[18] In other words, someone limited to third-order intentionality can only understand propositions of the form 'A → B → C' (where A, B and C are clauses in a proposition), whereas someone able to achieve fifth-order intentionality can manage one with the structure 'A → B → C → D → E'. Fourth, and most importantly, without the ability to communicate my ideas about this to someone else it is not possible to have any kind of formal religion. I might well believe in the existence of God, but that on its own doesn't equate to a religion; it is simply a belief. A belief becomes a religion only when at least two of us agree about its tenets. To do so, we both have to agree that a proposition about a religious fact is true.

Although it is obvious that mentalizing plays an essential role in our ability to think about the world, it is not at all obvious how many orders of intentionality are needed to achieve any of them. As we saw earlier, normal humans only have five orders of intentionality to play with. But do we need all five to conceive of, and hence believe in, God? Could we have religion with two or three orders of intentionality? This will turn out to be important when, in a later chapter, we come to investigate the timing of the origin of religion. So let me spell out the basic idea here.

Table 1 specifies the kinds of religious statements that we

can make with different levels of intentional competence. The sequence starts with first-order intentionality. All conscious animals are first-order intentional: they have beliefs in that they know what they are thinking. They cannot, however, have beliefs about other individuals' beliefs. A first-order being assumes that everyone else has the same knowledge as it does; it cannot appreciate that someone else might see the world differently, and so might hold a different belief about it. To have a belief about someone else's beliefs, you need second-order intentionality as a minimum. Even so, these beliefs must necessarily be factual beliefs about things or events in the world ('that hill is very high' or 'it's about to rain'). To be able to appreciate that you hold a belief about the existence of a *transcendental* world that cannot be directly experienced I have to go one step beyond the simple factual content of your mind, and that requires three orders of intentionality because I have to create a model of the model that is in your mind.

If I can graduate to third-order intentionality, I can *believe* that you *think* that there is some other world in which God exists. The important point here is not just that you have a belief about some physical fact ('I believe the tree in front of me exists') but that you have a belief about an invisible world that you have to be able to imagine. It's a two-step process, involving two orders of intentionality. At this point, we now have what I would call a simple religious fact – a belief about the existence of a transcendal world, but not about the impact that world would have on us in our world. To be able to imagine that God also has an intentional mind, I have to be able to achieve a further order of intentionality. Once I can do that (with fourth-order intentionality), I can imagine that God has

Intentionality level	Possible statements of belief	Form of Religion
1st	I *believe* that [rain is falling]	not possible
2nd	I *believe* that you *think* [rain is falling]	not possible
3rd	I *believe* that you *think* that God *exists* [in a transcendental world]	religious fact
4th	I *believe* that you *think* that God *exists* and *intends* to punish us	personal religion
5th	I *believe* that you *think* that we both *know* that God *exists* and *intends* to punish us	communal religion

Table 1
Forms of religious belief that are made possible by different levels of intentionality.

intentions that might affect our world. At this level, we have what I call *personal religion*. It is a personal belief that only the believer is committed to; when I think about your belief in this respect, however, I do not have to accept that it is true. Only with fifth-order intentionality is it possible to formulate a proposition about God's intentional status that we can *both* sign up to. At this point, we are both committed to our belief in God's intentions, and so we can have a genuinely *communal religion*. This seems to be a real Rubicon, or phase shift. We will see why this distinction is important in Chapter 7.

To explore the mentalizing bases of religious belief in more depth, nearly 300 people were asked to complete a set of questionnaires that measured their mentalizing skills, the effectiveness of their agency detection mechanism, their schizotypal tendencies and their religious beliefs and behaviours (religiosity).[19] Agency detection is the tendency to attribute human (or at least sentient) traits to non-living matter (see Chaper 1), and is often measured by peoples' willingness to give intentional or anthropomorphic descriptions when watching abstract shapes moving randomly on a screen. Examples include using comments like: 'The circle is chasing the square' or 'The triangle is threatening the circle' when in actual fact the shapes are moving randomly. Schizotypal thinking is the tendency to have unusual perceptual experiences (seeing ghosts or hearing voices) and disorganized thought processes, and has been explicitly linked to religiosity. In its extreme, clinical form it manifests as schizophrenia, a condition that often involves perceptual and mental-state misattribution – attributing your thoughts to others or their thoughts to you, or, in extreme cases, hearing God telling you what to do.

The results of this study suggest that mentalizing positively influences religiosity quite independently of agency detection and schizotypal thinking, both of which are extremely closely correlated. In fact, people who are predisposed to schizotypal thinking tend to have an unusually active hyperactive agency detection mechanism. This suggests that you can be religious either because you are prone to seeing visions or because you can reflect deeply on the mental states of God in his transcendental world. This is interesting because it suggests there might be two types of religious people who engage in two very different types of religion – reactive religion and reflective religion, or as I put it in the Chapter 1, shamanic/immersive religion versus doctrinal religion.

The mental-state side of this story was explored by another research group.[20] Their hypothesis was that if mentalizing ability was important for religious belief, then people who lack theory of mind (as is the case for autistic individuals) should be less religious. In addition, they pointed out that since males are much more likely to suffer from autism than females, men should be less religious than women.[21] In fact, not only are males much more likely to be autistic than women, but, as we have found in every one of half a dozen studies, men have lower mentalizing skills than women even in otherwise normal, neurotypical adults. As predicted, they found that autistic young adults (these would most likely have had Asperger syndrome rather than full-blown autism) were less likely to believe in God than neurotypical adults of similar age, when controlling for IQ and gender. In fact, they were barely 10 per cent as likely to believe in God as normal individuals were. In addition, when testing for the influence of parental ratings of adolescent mentalizing skills and IQ on belief in God, only mentalizing skills had a statistically significant effect.

In a follow-up study using a larger Canadian sample, they compared the influence of empathy and systematizing as intervening variables between autism and belief in God. Empathy is, of course, the ability to adopt someone else's perspective and to feel emotionally sympathetic to their feelings; males perform relatively poorly on this compared to females. In contrast, systematizing is a tendency to live in a very organized, rule-based mental world, and is often associated with a tendency to collect things and keep them in organized displays (for example, stamp-collecting, bird spotting, trainspotting); it is more typical of men than women, and is strongly correlated with autism. The two dimensions do not correlate with each other. Once again, autists were much less likely to believe in God than normal individuals, even when controlling for gender. However, this relationship was strongly mediated by mentalizing, and not at all by systematizing tendency. In other words, being diagnosed as autistic might be associated with both poor mentalizing skills and high systematizing tendencies, but only mentalizing skills influence whether or not you believe in God. Men's lower mentalizing skills compared to women's also significantly predicted their lower likelihood of believing in God.

These results were further confirmed in two large American adult samples where the researchers were able to control for age, gender, education, income and frequency of attendance at places of worship. In this case, they used willingness to endorse a personal God as their outcome measure. Each standard deviation[22] increase in autism score resulted in an 80 per cent reduction in belief in a personal God, with mentalizing ability again being the only mediator of this relationship. Neither systematizing nor the two personality dimensions they looked at (Conscientiousness and Agreeableness) had any influence on belief in God. Independently of this, males were half as likely as women to believe in a personal God. It seems that women's superior mentalizing skills predispose them to be more religiously engaged than men typically are.

Religion on the Brain

Whatever religion might it, it is obviously something that happens in our minds, and hence is something that happens in the brain. By far the most spectacular claim about religion and the brain was made in the late 1990s by the neuroscientist Andrew Newberg and the anthropologist Eugene d'Aquili. They scanned the brain of a trained Buddhist meditator while he was in trance and found reduced activity in the left posterior parietal lobe just above and behind the left ear, and significantly heightened activity in the prefrontal, and especially the orbitofrontal, cortex. The deactivation in the left parietal lobe attracted their particular attention because this area is associated with our sense of spatial self. They suggested that when the parietal lobe neuron bundle is disengaged by going into trance, a series of impulses are sent via the limbic system to the hypothalamus, which then sets up a feedback loop between itself, the attention areas in the prefrontal cortex and the parietal lobe itself. In effect, we have what is sometimes known as a 'reverberating circuit' that acts like a ratchet. As the cycle builds, it leads to a shutdown of the spatial awareness bundles, generating a burst of ecstatic liberation in which, depending on their particular religious persuasion, the adept experiences a sense of being united with the Divine Principle, the 'Infinity of Being' or God himself. Hence the term the 'God spot'.[23]

However, it seems to me that there is something rather more interesting in these results than Newberg and d'Aquili realized. The clue lies in the fact that they explicitly identified the hypothalamus as being involved in the reverberating circuit that brings on a trance state. The hypothalamus is one of the sites from which endorphins are released into the brain. In addition, the orbitofrontal cortex is especially densely packed with endorphin receptors and is deeply implicated both in the experience of emotions and in the management of social relationships. That burst of calming nothingness that comes at the point where you tip into trance may be nothing more nor less than an intense opioid surge. At the time Newberg and d'Aquili were doing their research, the relevance of the endorphin system for anything other than pain had not been appreciated. The important point, perhaps, is that these effects can be generated by what amounts to mental self-stimulation by a trained adept.

Although the Newberg–d'Aquili findings have not received universal approval, there have been further studies since to suggest that when people are engaged in religious activities, specific brain regions are differentially activated. In one such study, subjects' brains were studied while they were reciting passages that were either a religious text (a psalm), a children's nursery rhyme or the instructions for using a cashcard in a phone booth. For people who self-reported being actively religious (in this case, Christian), there was increased activity when they recited the psalm in broadly the same areas as Newberg and d'Aquili had highlighted (the medial parietal lobe, the dorsomedial prefrontal cortex and dorsolateral prefrontal cortex, both of which are adjacent to the orbitofrontal cortex).[24] In another study, this time of devout Mormons, elevated responses were consistently associated with peak self-reported religious feelings during four religious activities (prayer, reading scripture, reading Mormon tracts and watching a short religious video presentation). These elevated responses occurred in the nucleus accumbens, the ventromedial prefrontal cortex and the frontal attentional cortex.[25] The first two brain regions are associated with strong endorphin receptor activation in response to both pain and friendship.

Both the clinical and the neurobiological evidence suggest that a predisposition to religious experiences (such as hearing voices, mystical experiences, and glossolalia or speaking in tongues) involve a neural network composed, in particular, of units in the right prefrontal cortex (notably the orbitofrontal, dorsomedial and dorsolateral prefrontal cortex), the right temporal pole (the tip of the temporal lobe) and the limbic system (in particular, the amygdala and the hippocampus), along with the dopamine and serotonin neurotransmitter systems.[26]

In addition, the clinical evidence consistently reveals that temporal lobe epilepsy seems to trigger extreme forms of religiosity and a dysphoric sense of self (out-of-body experiences, space–time distortions or feelings of intense meaningfulness). Even transient microseizures deep within the temporal lobe that produce no overt clinical manifestations can have these religious effects. Many of the psychoactive drugs that trigger mind-altering religious and non-religious experiences (including LSD, psilocybin, mescaline and DMT) reduce serotonin production by suppressing activity in the raphe nuclei in the brain stem.[27] This seems to reduce the capacity of the frontal lobe to censor perceptual input, giving rise to perceptual distortions, a fragmented sense of self, enhanced spiritual awareness and mystical experiences. This, in turn, leads to increased activation in the dopamine system, simultaneously creating a sense of elation and pleasure.

The temporo-frontal-limbic network that has been identified as underpinning religiosity and religious experiences looks suspiciously like the default mode neural network that plays such a central role in both mentalizing and managing our social relationships. Given that most religious people believe they have a personal relationship with God, this may not be a coincidence. In addition, these brain regions are densely packed with endorphin receptors. In other words, it may be no surprise at all that there is a neural circuit in the brain that becomes active when we are in religious mode. It looks as though the theory of mind network might play an important role in religious experiences, especially when the activity of the endorphin and serotonin systems are involved. Religion is, after all, an intensely social phenomenon in precisely the sense that, at its mystical heights, it involves a direct interaction between two minds – yours and God's.

My aim in this chapter has been to explore the psychological underpinnings of primate (and hence human) social relationships and the neurobiological mechanisms involved in social bonding. There are three separate strands woven together.

One is the psychology of the bonding process itself, with its twin roots in the endorphin system and the cognitive machinery that underpins mentalizing and homophily. The second is how these mechanisms that bond close friendships have been extrapolated to bond larger communities. The third is the implications that the cognitive components, in particular mentalizing, have for our capacity to handle what are in effect the doctrinal concepts of religion. In the next chapter, I will say more about the role that the second strand plays in specifically religious contexts. Or, to put it the other way around, the way religious rituals have been designed to exploit the bonding mechanisms, and in particular the endorphin system. I shall return to the third strand in Chapter 7 when we come to consider the timing of the origin of religion.

CHAPTER 6
Ritual and Synchrony

Rituals form the bedrock on which most, if not all, religions rest. They provide the centrepiece for religious services in the doctrinal religions, while in the shamanic religions they identify the practices that need to be carried out for propitiating gods, creating good luck or entering trance. Two important features of rituals are that they are often highly synchronized (the entire congregation kneels, sits or sings at the same time) and that they usually have to be carried out in a precise manner and a set sequence. Performing the ritual incorrectly usually nullifies its effect: if the gods are not satisfied by the performance, they won't respond in the hoped-for way.

Robert Bellah, one of the great experts on the sociology of religion, argued that rituals change how humans experience the world, and have been selected for precisely this reason.[1] We know, for example, that mood can influence how we see a neutral stimulus. Some evidence to support that comes from a study of subjects who listened to sad music: they subsequently rated sad faces as more sad, and happy faces as less happy.[2] Another study found that people asked to write about an intensely positive experience on each of three successive days rated their mood on the followings days as more positive, and paid fewer visits to clinics, than those who had been asked to write about a neutral topic.[3] These effects can even be detected in brain studies: higher activation in the visual cortex after positive mood induction, and decreased activation in the prefrontal and temporal cortices to the same stimulus after negative mood induction.[4]

Bellah suggested that rituals have their origins in the play behaviour of animals. Play in animals and humans has a ritualized form in terms of the way it is formed out of repetitive patterns of behaviour. In animal play, the combination of rapid, vigorous, often jerky movements combined with a great deal of physical contact, mouthing and rough-and-tumble is about as good a trigger of the endorphin system as it is possible to get. That not only creates a psychological ambience of warmth, pleasure and trust, but also reinforces affiliative relationships, turning an otherwise neutral world into a positive social one, much as laughter does in humans.

Many human social rituals, and even some religious ones, have a similar playful ambience. One such example is the Hindu festival of Holi, the spring festival of love and colours in which celebrants drench each other in coloured flour or water. It is a week-long occasion of joy and fun that celebrates the end of winter and the beginning of a new year. At least according to one tradition, it commemorates the divine love of the goddess Radha for the god Krishna. The joy and laughter occasioned by such rituals will inevitably trigger the endorphin system and create a sense both of pleasure and of communal bonding.

What's in a Ritual?

Although rituals can take an almost infinite variety of forms, they condense down into three broad types in terms of the effort involved. Low-effort rituals typically involve a brief action at a specific place or time (genuflecting or crossing oneself when entering a church, or kissing the statue or tomb of a saint). Medium-effort rituals typically involve taking part in services (for example, singing, kneeling to pray, yogic meditation). Extreme rituals incur significant physical pain for those taking part. Low-level rituals are usually performed alone; medium and extreme rituals are more explicitly social, often communal (in the sense that the entire congregation at a service acts in the same way at the same time or, in the case of many extreme rituals, the ritual takes place in public before onlookers).

Rituals are obviously defined by the fact that they have meaning. There would be little point in flagellating oneself simply for the sake of it. But flagellation with religious meaning puts the experience on a completely different psychological plane. In the most extreme cases, the meaning will be specific to the particular religion or culture. Many of the low-effort rituals, such as the humble manner in which we approach an altar or the statue of a god, may be near universal.

One of the best known examples of an extreme ritual is firewalking. It is practised in Fiji (where it became a tourist attraction in the early 1900s), some parts of Polynesia, Spain and Greece, although there are historical references to it in India as early as 1200 BC. As a form of trial by fire, devotees walk barefoot across a pit of glowing embers – which obviously seems like it ought to burn the skin, but in fact doesn't providing you walk at a steady pace and the embers have cooled down to around 500°C. Snake-handling among some Pentecostal sects in the Appalachian Mountains is somewhat similar, since the snakes used are usually rattle-snakes and can (and very occasionally do) deliver a deadly bite. A number of religions engage in mass rituals that incur serious pain. During the South Asian Tamil Hindu festival of Thaipusam, devotees of the god Murugan carry an offering or a burden (*kavadi aattam*) to his temple, often heightening the pain of doing so by piercing their skin with skewers. An-other example is provided by the re-enactments of Christ's Passion and Crucifixion on Good Friday in some parts of the Philippines. Penitents volunteer to be crucified (with four-inch steel nails driven through hands and feet). Some people (men and women) volunteer to do this annually.[5]

Self-flagellation has a long history in connection with re-ligion. Though the practice is now banned, the Shia Islam festival of Ashura (commemorating the martyrdom of Mo-hammed's grandson Husayn in 680 at the Battle of Karbala in modern-day Iraq) was traditionally associated with this form of self-punishment as part of an intense communal form of grieving for Husayn's death. Those taking part would fla-gellate themselves with bladed chains as they paraded to a holy site, usually in synchrony and in time with their march-ing feet. Mortification of the flesh (self-flagellation using a seven-corded scourge known as 'the discipline') is a common practice in the western Christian monastic tradition, though commonly done in private.[6]

Other common forms of ritual that involve the infliction

of pain include wearing uncomfortable clothing like a hair-shirt, fasting, and performances like the Sun Dance of the American Plains Indians and the *okipa* ceremony of the Mandan and Lakota tribes of the America Northwest. Some of these rituals function as signals of tribal or community membership, but others are associated with a purely religious function, although the distinction can become blurred.

Most rituals, however, are of a rather more benign kind. Almost all of these involve elements of behaviour that form a central part of the mechanism of social bonding. Although it is rare to find all of them present in any given religion, religious services typically include some combination of the following: singing, dancing, hugging (the Kiss, or Sign, of Peace), rhythmic bowing (the *shuklen* in Hasadic Judaism), emotional storytelling (rousing sermons, readings from scripture, self-disclosures), communal meals (literally in religions like Sikhism where a communal meal often follows a major service, or the *seder* Passover meal in Judaism and communal meals at the end of Eid in Islam; and metaphorically in the Christian Communion service when the Host is given out to commemorate the Last Supper before Christ's Crucifixion).

Rhythmic singing and dancing play a particularly important role in many religious rituals. In the Ethiopian Coptic Church, the *dabtara* (deacons) dance formally before the altar, representing the Ark of the Covenant before which, as the Bible tells us, King David danced. In fact, what they actually do is a form of slow swaying while tapping the ground with prayer sticks, often accompanied by chanting, drums and sistra. Similarly, the nineteenth-century Shakers were famous for the slow dances that formed a central part of their services. In both these cases, the dances have an hypnotic effect not unlike the slow rise and fall of Gregorian chant in the monastic tradition of the Catholic Church. Chanting also forms an important part of Buddhist services, often in a very monotonous style and in a very low vocal register – in some forms of Tibetan Buddhism, in a vocal register (throat- or overtone singing) so low as to be beyond the range of untrained individuals.[7]

Rhythmic sensory stimulation, combined with low vocal tones, plays a particularly important role in the Sun Dance rituals of the American Plains Indians and the Spirit Dance of the Salish of the Northwest Coast.[8] William Grey Walter, one of the founding fathers of neuroscience, showed in a seminal series of studies in the 1930s that an intense, steep-fronted sound such as that produced by a drum maximizes the sensory stimulation of the inner ear hearing mechanism.[9] Then, in the 1960s, studies of the phenomenon known as auditory driving (the process by which particular sounds induce trance states) showed that this effect is best produced by a low frequency, high amplitude sound, such as that produced by a drum rhythm of three, four, six or eight beats per second.[10] Sun Dances were always preceded by several days of fasting and dehydration, as well as physically exhausting exercise (for example, long runs, bathing in cold streams) and sensory deprivation, while the ceremony itself involved self-inflicted torture and strenuous dancing to low-frequency chanting and rhythmic drum beats at around three beats per second – memorably enacted by Richard Harris in the 1970 film *A Man Called Horse*.

The central role of ritual in most religious services raises the question of why it should be so important. Some scholars have suggested that rituals express a sense of belonging – by

knowing the way things *should* be done, you demonstrate
that you are a member of the community. Like knowing
the right way to speak, the right words to use, the right folk
tales, the right way to behave in public, the right clothes to
wear, and having the right kind of hairstyle, the correct performance of a ritual demonstrates that you know the secret
formula of membership. We might think of this as the shibboleth hypothesis – recalling the biblical account of how the
Gileadites identified their enemies the Ephraimites by asking
them to pronounce the word *shibboleth* (which means 'grain'
in Hebrew), because the two tribes pronounced the first syl-
lable differently (*sib-* versus *shib-*). In this respect, rituals as
signals of community membership clearly hark back to the
Seven Pillars of Friendship (Chapter 5).

An alternative suggestion is the costly signalling hypothesis. The more time, inconvenience, money or pain you are
prepared to give, the stronger must be your desire to be a
member of the community. By being prepared to pay the price
of performing the ritual, you publicly demonstrate your commitment to the other community members, making it psychologically more difficult to leave the community later. Recall
that, in the study of nineteenth-century American religious
communes, the more things that aspirants had to give up
(swearing, alcohol, meat, private property, sexual intercourse)
in order to join, the longer the commune lasted. Although this
attitude is always open to the *Concorde* fallacy (you keep going
because you paid so much to get started),[11] nonetheless there
will eventually come a point at which the costs outweigh the
benefits by so much that continued membership is no longer
worthwhile. In practice, this may be well beyond the stage at

which it might have been economically wise to withdraw. And that may be the point: it makes you stay longer in the community than you might otherwise have done.

Two other possibilities are the prosociality hypothesis (taking part in rituals makes you more willing to act prosocially towards other members of your community) and the community-bonding hypothesis (rituals help create a sense of community). It may be no accident that in Islam beggars should not be denied alms on a Friday – the day on which everyone is, of course, enjoined to attend mosque and take part in the rituals of the service. Having taken part in the rituals of prayer, people may be psychologically more willing to give alms than they are on any other day. That might be because the rituals of prayer make us feel more generous towards all and sundry, or because they make us feel we are all members of the community (some of whom are less fortunate and deserve our support).[12]

Although these various hypotheses have often been thrown into opposition with each other, the lesson we learned in Chapter 1 is that it isn't necessarily the case that if one is right then all the others must be wrong. In some cases, this may be because the explanations are simply different ways of expressing the same thing. The difference between the shibboleth and costly signalling hypotheses may be simply one of degree: both mark you out as a member of the community, but one is passive and other active. In other cases, it may be that the two explanations are acting at different explanatory levels (in the sense of Tinbergen's Four Whys). There is, however, something more fundamental that all these explanations overlook, and this is the fact that most rituals probably trigger the endorphin system.

Inducing pain certainly triggers endorphins, since endorphins are part of the brain's pain management system. However, rhythmic movements such as those that occur in jogging and dancing are also extremely good at triggering endorphins, and may actually be even more effective than outright pain since the endorphin system responds best to low-level persistent pain (as when jogging). Many of the less painful rituals, and especially those rituals explicitly involved in services, have a rhythmic quality and so may be very good at activating the endorphin system. I'll come back to this in a later section. First, let us look in a little more detail at the neuropsychology involved.

The Neuropsychology of Ritual

There is now considerable evidence that behaviours like singing, dancing and emotional storytelling trigger the uptake of endorphins in the brain, and that this in turn enhances a sense of bonding to those with whom we perform these actions. In addition, there is good evidence that the induction of pain enhances the sense of group belonging, providing prima facie evidence that this mechanism is involved in extreme rituals.

In one series of experiments, small groups of 2–5 strangers were asked to undergo either a painful or an equivalent non-painful task together, and then asked to rate their feelings of positive and negative affect as well as their sense of belonging to the group. The painful tasks involved either collecting discs from the bottom of a bucket of iced water or adopting the Roman Chair position (the wall-sit task). The non-painful versions of these tasks were to collect the discs in a bucket of room-temperature water or to stand on one leg for a minute (with the option of switching legs if it became painful). Collecting the discs was simply a decoy to make the task seem as though it had a purpose. There were no differences in either positive or negative affect between the two conditions, but those who endured pain together felt more bonded to each other than those who had performed the non-painful version of the exercise, even when controlling for age, sex and group size. In two follow-up experiments, participants were invited to play a standard economic game after completing the pain task. The economic game was a public good task where players contribute some proportion of their fee to a common pot in the hopes of getting an enhanced reward back, depending on the size of the contributions made by the group as a whole. Once again, there were no differences in affect, even though those in the groups that had experienced pain rated the task as having been more painful. Nonetheless, those in the pain groups made significantly larger donations to the common pot than those in the no-pain groups. In a third experiment, pain was induced by asking participants to eat a very hot chilli pepper, while those in the no-pain groups were given a boiled sweet to eat before deciding how much to donate. Once again, those in the pain condition were more generous in their contributions to the common pot than those in the no-pain condition.[13]

To explore the role of the endorphin system in an explicitly religious context, conventional Christian church services (covering the full spectrum from evangelical to Anglican) in the UK and Umbanda Afro-Brazilian trance-based services in southern Brazil (see Chapter 2) were sampled. Pain threshold and self-rated bondedness to the group increased after both kinds of services. However, the change in pain threshold was much less strong for the UK churches compared to the Umbanda groups, perhaps because the Umbanda services were much more intense and uplifting. Overall, change in social bonding was significantly predicted by the change in pain threshold, even when controlling for country, individual sense of connectedness to God, frequency of attendance at services, age and gender.[14]

To check whether this effect was due to a religious component to the ritual or simply to the effect of physical movements, a lab-based study was set up in which conditions could be more carefully controlled.[15] Hatha yoga was used because yoga classes could easily be transposed to a lab setting without making them seem overly contrived since many classes of this kind are run for students in university facilities. Also, exactly the same exercises could be presented as either religious or secular, which helped to minimize the number of differences between the two conditions. The classes were run by the same person, the professional yoga teacher and author Swami Ambikananda Saraswati. She presented one set of classes with relevant yoga philosophy and theory to explain the exercises (the religious condition) and the other set as purely secular (simply a set of physical exercises that influenced general wellbeing). For both conditions, the sense of social bonding to the rest of the group increased over the hour-long class and over successive weeks, although the difference between the two kinds of class was modest. There was, however, a significant difference between the two conditions in whether participants felt an increasingly closer connection to some higher spiritual force as the course progressed, with the spiritual group rating themselves significantly above the secular group. This was not affected by the participants' underlying degree of spirituality or religiosity, as this remained constant across the experiment. It was simply an outcome of doing the exercises.

To check whether the increase in pain threshold observed really was due to endorphin activation, a follow-up experiment was run on one yoga class and several Umbanda services in Brazil. In each case, half the participants were given an endorphin blocker (naltrexone) and half were given a placebo.[16] Since the endorphin blocker given before the service locks onto the endorphin receptors in the brain, the endorphins activated in the subsequent service have nowhere to go, so pain thresholds and the sense of bonding should be lower for those given naltrexone compared to those given the placebo. Those who took the naltrexone did feel less bonded to the other members of their group after the service than those who were given the placebo (Figure 6). Those given the placebo showed the standard increase in bonding we expect when the endorphin system is activated.

A follow-up study, run on Sunday Assembly meetings, tried to determine how important a religious or transcendental perspective might be for the feelings of community bonding. The Sunday Assembly movement was launched in London in 2013 to provide a secular version of traditional Sunday church services. A typical service will consist of well-known secular songs (usually with a band and, in larger assemblies, even a choir), a poetry reading or similar, an inspirational talk by a member of the assembly, perhaps a TED-style lecture by a visiting speaker, and a time for quiet reflection, plus the usual paraphernalia of community notices and perhaps a collection

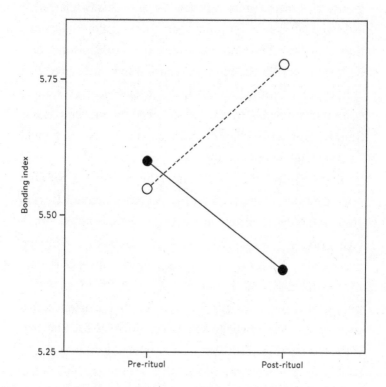

Figure 6
Effect of administering the endorphin blocker
naltrexone (filled symbols) or a placebo (unfilled symbols)
on the sense of bonding before and after a religious
service. Sense of bonding to the other members of the
congregation was rated by each subject using the Inclusion
of Other in Self (IOS) rating scale.[17]

plate for meeting expenses and good causes. There may be refreshments or even a communal meal afterwards. The groups that meet regularly in this way are usually referred to as 'chapters' so as to set them apart from religious congregations. Smaller ad hoc interest groups of 5–15 people may also be formed within the chapter. These might be related to a craft or some external activity like beer-tasting or a voluntary community activity. In the decade since the movement was founded, forty-five chapters have been established in eight (mainly Anglophone) countries around the world.

In many ways, the Sunday Assembly movement parallels several earlier attempts to create secular or humanistic religions, including the Humanistic Religious Association founded in London in 1853 and the Religion of Humanity (famously described by Aldous Huxley as 'Catholicism minus Christianity') founded around the same time by the French positivist philosopher Auguste Comte. Though still in existence, neither of these has proved to be especially successful. This may suggest that religion without a transcendental dimension and belief in a spirit world just doesn't work quite as well. For this reason, the Sunday Assemblies provide an ideal context in which to test how important the spiritual component of rituals is compared to their purely mechanical properties.

The experiments run on the Sunday Assembly chapters yielded rather similar improvements in social bonding to those observed following conventional church services, though church members did start at a significantly higher level than Sunday Assembly members (perhaps suggesting an added cumulative benefit from having a religious dimension). Neither personal spirituality nor level of religiosity influenced change in bonding as a result of attending a service, irrespective of whether the meeting was secular or religious.[18]

Another study asked Sunday Assembly members drawn from all around the world to complete a series of surveys that measured wellbeing over a six-month period. The results suggested that members benefited by a 16 per cent increase in the number of close friends drawn from within their chapter. The most robust finding, however, was that the more time members devoted to small group activities within their chapter, the greater their sense of wellbeing – at least in the case of men, but not women.[19] This last result probably reflects the fact that, as we have shown in our studies of friendship formation, social bonding in men is activity-based and clubbish, whereas in women it is conversation-based and more dyadic.[20]

Taken together, these various studies suggest that attending a religious service and engaging in the rituals involved does activate the endorphin system, and this enhances the sense of bonding with those with whom one engages in the ritual activity. Although neither the elevated pain threshold nor the heightened sense of bonding may necessarily be due to the religious context as such, the rituals are given *meaning* by the religious context and this may enhance their effects. One other reason why the religious context may be important is that it provides the incentive for continuing to attend services or take part in rituals on a regular basis.

The Role of Synchrony

In many ways, the most salient feature of rituals is that they are invariably performed in synchrony. The sections of a service move in close order: everyone stands, kneels, sits or prostrates themselves at the same time. Ritual actions like crossing oneself are done together. The singing is done in time. Prayers are recited in unison. Where there is dancing, the dancing is synchronized. There is something mesmeric about synchronized actions that adds measurably to the sense of communality.

I first became aware of the significance of synchrony through a study we did of coxed-eight rowing crews. We studied these not in boats, but in the gym using the rowing machines, or ergs, that rowers train on. We first tested our subjects (all top athletes from an elite rowing team) on their own and then, the following week, rowing in unison together as a virtual boat. The physical effort of rowing produced an endorphin effect (at least as measured by elevated pain thresholds after the task), just as might be expected; but rowing in synchrony ramped this effect up by 100 per cent compared to when they rowed alone, even without any increase in the effort involved (as we could tell from the ergs' computers).[21] Something about rowing in synchrony increased the endorphin output. We still don't know how or why this happens, but our rowing study has been replicated by others and we have shown exactly the same effect in a series of studies using dance moves.[22]

Since these studies were done, a number of other studies have looked at synchrony in more detail. One asked people to perform a set of simple arm movements alone or in or out of synchrony with a confederate and showed that, when the subject and confederate were in close synchrony, pain thresholds rose and the subject trusted the confederate more; at the same time, synchrony independently increased the sense of bonding between them, and that in turn enhanced liking and cooperation.[23] Another study assembled large groups, each of 40–50 people, in a sports arena and asked them to march around the arena following a research assistant who walked at a fast (high arousal) or slow (low arousal) pace. Half the groups were instructed to march in step with the assistant (synchronized group) and the other half were allowed to walk however they wanted (unsynchronized group). After the exercise, subjects from the high arousal (fast marching) group stood closer together and performed a cooperative task more efficiently than those in the low arousal (slow marching) condition, with synchrony enhancing this effect in the high arousal group but not in the low arousal group (as we had previously found with dancing).[24] Similar effects have even been shown when a group was asked to read a list of random words in or out of synchrony with each other, suggesting that even the act of recitation in unison increases the level of cooperation within a group.[25] Once more, the unison singing of Gregorian chant comes to mind.

One thing that does seem to be important is that the synchrony involves a task that is clearly goal-directed – in other words, has a clear purpose. This was first demonstrated in a simple experiment in which groups of four people performed a simple action in synchrony either with each other (synchrony with a social goal) or in time to a metronome (synchrony without a social goal). Groups in the synchrony-with-goal condition were significantly more generous in their contributions to the common pot that those in the other conditions. Having a common focus also ramped up the level of cooperativeness over and above that due simply to synchrony.[26]

The significance of this for religious rituals was examined in a more naturalistic study of nine groups representing different religious and social interests. [27] The nine groups divided into three natural subsets: three exact synchrony groups (a yoga group, a Buddhist chant group and a Hindu devotional singing group) where the activity occurs in unison, four complementary synchrony groups (a capoeira group,[28] a drumming circle, a choir and a Christian church group) where the activity is highly coordinated but not necessarily in full synchrony, and two unsynchronized groups (a poker club and a running group). Each group was asked to perform its normal activity and then played a standard public good game. Once again, synchrony predicted both the sense of belonging to the group (prosocial sentiment) and trust, but only synchrony and sense of belonging in combination predicted that a sense of sacred values was associated with the activity, which in turn predicted cooperativeness (as indexed by donations in the public good game). Neither the frequency of the group activity nor its duration had any effect on the level of cooperation. Once again, having some kind of religious purpose seems to ramp up the effect of engaging in a synchronized ritual.

Singing provides a particularly interesting example of ritual, and most religions use singing as part of their services. In most cases, this is done in unison, with polyphonic singing usually being confined to concert-type performances by trained choirs. One feature of communal singing that seems to have been completely overlooked is the fact that male and female voices are exactly an octave apart, allowing unison to be recreated out of voices that differ in register. This phenomenon is known as *octave equivalence*. Women and children have the same vocal register, but male voices drop after puberty, stabilizing around the age of twenty or so at an octave lower. While the lower male register is conventionally attributed to the effects of sexual selection (lower voices imply a larger body, and hence greater competitiveness in conflicts for access to reproductive females, in turn making males with deeper voices more attractive), this does not explain why the difference should be exactly one octave. In fact, male voices are considerably lower than would be expected for their body size: if voice pitch was directly proportional to body size, human males would be ten foot (three metres) tall. Octave equivalence seems to be specifically designed to bring male and female voices back into unison in order to engineer communal bonding in (relatively) large groups.[29] It seems that singing in tonal unison creates a 'sweet spot' that triggers a sense of 'thrill' (the tingling down the spine sensation) that feeds into the sense of belonging – the very effects that Gregorian chant seems to be so successful at creating.

Taken together, these studies suggest that rituals trigger the endorphin system, and hence play an important role in creating a sense of belonging, of community bonding. Synchrony seems to play an especially strong role in this respect by exaggerating the magnitude of the endorphin effect, though it is not entirely clear how or why it does so. In this respect, rituals are much like laughter, singing and dancing in more conventional secular contexts. Although the meaning or religious significance of a ritual on its own seems to be of much less importance than we might have anticipated, in combination with synchrony it gives added value and significantly increases the bonding aspect of rituals.

CHAPTER 7

Religion in Prehistory

Behaviour and the mind do not fossilize, so it is impossible to know what religion looked like in deep prehistory. The archaeological record provides glimpses, of course, but at best this is simply the casual residue of whatever rituals may have been performed. We cannot always tell whether a bowl was used to make a ritual offering to a god or for serving an everyday meal. Does a carved stone statue represent a deity worshipped in a shrine or was it simply a decorative addition to someone's dwelling that they just happened to like? If it comes to that, we cannot always tell whether a building was a living space or a ritual space. Indeed, in many small-scale contemporary ethnographic societies, the two are not always distinguishable. Even today, most Japanese homes have a shrine for the family ancestors in the main living room. Does that make the building a domestic dwelling or a religious site?

Nonetheless, the archaeological record is the only direct source of information we have on the religious beliefs of our distant ancestors. So, how far back can we trace the evidence for religious belief? What did religion look like in deep time? Were our predecessors, the Heidelberg folk and their Neanderthal cousins, actively religious?

Grave Evidence

Archaeologists have rightly been cautious about over-interpreting the evidence for religion. They have tended to rely on symbolic meaning as the only reliable touchstone for this. Burials accompanied by grave goods, for example, must imply belief in an afterlife, otherwise why would you bury the dead in a deliberate, respectful way (as opposed to just dropping them down some convenient fissure)? More importantly, why would you bury them with an array of everyday items if you didn't suppose they might need these in whatever world they had gone to?

For archaeologists, evidence of deliberate burial includes one or more of the following: that the body was fully articulated (that is, it hadn't been torn apart by predators), that the bones are stained with red ochre or flower pollen (suggesting the body had been laid to rest with a covering of ochre or flowers), that it had been buried in a deliberately excavated hole or had been carried deep into a cave where neither predators nor streams are likely to have carried the body, and that artefacts were included in the grave in a deliberate rather than accidental way (for example, being placed in the dead person's hand, or alongside the body). As usual, this is a 'severally and jointly' criterion: some, but not necessarily all, these conditions have to be satisfied.

Deliberate burials accompanied by grave goods such as worked ivory or shell ornaments, like those found at Sunghir that I mentioned in the Introduction, are relatively common in Upper Palaeolithic sites from 40,000 years BP (Before Present), and are found all over Europe. These sites are all associated with anatomically modern humans, that's to say our own species. So we can be reasonably confident that they are likely to have thought in broadly similar ways to us. Evidence for burials earlier than this mainly derive from Neanderthals, most dating within the last 100,000 years (so well after the appearance of our own species sometime around 200,000 years ago, or perhaps a little earlier). These include the sites at Shanidar in Iraq (dated to 70,000 years ago), Kebara in Israel (around 50,000 years ago) and Krapina in Croatia (about 120,000 years ago), as well as various sites in Spain and southern France dating from around 70,000 years ago. All are in deep caves. In most cases, the claim that these are deliberate burials is based on the positioning of the body and the presence of red ochre; they are rarely, if ever, associated with grave goods, however. In several of the French sites, there are cut marks on the bones, suggesting that they had been stripped of their flesh before burial (excarnation, a mortuary rite also practised by some historical human populations) – although this has also been interpreted as evidence for cannibalism.

The cave site at Shanidar in the Bradost Mountains of Iraqi Kurdistan is one of the iconic human fossil sites. Between 65,000 and 35,000 years ago, this large hillside cave was occupied at irregular intervals by bands of Neanderthals. Later, after the Neanderthals went extinct, the cave was used intermittently by modern humans around 10,000 years ago. So far, the skeletal remains of ten different Neanderthals have been excavated from the site. The first of the skeletons to be discovered attracted considerable attention because it was an elderly man who had sustained major injuries during life: the left side of his face had been crushed by a heavy blow, leaving him blind in one eye, his right arm was withered beyond use and he seemed to be suffering from a degenerative bone disease. These injuries led to rather exaggerated claims about the altruism of Neanderthals on the grounds that someone so disabled could only have survived if they had been looked after by the group. In fact, there are plenty of examples of disabled monkeys and apes surviving in the wild without the help of their group-members, so this claim is probably unjustified.[1] Some of the Shanidar burials are associated with large quantities of fossilized pollen from a yellow flower which was assumed to have been laid on the bodies at burial – though it has subsequently been suggested that these may have been brought into the burial site by burrowing rodents. The sheer number of skeletons now excavated from the site has been used to argue that the cave was a burial rather than a living site.

At least two cave-site multiple burials associated with anatomically modern humans (Skhul and Qafzeh in Israel) are even older than Shanidar, having been dated to around 90–100,000 years BP. In contrast to the Shanidar burials, these really do seem to have been deliberate, since several of the skeletons are associated with pierced marine dog-whelk shells (probably from necklaces) and animal bones. An apparently deliberate double burial of a woman and child at Qafzeh is probably the earliest of these, although the claim for any religious significance is based solely on the fact that they have been buried together.

Even if we accept all of these cases as deliberate burials, they take us back only around 100,000 years or so – long after own species first appeared. Further back in time, the evidence becomes much more murky. There is circumstantial evidence for deliberate burials at some southern European sites dating to around 400,000 BP, when archaic humans such as Heidelbergs or early Neanderthals occupied Europe. A particularly impressive example is the Sima de los Huesos ('Pit of Bones') in the complex of caves at Atapuerca in northern Spain. Here, the remains of at least twenty-eight Heidelberg men, women and children were found deep underground at the base of a narrow 13m-deep shaft at the far end of a cave system that, even now, is only accessible with difficulty. The fact that the remains are jumbled together at the bottom of the shaft is consistent with them having been dropped down it. It is not difficult to imagine that a species that believed in an afterlife might see such a shaft as the entrance to the underworld, and so hasten their dear departed into the next world by dropping them into it. However, given the length of time the cave was occupied, it is possible that they fell down the shaft in individual accidents when venturing into the cave with only the aid of dim lamps to guide them – or become lost in the dark after the lamp ran out of oil. If they were concussed by such a long fall, their companions would not have known what had happened to them, and would no doubt have been very reluctant to climb down a hole with no obvious end.

Another important source of information on the cultural behaviour of early humans has been the extensive variety of their cave art, especially in the limestone caves of southwest Europe. This comes in two forms. One is a remarkable variety of sketches and drawings on cave walls; the other comes in the form of artworks like the famous Venus figurines (Figure 7). Although both date only from the last 30,000

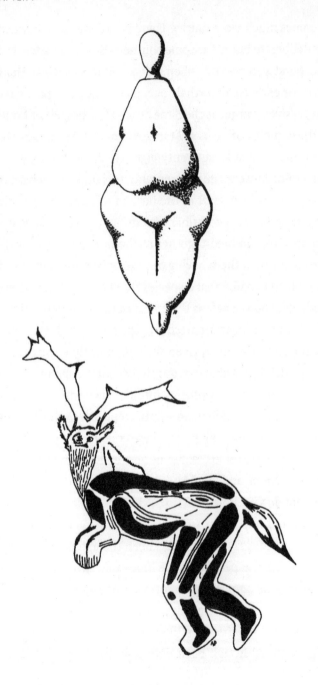

years, they do, nonetheless, provide important insights into the minds and behaviour of Upper Palaeolithic anatomically modern humans.

The cave paintings consist of a curious mix of beautifully drawn animal figures, stick people, lines, dots, finger-engravings and handprints (in the latter case, by the thousand, including those of both children and adults, some created by pressing a paint-daubed hand onto the cave wall, others by blowing paint onto the hand to create a negative image). Sometimes, these paintings are overlain on each other as though later artists have scrawled over the daubings of earlier ones. Others are beautifully articulated with the rock surface so that an animal seems to be in 3D. The many animal drawings have been attributed to hunting magic, mainly because some of the human stick figures associated with them seem to be engaged in spearing the animals. Of more interest, however, are the other human and abstract figures.

The cave painting known as 'The Sorcerer' from Les Trois Frères cave (12,000 BP) depicts an ambiguous figure with

Figure 7

Left: The ivory Venus of Lespugue, from Rideaux cave in southern France, dated to 25,000 years ago. More than 200 similar figurines dating to the period 35,000–11,000 BP have been found, mostly in Europe and the Middle East, with one from as far away as northern India. Their symbolic meaning and function remains unknown, though it has been suggested that they were fertility goddesses. Right: The cave painting known as 'The Sorceror' from Les Trois Frères caves in the valley of the River Volp in the French Pyrenees, dated to 12,000 years ago. It has variously been interpreted as a dancer wearing a deer mask with horns (much as San Bushmen still do in their eland healing dance) or a therianthrope (a half-man/half-beast inhabitant of the spirit world). (Drawings ©2007 Arran Dunbar.)

human body and limbs and a deer's head, complete with antlers (Figure 7, right panel). Though by no means unique, this is without question the most spectacular of the human-oid figures known as therianthropes (animal–humans). San bushmen wear animal headdresses of just this kind during their eland healing dance, often executed at the time of a girl's first menstruation. Grotesque masks are also common in tribal religious ceremonies in both West and East Africa, especially among the Bantu.

Venus figures (Figure 7, left panel) are stone or ivory (very occasionally ceramic) female figurines, most with decidedly Rubenesque physiques, that are found widely in Upper Palaeo-lithic European sites. Around 200 are known, most of them from about 150 caves in southern France and northern Spain. They vary between 3 and 40 cm in height. All have one thing in common: they lack feet, with the legs usually tapering to a point. Although most date from (and in many ways define) the 5000-year period between 21,000 and 26,000 BP known as the Gravettian, the oldest dates from around 35,000 years ago – very shortly after modern humans arrived in Europe from the southern Russian steppes. Perhaps inevitably, given their large breasts and hips, they are often interpreted as fer-tility goddesses. Their uniformity across Europe has led to the suggestion that they are representations of a specific Supreme Female Creator deity. However, realistically, we have no idea what their meaning or function might have been.

It has been suggested that the cave paintings are records of experiences in the spirit world made during trance.[2] If so, the, the half-animal/half-human therianthropes like that in Figure 7 could be interpreted as ogres keen to prevent the

Figure 8

San cave art from the Drakensberg Mountains, South Africa, dated
to c. 2,000 years ago, apparently depicting a trance dance. On the
right are clearly a group of women who seem to be clapping (as
women do during the dances). On the left, a group of men appear to
be dancing, with the central figure leaning on his dance stick and the
leftmost figure collapsing in trance. (Drawing ©2007 Arran Dunbar.)

dancer's spirit from finding the exit back to the physical world (see Chapter 2). Some of the more obviously human representations are particularly interesting in this respect, because they look very much like dancing groups. Figure 8 is a more modern, but quite typical, example from a southern African rock shelter painted by San Bushmen some 2,000 years ago. This is quite unequivocally a group of trance dancers: the women, with their pendulous breasts, are grouped on the right, clapping to provide the rhythm as they sing (as they do in San trance dances), while the men dance on the left. One of the men is even using a dancing stick to lean on, just as modern San do, while the figure on the extreme left appears to be collapsing in trance.

Magic Mushrooms in Antiquity

We are on somewhat firmer ground once we get to the more recent archaeological record. There is a great deal of archaeological evidence suggesting that psychoactive substances were consumed by indigenous populations in the Americas, Europe and Asia in prehistoric times.[3] Traces or seeds of mescalin, peyote, San Pedro cactus, coca, betel nut, *Psilocybe* and fly agaric mushrooms, opium, cannabis, morning glory (whose seeds contain the same ergoline alkaloids as LSD), nightshades (including henbane, belladonna and mandrake), hallucinogenic snuffs and alcohol have been found in living sites in both the Old and New Worlds dating back at least as early as the seventh century BC. Many of these found their way into the herbal remedies of medieval and early modern Europe, but they are also still widely used by local ethnographic cultures for both medicinal and ritual purposes. On his first voyage, Columbus reported that the native Carib Indians on the island of Hispaniola inhaled a powder (now known to be *cohoba* from the powdered seeds of the *Anadenanthera peregrina* tree) through reeds inserted into their nostrils, as a result of which they lost consciousness.

Betel nut is widely chewed throughout South Asia as a stimulant. Archaeobotanical evidence for it has been dated as early as 11,000 BC in Southeast Asia, with evidence for teeth stained from chewing betel from burials in the Philippines dated to 2660 BC. Poppy seeds, suggesting the consumption of opium, are found widely in European Neolithic living sites from 5000 BC onwards. Analysis of bone from an adult male burial from the fourth millennium BC at Gavá (near Barcelona, Spain) revealed evidence of habitual opiate use. Opium appears to have been used in religious contexts in Cyprus during the second millennium BC, and may have been used in Mesopotamia for similar purposes around the same time; it was certainly widely used in the pre-Islamic Arab world. It was a closely guarded secret of some Egyptian temple priests during Pharaonic times. Cypriot-made opium jugs have been found in Egyptian tombs and elsewhere in the Mediterranean, suggesting there was an active trade in psychoactive drugs and the paraphenalia required for their use. Instructions for the production of opium are inscribed on Sumerian tablets from the temple at Nippur dating to the third millennium BC, and are mentioned in accounts of the Persian conquest of Assyria and Babylon in the sixth century BC. It turns out that the blue water-lily flowers that frequently appear in Egyptian tomb paintings, and covered the body of the boy-pharaoh

Tutankhamun, also produce a calming euphoria when steeped in wine for several weeks.

The archaeological record for alcohol is even deeper. Fruit wines (often with honey or rice components, and herbal flavourings) were being produced and drunk as early as 7000 BC at the Neolithic site of Jiahu in China's Yellow River valley.[4] Wines are technically easier to produce than beers, so it may be no accident that the earliest evidence for alcohol production seems to have involved wine-like beverages. At Göbekli Tepe in southeastern Turkey (upper Mesopotamia), stone fermentation vessels of enormous size (160 litres in solid stone) date from 7000 to 8000 BC.[5] The fermentation residues recovered from inside them have allowed chemists to determine the original recipes. Although the domestication and cultivation of barleys and wheats in the Fertile Crescent was originally assumed to have been for the production of bread, in more recent years archaeologists have suggested that they may in fact have been cultivated first for the production of beer. These primitive einkorn and emmer wheats and wild barleys had a different gluten structure to modern cereals, as a result of which they make a very poor form of unleavened bread at best. However, they make an excellent gruel that would have provided the perfect mash for brewing. The fermentation of honey to make mead was widely known historically among the San bushmen, and there is circumstantial evidence for its production in Border Cave, South Africa, as early as 40,000 years ago.[6]

Evidence for the presence of psychoactive substances in deeper time is a great deal more circumstantial. There have been claims that Shanidar 4, a 30-year-old male Neanderthal from the Shanidar cave, was a shaman, mainly because his body was covered in fossilized clumps of pollen from a variety of local plants: these included cornflower, ragwort, grape hyacinth and hollyhock, all of which are known for their medicinal value as diuretics, astringents and anti-inflammatories, as well as being stimulants. Although this claim has been disputed, the fact that these plants appear to have been widely available nearby makes it plausible that humans would have discovered their medicinal and other properties and made use of them.

All this evidence for the presence of psychoactive drugs in the archaeological record provides us with a smoking gun for trance experiences, and hence shamanic religions. However, the archaeological record dates back with any certainty only to the beginning of the Neolithic some 10,000 years ago, and even the evidence from graves will only take us back another 30,000 years at most. Any earlier records are lost in the mists of time. In terms of deep time, there is nothing much this line of enquiry can add to that of the evidence from graves. To try and get us back further in time, the next two sections consider two indirect approaches that might provide more promising insights.

Reconstructing Early Religion

Ever since the Victorians first became interested in tribal societies and their religions, scholars have used ethnographic evidence to reconstruct ancestral religions. This led them to infer that animist or shamanic religions were typical of the earliest forms of religion. However, these conclusions suffer from a statistical problem that arises when two cultures inherit a particular trait from a common ancestor: counting both of them as independent cases artificially inflates the sample size, potentially making it easier to get a significant result. Over the last decade, new statistical methods have been developed that allow us to use language family trees to construct the family tree of cultural evolution.[7] This allows us to compensate for the likelihood that any two cultures inherited their religious traits from a common ancestor. In principle, this cultural family tree reaches back to the time when the ancestors of all the contemporary language families converge on a common ancestor – in effect, the time at which there was only one language (or, at least, only one language that produced surviving descendents). At present, it is uncertain how far back that actually goes. Nonetheless, although the language families probably only take us back in the order of 100,000 years, they map surprisingly well onto the genetic family tree of the different contemporary tribal groups.

In one such study, six religious traits were mapped across thirty-three contemporary hunter-gatherer societies distributed across southern Africa, South and East Asia, Australia and the Americas, and then the ancestral states of these traits reconstructed statistically. The six traits were: animistic beliefs, shamanism, ancestor worship, belief in an afterlife, belief in local gods who keep to their own domain, and belief in High Gods who interfere in human affairs (Moralizing High Gods). The study found that animism is likely to have been the oldest of these traits, being present, uniquely, in all the cultures in the sample, despite their wide geographical distribution. On the other hand, belief in an afterlife is by no means universal and, along with shamanism and ancestor

worship, appears to form a suite of traits that evolved together later. In contrast, belief in High Gods seemed to
be completely divorced from all the other traits (very few
hunter-gatherers actually believe in High Gods); instead, it
seems to be a trait exclusively associated with the rise of
agriculture and pastoralism.[8] Other studies have suggested
that taboos, ritual mutilation and premarital constraints on
sexual behaviour appear to evolve fast as a suite of traits in
a way that is unrelated to culture; they often seem to be bor-
rowed between cultural groups.

These analyses reinforce the suggestion that the earliest religions were relatively simple, with a strongly animist form and
little else. More importantly, perhaps, the data suggest that the
other traits did not appear piecemeal, one at a time; rather
they appeared in clusters, suggesting that the elements included in a cluster might be related to each other. This seems to
have involved first adding belief in an afterlife, ancestor worship and shamans as a cluster, with belief in Moralizing High
Gods (the one trait indicative of doctrinal religions) appearing
after the adoption of agriculture in the Neolithic. This seems
to suggest that the original insight that shamanic religions appeared first and doctrinal religions later (see the Introduction)
was right. However, this is about as far as this approach will
take us, and for the moment at least it won't allow us to put
dates around particular stages.

Inferences from Very Deep Time

There is, however, an alternative approach that might help
out. It is rather left field, but then so are most novel dis-
coveries in science. It involves a two-pronged attack on the

problem in that it uses two separate anatomical indicators (one for mentalizing and the other for speech) to triangulate the earliest possible time for the origin of religion by determining when language evolved. This gives us a minimum estimate of when religion might have evolved because, while we can have language without religion, we cannot have religion without language.

Palaeoanthropologists have typically adopted three alternative positions on when language evolved. All of them rest, explicitly or implicitly, on the definition of 'modernity' (that is, when our ancestors became fully modern 'like us'). For some, this clearly means that these humanlike traits appeared with the australopithecines, the earliest identifiable members of our lineage who appeared after we separated from the other African great apes around 6–8 million years ago. In reality, as we shall see, australopithecines were just bipedal apes who were no more likely to have evolved language than the chimpanzees or gorillas have. In fact, if australopithecines did have language, then we have some seriously tricky explaining to do to account for the fact that such small-brained apes had language when contemporary apes with brains of similar size do not.

Others have opted for the first members of the genus *Homo*, the genus to which modern humans (*Homo sapiens*) belong. If *Homo rudolfensis* and *H. ergaster* (the two earliest representatives of the genus that emerged in Africa) had fully modern language then it would place the origins of language sometime around 2.5 million years ago. Yet others, mindful that language should be marked in the archaeological record by evidence for symbolic thinking, have even opted for 50,000 years ago, corresponding to the Upper Palaeolithic Revolution in Europe (the period during which all the cave paintings and Venus figurines first appeared). Later, this was extended backwards to around 100,000 years ago to accommodate the fact that, though the archaeological record is much poorer, the Upper Palaeolithic Revolution in fact had its beginnings in Africa some considerable time before modern humans (that is, our species) arrived in Europe some 40,000 years ago.

That all of the human lineage species, back to the australopithecines, would have communicated among themselves is not in doubt – after all, there are no living monkeys or apes that do not communicate among themselves, often in quite sophisticated ways. The issue is language that is sufficiently sophisticated to express symbolic concepts and, perhaps more importantly, the capacity to refer to past and future, since this is something that no animal is able to do. What allows us to express tense (past, present and future) is the capacity to mentalize. Without that, we cannot abstract ourselves far enough back from the tyranny of the present to conceive of past and future on any scale beyond yesterday and maybe tomorrow. Nor could we ask whether it is possible for another (transcendental) world to exist. We know from the neuroimaging studies discussed in Chapter 5 that mentalizing competence (how many orders of intentionality you can manage) is directly correlated with the absolute volume of the brain's mentalizing, or default mode, network, so this capacity is likely to have increased over time as our ancestors evolved ever larger brains. We also know that the volume of the frontal cortex in particular increases across monkeys, apes and humans in a way that maps linearly onto their mentalizing competences – something recently confirmed in a very neat set of experiments that tested monkeys and apes on a specially devised mentalizing task.[9] So this relationship between mentalizing abilities and brain (or brain region) size holds across primate species, as well as within humans.

I argued in Chapter 5 that fourth-order intentionality was the minimum for supporting personal forms of religion, but that fully developed religion as a communal practice is impossible without fifth-order intentionality (the level characteristic of normal adult humans). Religion might have evolved later than language, indeed quite a bit later, but if language is needed to explain the nature of symbolism or the existence of a world we cannot see to someone else, then religion cannot possibly evolve *before* language. This does not mean that human species that only had fourth-order intentionality were not religious in the sense of having a predisposition for personal religious *experiences*. Rather, it means is that they would have had difficulty engaging in the kinds of linguistic exchanges necessary to create a truly *social* (or communal) religion involving complex theological ideas and meaningful rituals to which everyone in the community subscribes. Evidence for the timing of the evolution of language thus sets a lower limit on the timing of the origin religion *as a communal practice*, even though people might have been moved by personal experiences prior to that.

One everyday reflection of this is the fact that the complexity of the stories you can tell (and enjoy) is determined by your mentalizing competences. In one of our studies, subjects were shown the same story written in sentences limited to either third- or fifth-order mentalizing. People who naturally function at third order preferred third-order stories, whereas people who can function comfortably at fifth order found such stories rather boring; they preferred fifth-order stories because they found them cognitively more challenging.[10] Part of the reason for this is simply that mentalizing competences seem to determine in a fairly straightforward way the grammatical complexity of the sentences that you can interpret – how many subordinate clauses you can work with, for example.[11] The higher the order of intentionality you can manage, the more complex the sentences you can unpack. This will then obviously affect the complexity of the stories – and hence religious statements – you can make.

Figure 9 plots mentalizing ability predicted from cranial volume for the various species in the human lineage, listed in order of the time period when they lived. The equivalent values for Old World monkeys and great apes (orangutans, gorillas and chimpanzees) are plotted separately on the left-hand side of the figure for comparison.[12] Second-order intentionality (basic theory of mind, which normal human children acquire by the age of five) is indicated by the dashed line, and fifth-order intentionality (the norm for adult humans) is indicated by the horizontal solid line. Apes are the only non-human primate capable of theory of mind (second-order intentionality). It will be apparent that none of the australopithecine species do better than the living apes, confirming their status as bipedal great apes. The appearance of early *Homo* (the earliest members of our genus, *H. rudolfensis* through to *H. erectus*) marks an increase to third-order intentionality, with the later archaic humans (*Homo heidelbergensis* and *Homo neanderthalensis*) rising to fourth-order.

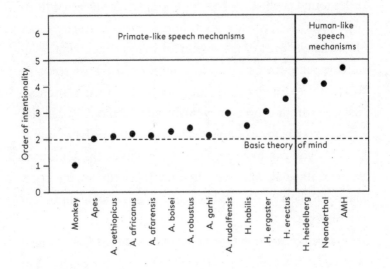

Figure 9

The evolution of mentalizing abilities, indexed by achievable order of intentionality, from monkeys to fossil populations of anatomically modern humans (AMH). Sources for the data are given in the endnote below. The plotted values are mean values for individual species based on all specimens for which cranial volumes are available. Level 2 mentalizing (conventional theory of mind: dotted line) marks the level achieved by great apes and human children (in their first big psychological breakthrough); level 5 (solid horizontal line) indicates the mentalizing competences of adult modern humans. The solid vertical line demarcates the point at which the anatomical markers for the human capacities for speech first appear.[13]

Only our own species (anatomically modern humans, *Homo sapiens*) has a brain large enough to allow fifth-order intentionality, the level required for language as we know it. In essence, this means that while archaic humans (Heidelbergs and Neanderthals) may well have had language in some form, it would not have been as complex as that of modern humans. Fourth-order language would be something like that of young teenagers: competent, and certainly adequate for a rich social life, but not good enough to develop and convey especially sophisticated ideas. It is unlikely that early *Homo* had any significant language capacity.

The scale of this difference is reflected in the complexity of the statements that could be made about religion (see Table 1). Archaic humans, who can achieve fourth-order intentionality, would certainly have been able have beliefs that we would consider religious, but they would have had difficulty converging on a communal religion. A species with fourth-order mentalizing would be able to imagine something about a spirit world, but only with fifth-order intentionality would they have been able to hold *communal* beliefs, and hence religion in its fullest modern sense. It seems that this only became possible with the appearance of modern humans around 200,000 years ago. Even if, as would surely have been the case, some individual Neanderthals had bigger brains than ours (as some did) and so might have been capable of quite sophisticated beliefs about the spirit world, it is unlikely that they would have been able to persuade the rest of their fellow Neanderthals of the absolute truth of their claims – not enough of them had brains large enough to grasp what their intellectual Einsteins were trying to explain. It seems that only anatomically modern humans (our own species) had the mentalizing capacities to have been able to do that. In other words, only modern humans could be meaningfully religious. This sets the earliest date at which any form of religion in its recognizable modern form could have arisen to around 200,000 years ago when our species appeared for the first time.

The second strand of evidence concerns the time course of the anatomical markers for speech – or at least vocal articulation and hearing. Speech requires two key capacities: the ability to produce long exhalations without having to take a breath and the capacity to control the articulation space in the mouth and upper throat by altering the position of the jaw, tongue and glottis. These are under the control, respectively, of the thoracic nerves in the upper chest and the hypoglossal nerve in the base of the skull. Both of these nerve bundles are much larger relative to body size in modern humans than in any of the monkeys and apes, so we can ask when this increase in size occurred.

Three other anatomical markers are of interest for speech. One is the position of the hyoid bone that anchors the top of the larynx to the base of the tongue. In monkeys, apes and human infants, it lies high in the throat (which allows them to breath and swallow at the same time without drowning themselves), but after weaning its drops low in the throat in humans (as a result, adults cannot drink and breathe at the same time). This low position is what allows us to produce certain vowel sounds, and vowels are crucial for human language. The other two indices are components of the inner ear, and hence our ability to hear fine distinctions in others' speech. These are the area of the base of middle ear bone known as the stapes and the size of the cochlea (the curled-up organ in the inner ear), both of which determine the range of sounds that can be heard. Both are relatively larger in modern humans than in monkeys and apes. They make it possible for humans to hear much lower sounds than apes can.

In fact, these five anatomical markers all appear to switch from primate-like to human-like with the appearance of archaic humans (*Homo heidelbergensis*) some 500,000 years ago. This is indicated along the top of Figure 9. It is important to appreciate that the capacity for speech is essential for language, but it is not the case that having speech necessarily means you have language. The capacity for speech (or controlled vocal production and the corresponding hearing capacity) is as necessary for singing as it is for speech, but singing does not need to have words – as is evident, for example, from jazz scat singing and Gaelic mouth music from the Outer Hebrides. It is perfectly possible, as the archaeologist Stephen Mithen has suggested, that singing evolved as a form of chorusing long before language appeared. In fact, this kind of wordless humming or chorusing might be precisely what Neanderthals discovered in the naturally echoing chambers of deep caves. It does not require superhuman cognitive abilities to realize that voices echo in large chambers and that this produces very positive endorphin effects, especially when they are in unison.

In sum, Figure 9 tells us while the capacity for speech probably evolved around 500,000 years ago with the appearance of archaic humans, it is unlikely that fully modern speech evolved before the appearance of modern humans around 200,000 years ago. Heidelbergs and Neanderthals surely had language in some form, but it could not have been as sophisticated as the language of modern humans. They might have had some inkling of a supernatural force, especially in their deep cave hideaways, but they wouldn't have been able to translate this into the kinds of complex theological statements needed to support religion in any formal sense. They might have expressed surprise and wonder at the atmospherics of these caves, and perhaps even gone into trance in the process. But it is unlikely that they would have been able to discuss the *meaning* of what they experienced in terms of a spirit world. Even basic animist religion is likely to have been beyond them, since that requires the ability both to conceive that rocks and springs contain spirits and to express this in a way that others could concur with.

Let me raise one last issue, because somebody is bound to do so if I don't mention it. In 2013 a new cave complex was discovered in South Africa that yielded a very large collection of fossils that were clearly part of the human lineage. The deposits were initially dated to around 300,000 years ago, making them very modern in the grand scale of human evolution. And herein lay the puzzle, because not only were they very small-bodied (and small-brained) but they also showed an eclectic mix of australopithecine and more modern *Homo* features. Although the individuals from this site share with modern humans a skeletal design associated with more efficient striding locomotion (one of the principal markers for the genus *Homo*), they also share some traits with the earlier australopithecines, including a remarkably small brain size for so late a species, and hands that were better adapted for climbing in trees than ours are. On these grounds, the fossils were ascribed to a new species, *Homo naledi*. More importantly, notwithstanding their ape- and australopithecine-sized brains, it was claimed that they had near-modern human cognitive abilities, mainly on the grounds that the only way the dozen or so bodies could have got down into the location where they were found deep inside the cave complex must have been if they had been carried down there in some kind of mortuary ritual. In other words, they must have has some kind of religion.

This claim, if true, completely contradicts Figure 9, since the species' ape-sized brain would imply that it would have been limited to second-order mentalizing like all the other great apes and the australopithecines. But if so, how could it have had both an ape-like cognition and modern human religion? The two are simply incompatible.[14] In addition, given that, anatomically, everyone would agree this is an early *Homo* and not an archaic human, it is most unlikely to have had the vocal tract anatomy required to support speech. In which case, it would not have had sufficient language competence to discuss the meaning and significance of its mortuary rituals, and so could not have made all the necessary arrangements for such complex funerary rites. The fact that so primitive a species survived so late is, of course, fascinating but hardly unknown.[15] That does not, in and of itself, mean they necessarily had fully modern cognition. The bottom line is that one should always be cautious of palaeoanthropologists' initial claims: they invariably get modified later as more detailed analyses of the fossils are undertaken. In the meantime, it is usually best to reserve judgement. The more important thing is the very consistent overall pattern exhibited by the much larger sample of fossil species in Figure 9.

Putting everything in this chapter together, what it seems to tell us is that while archaic humans might well have had language, it was not fully modern human language, and would not have had its level of subtlety. That means they would not have been able to convey high-level religious beliefs to each other. They could surely have told each other about what they had experienced during trance or in the mind-altering environments they experienced in deep caves. That might well have included fearing spirits and other unseen beings occupying natural features like caves. But it is very doubtful whether they would have been able to elaborate any meaningful theory about what it all meant.

Archaeologists have sometimes confidently asserted that Neanderthals had shamans and an intense religious life. Whether they actually believed in an afterworld – or an underworld – and, especially, one peopled by spirit beings whose influence on the present world could be mediated by shamans, seems, on the comparative ethnographic and cognitive evidence, unlikely. What may, however, be plausible is that archaics, and especially archaics like the Neanderthals who habitually used caves both as dwellings and, perhaps, to dispose of their dead, had discovered the magical properties of communal singing in echoing chambers and the way this can induce trance. Trance might provide evidence for some form of animism, but trance does not, in and of itself, imply the existence of shamans. It may simply be a communal ritual.

That said, the capacity to enter into trance is not, on its own, what modern humans understand by religion: something more is needed. In short, religion as we know it is unlikely to have evolved before the appearance of anatomically modern humans around 200,000 years ago. Religion is something that sets humans apart.

A Crisis in the Neolithic

From around 12,000 BP, new developments in the Middle East and elsewhere presage the arrival of the Neolithic, or New Stone Age. Settlements begin to appear in the form of clusters of stone-lined pit houses with clay floors. Initially, these settlements were small in size, but over a matter of a thousand years or so they increased in size dramatically. By 11,000 BP, Jericho amounted to some seventy dwellings, suggesting a population of around 300–400, and by 9,000 BP Çatalhöyük in Turkey was large enough to accommodate a population of 5,000–7,000 people.

Although the very earliest settlements do not suggest any significant change in style of religion, excavations at Göbekli Tepe and Çatalhöyük in Turkey suggest that by 9,500 BP, major new developments were under way. Some parts of these sites seem to have a religious or ceremonial function rather than being residential. At Göbekli Tepe, for example, there are several hundred massive pillars weighing 10–20 tons, many engraved with reliefs of animals. It has been estimated that it would have taken a community of 500 or more to move the pillars the 500 metres from the quarry to their final position. One does not go to these lengths for conventional dwellings. At Çatalhöyük, the dead were regularly buried under the floors of the houses. The walls were hung with the plastered skulls of animals, and some of the walls were painted with scenes of hunting and other activities. Stone-carved or clay-baked animal heads and human figurines are common.

The subsequent pace of development was remarkably rapid. By 3000 BC (5,000 years ago), the Naqada culture had developed into a formal state uniting Nubia and Upper Egypt, and the Akkadian empire had been established in Mesopotamia; the first of the Chinese empires, the Xia Dynasty, was established in central China less than a millennium later. This dramatic change in the demographic organization of populations would have had very significant effects on how individuals related to each other, and it is this, I argue in this chapter, that triggered the rise of doctrinal religions. To understand how and why this happened, we first need to consider the consequences of moving from a dispersed hunter-gatherer lifestyle to an urban one.

The Transition to Village Life

Traditionally, the Neolithic Revolution is associated with the mastery of cultivation, and a settled lifestyle has usually been seen as necessary for the provision of a work force for these purposes. This is almost certainly wrong, for three reasons. First, large work forces were not needed for agriculture until industrial-scale farming to service external markets developed, and these did not emerge until many thousands of years later. Subsistence-scale farming requires only the labour of a single family, even now. Second, archaeologists now agree that the earliest evidence for crop-growing predates the first Neolithic settlements by several thousand years. More importantly, during the early phase of settlement, a hunting and gathering economy was still the norm. Aurochs (wild cattle), gazelle and other wild animals were hunted and wild cereals gathered, although these practices declined over time with the domestication of cereals and livestock. Third, despite the widespread assumption that agriculture was good for you because it yields a significant improvement in nutrition for less effort, it seems that the opposite was in fact true. Evidence from physiological stress signs in skeletons and calculation of the energy throughput for hunter-gatherer and early farmer populations living in the same region show rather starkly that the farmers were under much greater nutritional stress than the hunter-gatherers.[1] Farming was extremely hard work and subject to the vagaries of climate as well as the depredations of wildlife and pests. It seems these populations had little choice: they could not pursue a hunter-gatherer life even if they wanted to but instead were obliged to live in settlements and put up with the significant costs of doing so. In short, people did not live in villages in order to develop agriculture, but developed agriculture in order to live in villages, at least once these settlements achieved any significant size.

Seeing the sequence this way round raises the obvious question as to why people made this sudden transition, and why they did so as rapidly as they evidently did. The answer appears to be defence against raiders.[2] Human populations seem to have been growing rapidly just before and into the early Neolithic, especially in the northeast corner of Africa and the Near East.[3] That raiding by neighbours was a problem is obvious from the fact that most settlements were built on hilltops or rocky promontories that provide a good all-round defensive position. In addition, the entrances to the houses in these early Near East settlements were almost always from the flat roof (a practice that persisted well into Biblical times in the Middle East), with just a few small, mainly inward-facing windows at ground level. Some of these settlements had substantial brick-built surrounding walls – recall the famous walls of Jericho which stood some 12 ft (3.6 m) high and 6 ft (1.8 m) wide at the base. These were costly to build in terms of manpower and hardly likely to be purely decorative.

The use of defensive positions was widespread throughout the Neolithic and into historical times. Well known historical examples include the thousands of Iron Age hill forts that dot the landscape of northwest Europe, the mesa-top villages of the Hopi and other pueblo Indians of the American Southwest, and the *conquistador*-period Inca hilltop cities like Machu Pichu in Peru. Although archaeologists have sometimes been surprisingly coy about admitting that these sites had anything to do with defence, in fact it is pretty obvious that this was why these settlements were built where they were. In fact, we know this is so from the historical record. At the end of the first millennium AD, the ancestral Anasazi Indians of the American Southwest deliberately moved their villages from the rather open, vulnerable positions they had previously occupied to more defendable positions on nearby mesas or ledges in canyon walls in direct response to increasingly intense raiding by Comanche and Navajo as these northern tribes began to expand southwards into their territory.[4] Many of the thousands of pueblo ruins in the area are on ledges in canyon walls that could only be accessed by rock climbs or the use of ropes, with overhangs that made them all but impregnable from three sides as well as above. We know from Spanish accounts that, during the Pueblo Revolt against their Spanish overlords in 1680, the Zuni abandoned their six large scattered villages and relocated to the 7,300 ft (2,200 m) Dowa Yalanne mesa (Corn Mountain), and remained there for three years until a peace treaty had been signed.[5] The Spanish records tell us that they had used this same refuge a century earlier in 1540 when the conquistador Vázquez de Coronado undertook an expedition to annex the lands north of their Mexican territories.

Similar observations come from Africa. Sir Kenneth Bradley noted that, while a young administrative officer in Northern Rhodesia (now Zambia) in the 1920s, a Chewa headman then in his eighties told him that his uncle, who had been headman many decades earlier, had moved their villages from the more fertile riverine plain where they had previously lived into the hills above because of marauding Nguni *impis* (war parties). After suffering a catastrophic defeat at the hands of Shakar's Zulu confederation during the Zulu civil wars of the 1830s, the Nguni Zulu clans fled north of the Zambesi River in 1833 and spent the following decades terrorizing the local tribes in what is now Zambia and Malawi. Many of the Chewa were enslaved by the Nguni. The neighbouring Tumbuka had also fled into the hills in the face of Nguni marauders and did not reoccupy their ancestral lands in the plains until after 1907 when the newly established British colonial administration put an end to Nguni raiding and slaving. Likewise, the Fali and other peoples of the Mandara Mountains on the Nigeria/Cameroon border had retreated from the richer plains into the less productive mountains for protection from the horse-based slaving parties of the Fulani, Wandala, Shuwa Arab and Kanuri that continued to harass them (for both domestic slavery and export across the Sahara to the slave markets of North Africa and Arabia) until as late as the 1920s – fully a century after the Atlantic slave trade had been suppressed by the Royal Navy.[6]

We tend to think of our prehistoric ancestors as living an idyllic life, quietly going about their business with only the occasional hunting expedition to excite them. In fact, nothing could be further from the truth. There has been a constant movement of peoples on every continent for at least the last 70,000 years, and as time progressed these migrations increasingly resulted in conflict between different tribal groups. That these interactions were serious is evidenced by the Crow Creek massacre that took place in South Dakota during the 1320s AD, when an entire village of Caddaon Central Plains Indians was massacred by their Mandan neighbours. Of the 486 bodies of men, women and children that have been recovered by archaeologists from this site, over 90 per cent had been scalped (as evidenced by cut-marks on the sides of the skulls). In addition, many had had their lower arms and tongues removed (another common form of trophy-hunting among Native Americans that persisted well into modern times). The Caddaons had been recent invaders from the south, and had clearly felt sufficiently threatened by the local Mandan that they were in the process of repairing their village's defensive dry moat fortification when they were overwhelmed.[7]

Similar massacre sites have been discovered in many parts of Central Europe, dating to periods around 7000 BC.[8] Most appear to involve massacres of entire bands of early European hunter-gatherers by farmers working their way westwards from Anatolia. The burial sites include men, women and children, with clear evidence of violent death from blunt instrument trauma to the side or back of the skull and casual rather than respectful disposal of the bodies. In around half the skeletons at one site, shin bones had also been deliberately broken before death (presumably to prevent escape).

At many of these burial sites, there is a conspicuous absence of young women, suggesting that these had been separated out and taken away as sex slaves – a practice that has been, and continues to be, characteristic of societies all over the world. Women of reproductive age were a major prize of raiding among Amazonian Indians even as late as the 1960s.[9] More remarkable is the fact that we can sometimes detect the genetic echoes of these events many centuries later. Eight centuries after Genghis Khan's conquests of Central Asia and Eastern Europe, around 7 per cent of all males currently alive within the geographic range of the thirteenth-century Mongol empire have the Y-chromosome genetic signature of the Khan and his generals.[10] Similarly, the genetic signature of the fifth-century Anglo-Saxon invaders is still evident in the contemporary English population: while the women on the east side of England have native Celtic mitochrondrial DNA, the men typically have Anglo-Saxon Y-chromosome (paternal) signatures.[11] We know from the historical records that the Anglo-Saxons operated a ferocious form of apartheid that, until the legal reforms of King Alfred the Great four and a half centuries later, actively discriminated against the Romano-British natives, including denying them legal status and allowing Saxon men to take both the property and women of the British natives with impunity.[12] Similarly, while 85 per cent of living Icelandic men have the expected Norse male genetic signature of the population that originally colonized the island, 50 per cent of Icelandic women have a Celtic maternal signature, reflecting the historically well-documented fact that the Norse regularly collected Irish and Scots slave girls on their way over to Iceland.[13] Indeed, slaving on the British mainland by Irish raiders continued until well into the twelfth century, notwithstanding explicit attempts to end it at the Council of London in 1102 AD.[14]

In other words, protection from attack by raiders has been a very serious issue for a very long time, and living in settlements provided the best defence. The problem, however, is that living in groups of any size is stressful. From time to time, the San Bushmen feel the need to dispel what they call 'star sickness'. This is a mysterious force that takes over a group of people, causing jealousy, anger, quarrels and the failure of gift-giving.[15] These pressures pull people apart and damage social cohesion. Trance dancing mends the social fabric because it releases hostility. In addition, the stresses created by social friction can have a dramatic effect on female menstrual endocrinology, causing temporary infertility. This is a general problem for all mammals and is a major factor limiting the size of the social groups of mammals in general, primates in particular and, by extension, humans.[16]

In an analysis of the causes of disputes among San in Namibia, the most common causes of complaint were the behaviour of inconsiderate trouble-makers, jealousy over possessions, persistent stinginess or failure to share, inappropriate sexual behaviour and the failure to fulfil obligations towards kin. Ostracism was the ultimate, albeit rarely used, sanction that, in such societies, was equivalent to a death sentence since individuals rarely survived when living alone. Most cases of ostracism involved behaviour, and especially sexual behaviour, that was considered socially disruptive. Under pressure from criticism by other members of the community, one woman who had had frequent sexual relationships with neighbouring Bantu men left the band and subsequently died. Another case involved the expulsion of a family in which the wife was frequently drunk and had promiscuous sexual relations with Bantu men; and, to cap it all, the children were unruly. Eventually, after the entire community had ganged up against them, the family left to live elsewhere. They were allowed back only after the woman had died.[17]

In any society, these kinds of petty, or not so petty, disagreements eventually boil over and lead either to direct violence or to accusations of witchcraft, which in turn invite retributive justice. Nearly a third of all recent historical deaths among the Gebusi horticulturalists of Papua New Guinea were homicides. While Gebusi men were more likely to be killed during intergroup disputes and raids, women were more likely to be killed as a result of within-community disputes, many of which involved accusations of witchcraft.[18] In hunter-gatherer societies, the proportion of deaths that are due to violence increases linearly with living-group size (Figure 10). In groups of fifty, violent deaths account for almost half of all mortality. No population can cope with demographic pressures on this scale. The flexible social arrangements of hunter-gatherers normally allow them to manage this so as to prevent things getting completely out of hand: if relationships become too fractious,

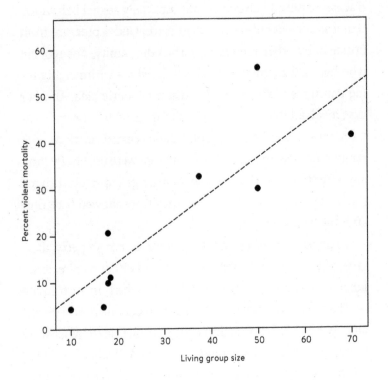

Figure 10
Percentage of adult mortality that is due to violence in
individual hunter-gatherer societies, plotted against the
average size of their living-groups. The dashed line is the
regression line through the data.[19]

a family can leave their camp group and move in with another group with whom they have connections. It may, hence, be no accident that the upper limit on living-group size in contemporary and historical hunter-gatherers is around fifty.

Because settlement results in the whole of the community or tribe being concentrated in one place, living in permanent villages and towns exacerbates this problem. Farmers living in villages of several hundred individuals experience significantly higher rates of homicide than hunter-gatherers, much of it due to within-community disputes.[20] In small-scale communities, fighting is much more likely to get out of hand because there is no police force to step in and resolve disputes. Once things get to this stage, views polarize rapidly along lines that have little to do with right and wrong and much more to do with personal and family loyalty. In a famous analysis of an axe-fight among Yanomamö Indians in Venezuela, the American anthropologist Napoleon Chagnon found that villagers rapidly sided with one or other of the main protagonists in a dispute and did so mainly on the basis of whom they were most closely related to or whom their own close relatives had sided with.[21] Fights force people to take sides one they becme serious enough to threaten injury or death, and that inevitably ruptures the delicate bonds that hold the community together.

The stresses of living together often emerge in conflicts between the women in the group. While studying the Siuai on Bourgainville Island in Micronesia during the 1950s, the anthropologist Douglas Oliver was told that villages invariably underwent fission when they exceeded nine households, mainly as a result of tensions created by quarrels among the women. The effects of this can even be detected within polygamous households. In tribes that practise sororal polygamy (all the wives are sisters), the women commonly live together under the same roof; however, when the women are not related, each wife usually has her own hut in the husband's compound. If they do not, relationships between them become too fractious.[22]

The need to find ways to reduce the levels of stress and internal violence as villages increased in size was crucial if humans were to live in larger settlements. Tribal societies that live in large settlements typically exhibit a variety of strategies to hold these disruptive forces in check. These include increased frequency of community bonding activities (dances, feasts), more formal marital arrangements involving the exchange of bridewealth between contracting families, a shift from a democratic social style to male hierarchies and formal leadership roles ... and a switch to doctrinal religions with more explicit rituals, formal religious spaces and religious specialists.[23]

The Rise of the Doctrinal Religions

Ritual spaces, symbolic representation of religious ideas, a priestly caste, gods and moral (as opposed to social) codes are all absent from modern hunter-gatherer societies but all appear very rapidly in urban settings during the course of the Neolithic. Some buildings at early sites like Jericho and 'Ain Ghazal (about 50 km east of Jericho) have been interpreted as having ritual functions on the grounds that they have unusual apsidal or circular shapes, are much smaller (sometimes just 2–3 m in diameter) than the other domestic buildings, and contain what appear to be basins and altars, as well as under-floor channels (to allow blood from sacrifices to drain out?). At 'Ain Ghazal, four of these 'ritual' buildings have been found spanning a 500-year period, only one of which was in active use at any one time.

Most of the domestic dwellings in these early Levantine Neolithic settlements are also associated with under-floor burials, with the bodies sometimes standing vertically, sometimes trussed into a crouching position. Some of these burials seem to have been so old that later householders were unaware of them and broke through, damaging the bones, when digging a grave for a later burial. Throughout the Levant as far east as Iraq there was a distinctive 'cult of skulls': in some cases, for example, skulls were removed from corpses and arranged around a central pit in a mortuary space on the edge of the village or in niches within a building. Some skulls had their faces reconstructed in plaster in eerily lifelike masks.

It is difficult to be sure when the various components of doctrinal religions first emerge. What we do know is that by 2000 BC in Sumeria, as well as around the same time in Egypt's Old Kingdom, we have evidence for a priestly caste. In some cases, these might be priestesses, many of whom were of noble birth, who often functioned as sacred prostitutes at temples. For example, Enheduana (the earliest poet known to us by name) was the High Priestess of the goddess Inanna and the moon god Nanna-Sin in the Sumerian city-state of Ur in the decades before 2250 BC. She composed the 153-line 'Nin-me-Šara' (Exaltation of Inanna) as well as a body of hymns of varying length, of which forty-two have survived. Enheduana was of royal blood, and seems to have been one of the *naditu* priestesses (temple slaves) recruited from high-born families. Inanna was worshipped in the Sumerian city of Uruk from as early as 4000 BC, but came to particular prominence and popularity as Ishtar, the goddess of love, beauty, sex, war, justice and political power, after the establishment of the Akkadian empire around 2300 BC. Known as the 'Queen of Heaven', she was not only the highest ranking deity in the Assyrian pantheon but continued to be worshipped until as recently as the eighteenth century in some parts of Mesopotamia.

This period also seems to coincide with the appearance of formal rituals. One characteristic of formal rituals is that they have to follow a prescribed script so as to be performed in exactly the same way on every occasion – otherwise they lose their 'power'. One of the earliest known examples of this are the so-called 'Pyramid Texts' that were carved onto walls and sarcophagi in the pyramids at Saqqara during Egypt's Fifth and Sixth Dynasties (2686–2181 BC). They specify prayers, spells and instructions to ease the deceased's way into the afterlife, many intended to be uttered ritually by priests. It has been suggested that the wording of some of these texts may even date back as far as the Second or Third Dynasties (2890–2613 BC).

The earliest forms of ritual seem to be associated mainly with propitiating gods whose interest in human affairs is often capricious and vindictive. In many traditional religions, the practice of making libations, offering farm produce or sacrificing animals is near-universal. Animal sacrifice was common in Old Testament Judaism right up to the time of Jesus, and, arguably, persists in modern Christianity in the form of harvest festivals where rural churches are decorated with produce from the field.

Ritual sacrifice may even extend to human victims. Sometime during the first century AD, Celts in the northwest of England gave a young man in his twenties a last ritual meal of charred bread, then garrotted him and cut his throat, finally depositing him naked in what at the time was a remote bog now known as Lindow Moss. Since the discovery of Lindow Man (or Pete Marsh as he is often irreverently known) in 1984, a total of 140 bodies have been recovered from bogs in Britain, all dating to around the same period. A large number of similar 'bog people' have also been found in Denmark, indicating that it was a widespread practice in northwest Europe at the time. Perhaps significantly, this period coincided with the beginning of the Roman occupation of Britain and continental Europe north of the Rhine, raising the possibility that these sacrifices might have been an attempt to propitiate the gods in the face of major societal disruption.

Religion and the Rule of Law

In the earlier sections, I suggested that there is a natural progression from informal religions in small-scale societies to formal religions in large scale societies as a way of managing the stresses involved. This development can be traced in some detail in South America. A reconstruction of village sizes on the Taraco Peninsula in Lake Titicaca, Bolivia, between 1500 and 250 BC (the period leading up to the formation of the Tiwanaku state) found that, in the early phase when the economy was largely subsistence agriculture, average village size was about 127 people and villages tended to split up when they

CHAPTER 8

reached 170 in size – at almost exactly the same size as they did three millennia later among the Hutterites in North America (Chapter 4). By 1000 BC, average village size had increased to around 275, with as many as a quarter of the villages containing more than 400 people. By about 800 BC, this had given rise to a fully fledged religious complex known as the Yaya-Mama religious tradition. This included a novel form of ceremonial public space (a plastered sunken court), decorated serving bowls, ceramic trumpets, incense burners, and a distinctive style of stone sculpture.[24]

The American Plains Indians provide us with another example because some of them switched from one state to the other and back again on a regular annual cycle. For most of the year, these tribes lived in small mobile bands of half a dozen families (perhaps 30–35 people), each with its own chief but little or no formal ceremonial. During the annual buffalo hunt, however, all the bands of a tribe came together in a single encampment of several thousand individuals. During this period, and only during this period, the chiefs of the individual bands formed an all-powerful council, with one member elected as the paramount chief. In addition, there were men's secret societies, religious ceremonial and a formal police force responsible for enforcing strict adherence to rules of behaviour. None of these occurred, or were needed, during the dispersed phase.

While the imposition of top-down discipline by a police force is certainly effective in managing disruptive behaviour among community members (especially the young males), it is always more effective to do this bottom up by making the individual feel committed to the community. In essence, this is how religions work at their best – by creating a sense of belonging through shared beliefs and shared rituals (the Seven Pillars of Chapter 5 again). In effect, the Seven Pillars constitute a totem pole at the centre of the village on which everyone can voluntarily hang their hats. If to this we add both Moralizing High Gods who monitor what humans are up to and religiously justified moral injunctions (such as the Ten Commandments), then we create a very powerful carrot-and-stick effect. In his analysis of the social and political correlates of Moralizing High Gods, Dominic Johnson found that these kinds of gods (the kind found only in doctrinal religions) are significantly more likely in societies that live in large communities and those that have 'jurisdictional hierarchies above the community level' (politically more complex societies in which an elite rules over the community).[25] In other words, organized religions seem to have been part of the machinery used to keep the lid on fractiousness so as to allow larger communities to exist.

Attempts to identify when and why Moralizing High Gods (that is, those that take an active interest in human behaviour) emerged have focused mainly on either economic or demographic contexts. As we noted in Chapter 7, Hervey Peoples found that belief in Moralizing High Gods was more or less confined to tribal groups with a pastoralist or agricultural economy – in other words, property-owning societies. In her view, Moralizing High Gods emerged as an adjunct to allow elites within society to maintain control over the product of others' labour, and this only became feasible with herding (most pastoralists typically have very large flocks and herds because they extol herd size as a measure of status) and intensive agriculture.

However, this explanation seems to put the cart before the horse: for most pastoralists, herding is a family business not a community arrangement and can be managed within the normal obligations of family relationships. The biggest problem that herders face is defence against raiding by other pastoralists. The mobility of stock animals means that pastoralists the world over face a constant threat of rustling that invariably results in significant loss of life (and women) as collateral damage. Banding together in communities large enough to provide sufficient numbers of warriors to protect and avenge these raids is the only viable solution. It is to ensure community cohesion for mutual protection that High Gods are necessary, not to arrange herding duties or prevent thefts within the community.

A number of recent analyses have focused on whether belief in High Gods emerged before or after the emergence of political complexity. Many studies differentiate between two separate phenomena: supernatural punishment and Moralizing High Gods. Supernatural punishment is usually associated with rituals to appease capricious deities who have little interest in the moral behaviour of humans, but require sacrifices and other forms of invocation designed to allay their wrath. An example would be the religion of the Aztecs, which required very large numbers of victims (typically war captives or slaves) to be sacrificed (sometimes by having their hearts torn out while alive) to deities such as Huitzilopochtli, the bloodthirsty god of war. The Aztec rain god Tlaloc was particularly fond of child sacrifices as he required their tears to make rain. In contrast, Moralizing High Gods usually take an active interest in the wellbeing and behaviour of their human worshippers, rewarding those that adhere to the rules they lay down (usually via some kind of revelatory process) and punishing (now or in the world after death) those who don't. The Abrahamic religions provide the classic examples. Religions with capricious deities tend to view the performance of the relevant rituals as a *communal* duty, with divine punishment being meted out indiscriminately on the whole of society. Moralizing High God faiths tend to view divine retribution as a *personal* matter, reflecting the individual's performance over the course of their life.

The close correlation between the emergence of human sacrifice and the suite of rituals associated with it, and the switch from simple to stratified societies in the Austronesian cultures that I mentioned in Chapter 3 provides an example of this process in action. Cultures that adopted sacrifice as a new ritual complex were able to switch to having stratified social structures, which in turn allowed them to increase the size of their populations. The analyses were very clear: sacrifice emerged before stratification. In effect, sacrifice and the rituals that make up doctrinal religions provide the gateway for increasing social complexity (and hence population size). In part, this comes about by imposing draconian discipline on those who transgress against the rules. If you don't develop the necessary rituals, your social groupings will necessarily remain small and dispersed. In this context, human sacrifice seems both to raise the psychological ante for being a member of the community and acts as some kind of transcendental threat (our god is *very* demanding, so beware lest you become the victim).

An alternative approach is to examine the actual sequence

of historical changes through time at a particular location. This provides a different perspective on the question because it allows us to map the acquisition of different rituals and beliefs onto the changes in the demographic and economic state of the community as it developed from a relatively simple settlement through a classic city state to a large empire. Several recent studies have used this approach to try to determine when High Gods emerged, and why.

One study collated data from over 400 societies covering the last 10,000 years and mapped the changes in social complexity either side of the appearance of beliefs in supernatural punishment and High Gods. Social complexity was indexed by a rather eclectic mix of traits ranging from population size, hierarchical and legal structures, infrastructure (such as canals and roads), a calendar, writing and metal coinage. The results suggested that rituals to avert divine punishment predate the appearance of High Gods by up to 2,000 years, and broadly predate or correlate with growing social complexity. High Gods typically appear as the society reaches its peak of structural complexity. In fact, the rate of change in social complexity seems to accelerate rapidly in the centuries immediately before the appearance of High Gods, and then stabilizes immediately afterwards. The data point to a population of around one million people as the key threshold at which High Gods appear, which might suggest that they are associated with empires rather than city-states.[26]

A smaller-scale study of the co-evolution of High Gods and social stratification provides some further light on this process, even though it was initially interpreted as yielding contradictory results. This study suggested that, in Austronesian societies, supernatural punishment is an immediate precursor of the evolution of social stratification, with Moralizing High Gods appearing *after* social stratification.[27] The apparent contrast between these two studies is in fact rather easily explained: the size of societies in the Austronesian study was an order of magnitude smaller than those at the crucial junction where Moralizing High Gods appear according to the previous study. Few of them had more than 100,000 members, compared to the figure of a million associated with the appearance of Moralizing High Gods. In fact, the Austronesian data lend clear support to the suggestion that Moralizing High Gods appear only when societies reach a very high demographic and structural complexity threshold. This suggests that there is a series of demographic glass ceilings at the high end just as there is at the low end. At each stage, a new mechanism is needed to allow the society to break through the constraint and increase in size to the next level.

The handful of major religions that now dominate the world all have their origins in the Yellow and Yangste River region in China, the Ganges valley in northern India and the eastern Mediterranean. Why all these large religions should have appeared at about the same time (the period known as the Axial Age during the first millennium BC) in these geographically widely separated locations has puzzled historians for a very long time. In fact, the best predictor of the switch to the Axial Age state turns out to be per capita annual energy production (essentially agricultural output), with a threshold at around 20,000 kcals per person identifying the transition point. This probably represents the level of production that creates agricultural surpluses sufficient to feed large cities at the centre of an empire (for example, Rome). The next-best predictor was population density (itself a correlate of energy surplus, of course). Although population size, the size of the principal city and the geographic size of the state individually had negligible effects, in reality these almost certainly form a single interrelated complex of variables.

The authors of this last study argued that increasing affluence spurs people on to develop more prosocial attitudes in order to protect the ownership of property. They suggested that the resulting emphasis on societal cooperation and the inhibition of selfish tendencies (for example, to prohibit stealing from others) precipitates a switch from a largely lawless society to one in which the rule of law applies and ideologies develop that encourage citizens to behave prosocially. These, they suggest, are reflected in the large-scale doctrinal religions that characterize the Axial Age, with their emphasis on good behaviour and individual responsibility for one's actions.[28] One problem with this claim is that it looks suspiciously like group selection: why would the downtrodden masses voluntarily acquiesce in protecting the wealth of the elite? Evolutionary biologists, as we saw in Chapter 1, are very nervous of any explanation that, intentionally or inadvertently, invokes group selection. Moreover, agricultural production alone cannot be an evolutionarily viable explanation. Evolution doesn't occur simply in order to allow more food to be produced. Production is either a proxy for something else, or a solution to a constraint that allows more sophisticated ideologies to emerge that maximize individual fitness.

Looking back over these three studies, two main conclusions suggest themselves. First, Moralizing High Gods were a very late development. Most of these transitions occurred in the first millennium BC, the period known as the Axial Age. All are associated with a dramatic increase in socio-political complexity, and this is invariably associated with a dramatic increase in the size of the population to a million or more individuals, with correspondingly greater difficulty in managing the stresses of living together. These stresses, as we saw in the previous section, include increased levels of violence, as well as theft, abuse and argumentativeness. Second, preceding this, there was often a long phase of ritual complexity and propitiatory worship based around belief in divine retribution that gave rise to a constant need to mollify the deities involved. This seems to have been associated with societies that number around 100,000 individuals. The earliest of these (in Anatolia and the Levant) date to around 6,000 BC, but most predate the appearance of High Gods by around 2,000 years (that is, they appear around 2,500 BC).

Although little is made of this, in almost every case the appearance of these forms of ritual coincide with a distinct upswing in social complexity soon after, as a result of an escalating increase in population size and its concentration in a handful of large centres (towns and cities). The increase in population size seems to have something to do with the climate and conditions for growing agricultural surpluses in these regions, while the rapid growth of cities is almost always fuelled by economic opportunities at the seat of wealth and power sucking in people from the rural provinces – an effect that continues right into the present day. Added religious complexity seems to be necessary to allow community size to increase to these levels. What we seem to be seeing here is evidence for a series of glass ceilings. Finding a solution at each step allows community size to increase to the next glass ceiling rather than imploding on itself through lawlessness and civil war; failure to find a solution means either that community size remains stuck at the lower level or that community fragmentation results in regression to a lower stable point.

One final relevant observation concerns the circumstances under which a priestly caste (religious specialists) appears in a society. In an ongoing project, Joseph Watts has used comparative methods to analyse ethnographic data on the presence/absence of religious specialists in different contemporary hunter-gatherer societies drawn from all around the world. He was mainly interested in whether religious specialists appeared when the environment was especially unpredictable – a context in which diviners and shamans might have played a role in predicting and controlling environmental catastrophes. His analyses suggest, however, that environmental unpredictability is not itself directly related to the presence of religious specialists. Instead, it seems that the factor that most directly influences their appearance is the presence of food stores. Food storage is indicative of food surpluses, implying that religious specialists appear when a society is sufficiently well-off to be able to set aside food for some individuals who can devote their time to being religious specialists. This suggests that a priestly caste – as opposed to individual shamans or healers – emerges only when agricultural production is high enough to give rise to populations of sufficient size to produce food surpluses. Of course, when populations reach this size, they are also likely to experience serious social and demographic stresses.

Monotheism and the Axial Age

It seems that the major doctrinal religions emerged in areas where population growth was high and large states were emerging, but why did these demographic conditions occur where and when they did? It is conspicuous that all the great world religions emerged within the very narrow latitudinal band of the northern subtropical zone that lies immediately above the tropics (Figure 11). Each of the subtropical zones occupies just 12 degrees of latitude, so the northern zone accounts for about 10 per cent of the world's occupiable land surface. Yet fourteen of the world's sixteen monotheistic and major state religions were founded within or on the edge of this zone. Of course, there is very little landmass south of the Tropic of Capricorn, and all the tribes that historically occupied the southern zones in all three southern continents (that is, prior to the Bantu invasions of southern Africa after AD 1400) were low-density hunter-gatherers. So it is perhaps no surprise that most of these religions originated in the northern zone. However, this still begs the question as to why this very narrow band of subtropical climate should have been responsible for so many major religions.

To answer this question, we need to take note of a more general relationship between latitude and a number of social and biological phenomena. It has been known for a long time that the tropics are a hothouse for pathogen evolution, mainly due to its equable climate, warmth and lack of severe seasonality. If you want graphic evidence of this, you need look no further than the cemeteries scattered across the tropics. In the eighteenth and nineteenth centuries, Europeans,

Figure 11
TK

who lacked natural resistance to the many local diseases, experienced life expectancies measured in months rather than years in the tropics of West Africa and South Asia.[29] As one goes north or south towards the poles, the increasingly long, cold winters put a break on most pathogens' ability to replicate and speciate. In effect, there is a cline of pathogen and disease prevalence that starts high on the equator and declines rapidly outside the tropics.

Diseases place such heavy pressure on human populations within the tropics that there will be strong selection for anything that reduces pathogen load.[30] Reducing the pool of

Figure 11
Place of origin of the main monotheistic and major state religions. Dashed line is the equator. The solid lines either side are the tropics, and the grey-shaded areas are the subtropical zones. (Map: www.Free-Printables.net)

★ Place of origin of the monotheistic religions in Africa: A, Atenism (pharaonic Egypt); B, Cushitic and Nilo-Hamite tribes originating in northern Sudan (Oromo: now inhabiting northwest Ethiopia; Maasai and others: now inhabiting Kenya and northern Tanzania); C, Igbo (southeast Nigeria, having migrated down from central Niger plain); D, Himba (a member of the Bantu linguistic family expansion now occupying northern Namibia).

★ Place of origin of major Abrahamic religions ('the People of the Book'): 1, Christianity; 2, Judaism; 3, Islam; 4, Mandaeanism; 5, Manicheism.

✵ Monotheistic religions in Asia (L to R): Zoroastrianism, Sikhism and, in Shang Dynasty China, Shangdi and its derivative Mohism.

▲ Other major states with polytheistic religions: Aztec (southern Mexico), Inca, including immediate Tiwanaku ancestors (Lake Titicaca, Bolivia), Hinduism and Shinto (Japan).

● Major non-theistic world religions: Jainism and Buddhism.

people from whom one might contract a lethal disease is largely a matter of reducing the number of people with whom one
trades or intermarries. And the easiest way of doing that is to
have a different religion to your neighbours. This is reflected in
the fact that the number of different tribal religions per area increases, and their average number of adherents gets smaller, as
a function of disease load (Figure 12a). This is reinforced by the
extent to which social attitudes increasingly favour the local
community (so it becomes more collectivist and less individualist) as disease load increases (Figure 12b). In other words,
people minimize social interactions with strangers and focus
their social lives around a small tribe-based community.

The tropics offer a number of features that make this cir-
cling of the wagons possible. The most important is that the
growing season is usually twelve months long. This means
that it is possible to have several crops over the year, allowing groups to be self-sufficient rather than having to trade with
each other. Trading depends on having a common language, so

Figure 12

Figure 12a: Number of tribal religions per country (controlling
for size of country) plotted against number of parasitic diseases
recorded for the country (based on data for 177 countries).[31]

Figure 12b: Degree of individualist (versus collectivist) attitudes
plotted against pathogen load (based on data for 67 countries).
The individualism index is the Hofestede worldwide survey of IBM
employees (0 = wholly collectivist; 100 = wholly individualist).
Pathogen load is the summed prevalence of nine major pathogens
(leishmanias, trypanosomes, malaria, schistosomes, filariae,
leprosy, dengue, typhus and tuberculosis).[32]

Figure 12c: The number of languages per 1,000 km² area spoken
in 74 tropical countries, plotted against the length of the growing
season (a measure of ecological predictability).[33]

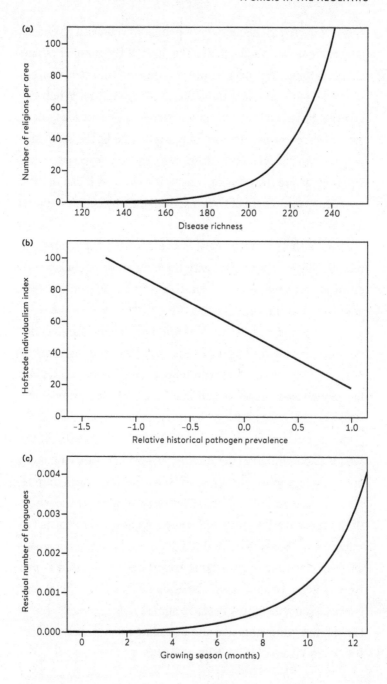

this is reflected in the number of people who speak a given language. Figure 12c shows this in the form of the number of languages spoken in a given country (adjusted for country area) plotted against the length of the growing season. When the growing season is short, as is the case at high latitudes, there are only a few widely spoken languages (that is, the same language is spoken over a very wide area); the closer you get to the equator (where the growing season is as long as it can be) the more languages there are, each spoken only by a few people in a small local area.

Notice that, as in the case of the density of religions, the relationship is exponential, with the number of languages suddenly increasing steeply once the growing season exceeds about six months – roughly equating to the edges of the tropics. At high latitudes, food is unpredictable, and survival depends on having trading networks over a wide enough area to ensure that at least one community accessible to you will be far enough away to act as a refuge from whatever disaster has befallen you. Since having a common language is crucial for negotiating trading arrangements of this kind, both the size of the language community (the number of speakers of a language) and the geographical area occupied by this language community increase proportionately. Contrast the fact that the whole of Europe, covering an area of some 4 million square miles (10 million km^2) boasts a mere three dozen or so distinct languages, each covering an enormous area, with the fact that Papua New Guinea, lying just off the equator, has 850 official languages in an area of just 180,000 square miles (460,000 km^2). Having the same language and the same religion ticks two of the Seven Pillars of Friendship (Chapter 5).

In effect, those living within the tropics try to isolate themselves from their neighbours not because there is any constraint on food availability but because of the increased risk of contracting novel diseases for which they have no natural immunity. They can only do this *because* the growing conditions are rich and food is superabundant most of the time. The pathogen load may be low at high latitudes, but the climatic seasonality, combined with much greater year-to-year variation in climate, increases the risk that people will experience crop failure, making a wide trading network more and more advantageous, the further from the equator you live.

There is an obvious trade-off here between the impact of disease and the capacity for food production. Population growth will be optimized by the difference between these two processes. At very high (that is, polar) latitudes, the environment is so poor that, historically, only hunter-gathering economies have realistically been possible, and population densities will always be low. Within the tropics, and especially near the equator, populations are constrained by disease rather than food, with population density held down by a combination of the disease burden and the socio-political fragmentation that attempts to mitigate this. Somewhere in between these two extremes, the balance will be more favourable. Figure 13 illustrates this by plotting the length of the growing season and the contemporary disease burden against latitude. The shapes of the two curves mean that the difference between the two will be greatest in the subtropical zone (between 23° and 35°) and just immediately beyond it. This suggests an explanation as to why the Axial Age religions all emerged in this narrow region:

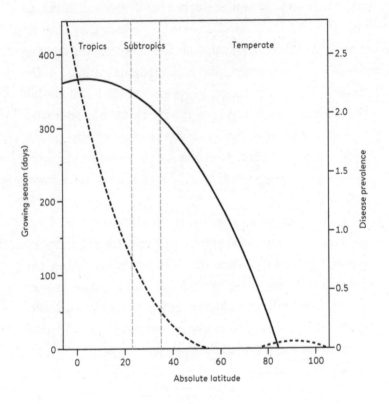

Figure 13
Length of growing season (solid line: number of consecutive
days when lake water temperature is >9°C) and current
disease load (long dashed line: vector-borne and parasitic
diseases) as a function of latitude. Short dashed lines
demarcate the subtropical zone.[34]

the length of the growing season was still reasonable, but the disease burden was very low, making the conditions perfect for rapid population growth.

This suggestion is made even more convincing when we remember that, due to climate warming, the climatic zones have moved dramatically since 2000 BC. Prior to this, the northern subtropical zone was much more luxuriant than it is now. The climate was wet and humid, and the central Sahara contained many substantial lakes and permanent rivers, with abundant fish, crocodiles and hippopotamus, as well as a variety of land mammals (baboons, rhino, warthog and gazelle) that are no longer found there. To take just one example, the current northern limit of the baboons' distribution is 850 miles (1,400 km) to the south of where it was in 2000 BC. In Ancient Egypt, Thoth, the god of virility and the dead, and also the scribe to the gods who invented writing, was often represented as a baboon-headed figure, reflecting the Egyptians' familiarity with the species; today the nearest populations of this unusually spectacular baboon (the hamadryas baboon) live in northern Ethiopia, some 800 miles (1,250 km) to the south. From around 4000 BC, conditions in the Sahara began to undergo progressive drying, with the present desert conditions appearing around 2000 BC.

Climatically and vegetationally, the northern part of Africa and the Levant would have been able to support significant human populations during the period of the Neolithic Settlement from around 8000 BC. The conditions would have been perfect for populations to explode and start to prey on each other, free from the disease burden imposed by the tropics further south. The sudden deterioration in the climate after 4000 BC would have caused significant inter-community strife as communities competed for declining resources. They may well have found it easier to raid weaker communities so as to make up their own shortfall.

That religion may help to bolster communal cohesion and cooperation in the face of external threats of this kind is suggested by a study of more than 190 tribal or social groups drawn from ninety-seven countries. The degree of 'religious infusion' (the extent to which religion permeates private and public life, for example by justifying prejudice and discrimination) correlates significantly with both the extent to which the society's worldview clashes with those of its neighbours and the extent to which they were in competition with their neighbours for resources and power. Analysis of the causal relationships between these variables suggested that religion exaggerated the causal link between incompatible values and willingness to discriminate against neighbours.[35] It may be no accident that Hervey Peoples found that Moralizing High Gods were unusually common among pastoralists. The subtropical zones were precisely where cattle, sheep and goats (in the north), and llamas and alpacas (in the south) were first domesticated. It may, equally, be no accident that all three of the Abrahamic religions had their origin in peoples who tended flocks and herds. Indeed, the East African Cushitic and Nilo-Hamitic tribes, most of whom are cattle herders, are also monotheistic. They originated in the Upper Nile Valley and spread southwards into Ethiopia and East Africa over the last millennium, arriving in central East Africa as recently as the mid-eighteenth century.

The evolution of all primate and human societies can best be understood as a series of glass ceilings imposed by constraints on fertility and reproduction generated by the stresses of being forced to live in close proximity. During the course of their evolution, some monkey and ape species evolved novel cognitive and behavioural strategies that enabled them to breach these glass ceilings so as to live in larger groups (mainly to allow them to occupy habitats that were more predator-risky). For primates, these solutions involved the formation of grooming-based coalitions, multilevel social systems and, in a few cases, social roles like policing.

As our human ancestors sought to evolve even larger social groups, this process necessitated finding novel means of community bonding (singing, dancing, feasting) and, once language had evolved, religion. Even so, these gave rise only to informally organized communities of 100–200 people. To allow communities to evolve significantly beyond this size required social structuring and the introduction of more organized forms of religion. Doctrinal religions effectively mark the last stage that made it possible for humans to move beyond small-scale face-to-face societies and develop the kinds of mega-polities in which we still live today. Even though each of these stages is associated with increasingly complex secular and judicial mechanisms for maintaining law and order, in itself the religious element represents a unique strand that is distinctively human. A Moralizing High God, of the kind found in many of the world religions, seems to represent a final stage of development that appears only when the civic units are very large.

Cults, Sects and Charismatics

All religions begin as cults, built around a charismatic leader. In most cases, these have been wandering holy men, very occasionally women. In some cases, new cults have arisen as a result of disputes between factions within an existing religion; in others, they have simply been inspired by individuals coming up with novel perspectives on life and theology, perhaps after time spent alone in contemplation. The distinction is probably trivial because almost no founder of a new religion exists in a cultural vacuum; all are embedded within an existing set of beliefs and practices that they either develop in new ways or react against.

Many of these charismatic individuals are influential only for brief periods of time during and immediately after their own lifetimes, their names lost to history as their memory fades and their followers drift away. A minority, like Siddhārtha Gautama (the founder of Buddhism), Guru Nanak (founder of the Sikh religion), Jesus Christ or the Prophet Muhammed, found religious movements that eventually came to dominate the world scene. Some, like St Francis of Assisi or St Ignatius Loyola (the founder of the Jesuits), leave formidable legacies in the form of religious orders that become the shock troops for their particular religion – in effect, cults within a doctrinal religion that retain theological orthodoxy. Often, however, cults are expelled from their parent religion for theological heresy or leave of their own volition.

Since cults are, invariably, a reaction against some aspect of the larger religious landscape within which they are embedded, most established religions have been ambivalent about them, often endeavouring to impose some degree of control over them once they have become sufficiently established to attract attention. In only a few cases have religions tolerated variety of expression and allowed cults (often based around local saints or deities) to flourish. Hinduism would be the most obvious example: its greatest claim to fame has been its extraordinary diversity of gods and religious traditions that happily coexist. Most major religions have taken a less tolerant attitude to theological deviance within their ranks. The medieval Cathars (or Albigensians) provide us with one of classic examples of this.[1]

It was the Cathars' theological views that most upset the religious establishment. They had strong gnostic leanings based on personal knowledge of God, took an anti-Trinitarian stance and believed in a version of reincarnation, many of these views having derived from the gnostic Paulician and Bogomil sects that flourished in Armenia and the Balkans in the ninth and tenth centuries. It probably didn't help that they promoted a remarkably egalitarian vision of society in which both sexes presided at services, as well as being vegetarians (killing anything was considered a sin).[2] Their main problem was that they became a formidable political force in southern France and northern Italy in the twelfth century – so much so that in 1209 Pope Innocent III launched the

Albigensian Crusade to suppress them. Many tens of thousands of Cathars lost their lives in Languedoc alone, mainly as a consequence of the entire citizenry of towns and cities being massacred as heretics after they had capitulated to the papal forces. So successful was the campaign that Catharism ceased to exist as a religious movement. Nonetheless, despite their demise, Cathar views continued to influence western Christian movements like the Beguines (an informal collective of lay women who lived together in semi-seclusion) into modern times.

In this chapter, I want to explore religious cults and sects in more detail for two reasons. One is that the significance of the process of cult generation has often been overlooked. Most studies have focused on the dynamics of individual sects as exemplars of new religious movements and seldom paused to ask why cults constantly seem to emerge. The second reason is one of the puzzling features of religions, namely the ease with which even the best of them spawn cults.[3] Why do they break up so easily into mutually antagonistic sects?

Mabel Barltrop and the Panacea Society: A Case Study

To provide some insights into the processes involved in the formation of cults, let me start with an example of a fairly typical cult, the Panacea Society. I choose this example for several reasons. First, despite its eccentricities and uncontroversial theology, it was never viewed as more than an idiosyncrasy by the local Church authorities. Second, it was very much of its time and provides us with a vignette of how themes from different sources become combined in the thinking of cult founders. Third, the Society is not well known, which means we can approach it in a more neutral frame of mind, unbiased by the views that often colour our attitudes towards the more familiar cults. Fourth, and in many ways most important, we are unusually fortunate to know a great deal more about the Panacea Society than is the case for older, more exotic cults whose origins are invariably buried in the mists of time and whose writings, if any, were suppressed by persecuting authorities. The fact that we have such good records in this case is in part due to the fact that most of those involved were well educated and kept meticulous records that are now housed in a small museum.[4]

Despite the comfortable orthodoxy provided by the Church of England, the late Victorian period witnessed a growing interest in an extraordinary range of unorthodox philosophies and cults, especially in England. Some, like Spiritualism, grew out of a longstanding national preoccupation with the occult that dates back to pre-Roman times (see the Introduction). Others, like Theosophy, developed out of a growing exposure to exotic eastern philosophies and religions, mainly those in India. Yet others were small-scale cults whose idiosyncratic views were an eclectic mix of conventional religions and homegrown beliefs. The Panacea Society, founded as a semi-enclosed millenarian community in Bedford by Mabel Barltrop in 1919, is one of these.

Mabel Barltrop was the widow of a Church of England clergyman. At the time of her husband's death in 1906, she had been a patient in the local asylum, diagnosed with melancholia (extreme depression), possibly brought on by her husband's chronic illness and his failure to find a permanent position.

Her own father had died when she was nine, leaving her semi-invalid mother to cope as a single parent. Now, as her husband's health failed, she faced the same prospect with four young children. After a second period in hospital suffering from depression and delusions, she became inspired by the teachings of the eighteenth-century rural prophetess Joanna Southcott, and came to believe that Bedford (where she was, fortuitously, living with her husband) was the original site of the Garden of Eden. After her husband's death, she bought a property in the town and established a community based on Southcott's teachings, with twelve female apostles (whose feet she ritually washed in imitation of Jesus washing the feet of his disciples).

Southcott had declared, at the age of sixty-four, that she was pregnant with the Shiloh (or Messiah) promised by the Old Testament patriarch Jacob in the Book of Genesis. When the baby failed to materialize, she withdrew from public view and died soon afterwards. One of Barltrop's women associates had a revelation that Barltrop was the Shiloh of the Southcott prophecies. As a result, Barltrop came to see herself as the infant incarnate and took the name Octavia, reflecting her self-proclaimed status as the eighth prophet in the Southcottian line.

Adopting a feminist theology based on Southcott's teachings, the Society aimed to challenge the male hegemony of the Church of England in particular, and of Christianity in general. In what would, at the time, have seemed like an outrageous assault on sacerdotal authority, Barltrop herself took on the priestly functions of presiding at Eucharistic services. Over the course of time, she began to see herself as the 'Divine Daughter' making up the fourth corner in a reconfigured Trinity: God the Father, the Divine Mother (formerly the Holy Ghost), the Divine Son (Jesus) and the Divine Daughter. Along with some of her close lieutenants, she developed a regular programme of automatic writing in which they took dictation directly from God every afternoon at 5.30 p.m. precisely. The writings would often be rushed to the early evening service to be read out to the expectant congregation.

By the 1930s, the community had grown to around seventy resident members, with as many as 1,300 additional 'sealed' members (those who had undertaken the necessary training and signed up to the commitments of membership) living elsewhere. An important benefit, provided free to anyone who asked, was the provision of a small strip of linen that had been blessed by Barltrop. The linen was to be soaked in a glass of water and the liquid drunk, or steeped in bathwater, with the promise that it would cure many diseases. Nearly 130,000 people around the world applied for linen strips during the Society's heyday in the interwar years.

Most of the resident members were older women, a number of them the disillusioned wives, widows, daughters or sisters of Anglican clergymen, many of whom fared rather poorly economically if their breadwinner died prematurely. In the later 1920s, a few men were allowed to join, including some active Anglican priests. However, it seems that the presence of men created additional tensions, not least the occasional romantic attachment. The latter usually resulted in the offending couple having to leave the community. An American was forced to leave on the grounds that he seemed to be making a bid to take over the Society *and* had been responsible for establishing a homosexual subculture among the men. One of the women, Emily Goodwin, who claimed to speak as the instrument of the Divine Mother, prophesied that he would die in New York. When news came back a few months after he had left the community that he had in fact died in New York, her status was assured and she quickly became Octavia's deputy.

The increase in the size of the community seems to have meant that managing relationships among the residents became a more taxing task. Once the community exceeded a few dozen people, Barltrop was obliged to produce a more formal set of rules that regulated in extraordinary detail the behaviour and activities of the residents, down to cleaning the lavatory after use and leaving hand towels neatly hung, ensuring that outdoor coats had loops so they could be hung on the hooks provided, and making sure that visitors left the premises. There were special instructions on how to make tea, and what to cook. Residents were obliged to engage in public self-criticism as well as report to the Divine Mother any anti-social or irksome behaviour by other members. The community remained largely shut off from society, with Barltrop herself never walking further than 75 yards from the house throughout her entire time in the community. Perhaps the saddest member of the community was her youngest offspring, Dilys, who was obliged to live in a claustrophobic community of older women from the age of twenty until her death in 1968.

After Barltrop's death in 1934, the community gradually went into decline, having failed to recruit enough new residents to replace losses due to deaths and departures. When the last surviving member died in 2012, the Society was closed down, the assets converted into a charity and the building into a museum. In many ways, the history of the Panacea Society is the classic story of a cult. Few survive for more than a generation or so after the death of their founder, if only because most are the product of their time and later generations fail to find their more arcane tenets and practices congenial. Subsequent leaders often lack the founder's charisma and commitment, and are unable to provide the direction that gave the original movement its fervour and momentum. In addition, growth in size creates organizational stresses that the community is often ill-equipped to cope with – in many cases, precisely because it was dominated by a single, temperamentally autocratic individual.

Nonetheless, the Panacea Society nicely illustrates many of the points made in this book. It began with a disgruntled member of a conventional religion, who in turn attracted a number of like-minded individuals. Since the founder was a woman, it may be no surprise, given the strong gender bias of conventional social networks,[5] that she attracted mainly other women to join her and that there are signs that when men joined the community it created some social difficulties. In this respect, it is notable that many of the nineteenth-century American millenarian cults either proscribed sex among their members or, as the Shakers did, obliged the two sexes to live apart in separate buildings. Among other common themes are the tendency for the founders of cults to see themselves increasingly as divine, invariably giving rise to claims that the founder's clothes and other everyday items have restorative powers. Initially, the Panacea community appears to have been quite informal in its arrangements, but its early success in attracting members soon meant that more formal structures were needed. As a result, it seems to have become more hierarchical, with Mrs Baltrop assisted by a small coterie of close lieutenants gathered around her. Mrs Baltrop's adoption of a divine persona (the 'Divine Daughter'), and her acquisition of a direct channel to God through automatic writing are classic devices, creating both a semblance of personal authority and a means of enforcing that authority.

The eventual demise of the community a generation after Barltrop's death reflects a common pattern. It seems to have resulted from the concatenation of two separate factors. One was that no serious efforts were made to proselytize more widely or encourage the planting of new communities elsewhere.[6] That might in part have been due to Barltrop's own reclusiveness and reluctance to leave the Society's site or preach to outside audiences. It was, however, reinforced by the second factor: the fact that none of her successors had the flair or charisma to modify the principles of the Society to accommodate a changing world. This contrast is illustrated by the split in the very early history of Christianity between the traditionalists who wanted to remain a sect within Judaism (mainly some of the original disciples) and those who wanted to broaden the sect's appeal to the wider Graeco-Roman world (mainly the outsider Paul of Tarsus). The former vanished without trace within a generation or so; the latter developed into a dynamic religion that gave us the Christianity we now have.

This raises two questions of interest. Why do some individuals become charismatic leaders? And why do other people become attracted to and follow these individuals?

Charismatic Leaders

What makes a charismatic leader, or gives someone charisma, is not entirely obvious. In large part, this is because charisma is actually something that is conferred on someone by their followers, not necessarily a property of the individual themselves. Charismatic individuals surely have attributes that others admire and which attract their followers to them, but it is not always clear what these properties are. Nonetheless, most charismatic individuals, religious and secular, probably share two related traits: they are convinced that they have some special ability or vocation (whether this be religious, political or physical – as in sporting or military prowess, or even just physical attractiveness) and they have a degree of presentational confidence. The latter is not the same thing as being an extravert, but rather that when they are in role (for example, giving a sermon or performing in some other way) they become animated by their convictions and, to their audience, dazzling.

For many religious charismatics, it is their spiritual message that underlies these two traits. Most claim to have special knowledge of God, or a mandate from God to lead people to salvation. In a surprising number of cases, they even claim to be God, or at least the Messiah sent by God. The medieval period was especially rich in such individuals. As early as the sixth century, the self-proclaimed 'Christ of Gévaudon' in southern France (together with his female companion, whom he named Mary) attracted a considerable following as both a healer and a diviner, as well as being bit of a Robin Hood character whose followers were encouraged to rob rich travellers to provide alms for the poor.[7] In the eighth century, Aldebert of Soissons declared himself a living saint. He even claimed to possess a letter from Jesus himself. He acquired such a large following that the local Church authorities appealed to Pope Zacchary in Rome to have him dealt with. In the twelfth century, the wandering preacher Tanchelm of Antwerp went one better and proclaimed himself God; he had such a large popular following that, when he decided to marry the Virgin Mary in a field outside Paris, some 10,000 of his followers were said to have attended.[8]

Examples from later centuries include James Naylor, an early Quaker, who, in the 1640s, rode into Bristol on a donkey with his band of women groupies (who believed he was the incarnation of Jesus) strewing the road ahead of him with palm fronds. In the 1840s, the Rev. Henry Prince was defrocked by his bishop for claiming to be the Prophet Elijah (he later elevated himself to God). He contracted several 'spiritual marriages' and acted as though possessed while taking services – behaviour that, incidentally, had such a dramatic effect on the size of what had previously been a very small rural congregation that two Sunday services were needed. To these, we can, of course, add Mabel Barltrop and, before her, Joanna Southcott. They were merely the tip of a very large iceberg.

Similar behaviour has been documented in other cultures outside Europe. In a study of Afro-Christianity in the Caribbean, Christopher Partridge observed that many of the nineteenth- and early twentieth-century ministers of the Native Baptist churches in Jamaica (Samuel Sharpe in the 1830s, Alexander Bedward in the 1900s, Marcus Garvey in the 1920s) were exceptionally charismatic.[9] Many of them succumbed to the belief that they were God or the Black Messiah – a Black Moses come to lead their people out of captivity to the Promised Land. Bedward, who claimed to be the reincarnation of Jesus Christ, at one point announced that he would ascend into Heaven in a chariot and duly sat himself in a chair perched in a tree to await his ascension. He was eventually consigned to an asylum where he died in 1930.

The motif of a member of the downtrodden poor rising up to save them from their oppressors also occurs repeatedly in Europe. The founder of the Skoptsy sect in Russia in the 1760s was a runaway serf, Kondratiy Ivanovich Selivanov, who referred to himself as the 'Son of God' and the 'Redeemer'. He too spent periods in a lunatic asylum and ended his days forcibly confined to a monastery to ensure that he did not influence any more susceptible peasants.

In many cases, this belief in a special mission seems to be associated with a period of intense personal psychological turmoil. Jesus famously experienced his temptations in the desert immediately before launching his ministery; Mabel Barltrop experienced her melancholic depressions brought on by anxiety over her husband's circumstances. In 1838, following the deaths of several of her children and her family's imminent bankruptcy, an illiterate Japanese farmer's wife named Nakayama Miki experienced possession by the god Tsukihi. Although subsequently reputed to be both a healer and a madwoman, she eventually attracted many followers and gave rise to the religious movement known as Tenrikyo that a century and a half later now boasts some 17,000 churches and two million members. Legend has it Siddhārtha

Gautama (the Buddha) was launched on his mendicant life-style as a result of being deeply troubled by the suffering he found in the world when he was eventually allowed outside the family palace to which his aristocratic parents had confined him in order to shield him from such knowledge. Intense religious experiences and crisis conversions seem to be a common response when the contradictions and tragedies of life create existential threats.

It seems that for a cult to get off the ground, the leader needs some degree of charismatic personality and a deep conviction that he or she holds the key to salvation. The merit of this deep conviction is that a cult leader who refuses to adjust their view eventually starts to attract sufficient support that the population as a whole swings behind them. Once a significant number of people fall behind the charismatic leader, a hierarchical structure with an elite inner circle around the leader emerges that acts both as a conduit between the leader and the followers and as a gatekeeper that control access to the leader.[10] At this point, the cult leader seems to acquire an additional mystique and distance that enhances their appeal: distance seems to magnify the sense of privilege when a follower is granted access. One is reminded of the inner circles around Mabel Barltrop and Bhagwan Shree Rajneesh of the Oregon Rajneeshpuram fame, but also, of course, of the twelve Apostles.

But why do some people end up as charismatic leaders and others not?

The behaviour of many cult leaders seems to border on the psychotic and the paranoid. Both the Rev. Jim Jones (of People's Temple and Jonestown massacre fame) and David

Koresh (of Branch Davidian and Waco massacre fame) were deeply troubled men who were exercised to the point of paranoia about internal rivals to their authority and the threat of raids by government agencies. During the 1970s, Ervil LeBaron became the leader of a breakaway polygamist Mormon cult that his father had founded in Mexico in the 1920s. He arranged the murders of at least ten members of the community (including his eldest brother Joel) with whom he had had theological or social disagreements. Several of the murders were carried out by some of his thirteen wives (many of whom he had married when they were under age).[11] During the 1980s, Jeffrey Lundgren was the leader of another breakaway Mormon cult in Kirtland, Ohio, but, after becoming paranoid about the loyalty of some of his cult members, organized the murder of an entire family (for which he was eventually executed by lethal injection in 2006).

During the 1970s, Rock Thériault established a small cult (the 'Ant Hill Kids') in the backwoods of Quebec based on Seventh Day Adventist beliefs. He exhibited extraordinary levels of controlling behaviour and violence towards anyone he considered was straying, spying on him or wanted to leave the cult: punishments included forcing members to break their own legs with sledgehammers, shoot each other in the shoulders and eat dead vermin. To demonstrate his healing powers, he subjected children and adults to amateur surgical procedures without anaesthetic. Directly or indirectly, one baby and three woman died as a direct result of his actions. Others sustained horrific injuries (in addition to having eight of her teeth forcibly removed, one woman had her arm amputated at the shoulder with a chainsaw). Despite all this, some of his followers remained loyal to him even after he was convicted and imprisoned.[12]

Several commentators have noted a common set of psychological experiences shared by mystics and psychotic individuals that include time distortion, synaesthesia, auditory and visual hallucinations, loss of self–object boundaries, social withdrawal, and transition from feelings of conflict and anxiety to a sudden 'understanding' that leads to a new sense of self. These states can often be associated with intense bouts of self-loathing. In a comparison of members of two new religious movements (Hare Krishnas and druids) with a sample of psychotic patients and normal controls, those belonging to the new religious movements were found to score higher on delusional ideation[13] than the controls, and at similar levels to the sample of psychotic patients.[14] The religious and secular members of the normal control group did not differ from each other.

In a detailed examination of the relationship between religiosity and psychological characteristics, the psychiatrist and anthropologist Simon Dien has suggested that schizophrenia and religious experience draw on the same cognitive processes in the brain. Up to 70 per cent of schizophrenics experience auditory and visual hallucinations. Religious delusions (hearing the voice of God, the taunting of demons, believing that you are the messenger of God, or even God Himself) are among the most common and persistent symptoms of schizophrenia, but especially so if the individual is religiously active. Schizophrenics are also more likely to express conspiracy theories, and to believe that they are being persecuted by people who are intent on doing them harm. However, while most cult leaders seem to exhibit these traits to some extent, they are rarely full-blown schizophrenics. Instead, they are perhaps better described as schizotypal personalities – those who display schizophrenic traits in attenuated form.

These psychological characteristics might well have their origin in neurological differences. Neuroimaging studies, for example, suggest that schizophrenics have larger ventricles (the spaces within the brain filled with ventricular fluid) and reduced grey matter in the temporal and frontal lobes. Temporal lobe epilepsy, and particularly microseizures deep within the temporal lobe, is common in schizophrenics, and is frequently associated with religious experiences and trance-like states. Padre Pio, for example, would often seem to become transfixed and lost in trance when saying Mass, causing the congregation to have to wait patiently until he emerged from his reverie. Similar behaviour was reported for many of the medieval Catholic saints.

A synthesis of the clinical and neurobiological evidence concluded that the same brain centres are overactive in schizophrenia, the manic phase of bipolar disorder and hyper-religious behaviour.[15] These include the basal ganglia and the amygdala and subcortical limbic system, the prefrontal cortex (especially the orbitofrontal and dorsomedial cortices, both of which are crucial for mentalizing and social relationships) and the right temporal lobe. In short, the default mode neural network again. When this circuit is stimulated you get religious ecstasy, and this is the case across many different types of religious practice and many different types of individuals. When this circuit is over-stimulated, you get religious aberrations. It seems that when the cortical units are activated, you get changes in belief systems, and when the midbrain units are activated you get changes in ritual behaviour (for example, compulsive performance of prayer and associated religious practices).

It is important to appreciate that schizotypal and schizo-phrenic personalities are not a particular category that individuals have or don't have. Rather, like most other personality types, they are simply one extreme of the normal distribution on which we all fall; it is simply that schizotypal individuals experience religious phenomena in more intense forms and hence may be particularly prone to the crises of identity that often seem to precipitate conversions and intense religious experiences.

It has been suggested that many charismatic leaders were orphans or raised in reduced circumstances. These have included the Prophet Muhammed, Confucius, Moses, St Teresa of Ávila and very possibly Jesus (since no mention is made of his father Joseph after Jesus was twelve years old). Being orphaned has also been true of a surprisingly large number of influential political leaders and thinkers (Aristotle, Genghis Khan, Robespierre, the Emperor Menelik II (the late nineteenth-century architect of modern Ethiopia), Jomo Kenyatta, Yasser Arafat, Chiang Kai-shek, Malcolm X), writers (Dostoyevsky, John Keats, Edgar Allen Poe, the French playwright Racine), artists (Michelangelo, Salvador Dali) and musicians (J. S. Bach, Anton Bruckner, Ella Fitzgerald, Louis Armstrong and John Lennon). Among the Cheyenne Plains Indians, war chiefs (who led the war bands during conflict) were invariably orphans: being orphaned meant being at the bottom of the social hierarchy along with slaves and war captives, with prowess in battle the only way of achieving any kind of success in life, including marriage.[16]

Learning early in life to cope and rise above the traumas of an impoverished, insecure childhood, and the need to challenge a self-sustaining society, may create the kind of psychological resilience needed to triumph in the face of adversity and ridicule. Whether the individual becomes directed towards political and intellectual ends or towards religious ones may depend on accidents of circumstance – the cultural environment, whom the individual happens to be influenced by, the degree of psychological trauma or even whether they attract followers.

It has commonly been observed that shamans, but also mystics in general, are often atypical individuals. They tend to suffer from psychopathologies that predispose them to enter trance. In many cases, they come across as physically and behaviourally odd, and many have found themselves certified as insane. Yet people believe in them. One reason why people believe in them may be that you need to stand out from the crowd for people to be willing to commit themselves to you. It is conspicuous that people often attribute superhuman powers to shamans. The same is true of Christian saints. Levitation or the ability to be in two locations at the same time are feats commonly attributed to such individuals. Among the Christian saints, such claims have been made on behalf of St Francis of Assisi, St Teresa of Ávila, St Josef of Cupertino and, in the twentieth century, even Padre Pio. Jesus, of course, walked upon the waters of Lake Galilee. The capacity to create miracles that defy the known laws of the universe and everyday experience is something attributed to such individuals in almost

CULTS, SECTS AND CHARISMATICS

all religions (and is, of course, one of the necessary criteria for being declared a saint in the Catholic Church). It is one manifestation of the cognitive science of religion's concept of the 'minimally counterintuitive' – something that breaks the known laws of physics, but not by too much (otherwise it becomes implausible).

What Motivates the Followers?

There is no more impressive evidence for the commitment that members of a cult or religion have than the fact that they are willing to die for their beliefs. In 1977, at the behest of their pastor, the Reverend Jim Jones, almost a thousand members of the People's Temple uprooted from California and went out to Guyana to build an entirely new community out of pristine jungle. Barely eighteen months later in November 1978, almost all of them committed mass suicide, feeding cyanide-laced grape juice to their children (numerically, about a third of the community) before taking it themselves. Similarly, in February 1993, seventy-nine members of David Koresh's Branch Davidian community died together at their Mount Carmel property near Waco, Texas, during a firefight with officers of the Federal Bureau of Alcohol, Tobacco and Firearms. Despite troubled psychologies and sometimes fractious relationships with their followers, Jones and Koresh (both of whom claimed divine or messianic status) engendered absolute loyalty in their followers.

As the decade wore on, at least three other groups of individuals belonging to various obscure latter-day millenarian or New Age cults committed voluntary suicide in California (the Heaven's Gate Cult), Switzerland and Canada (the Solar

Temple). In early 2000, 778 members of the Movement for the Restoration of the Ten Commandments (who, along with several defrocked priests and nuns, had recently seceded from the Catholic Church) variously committed mass murder and suicide in Uganda. Many of these cases do not seem to involve commitment to an ideal or religious belief as such, but rather commitment to a charismatic leader.

The Californian Heaven's Gate cult reminds us of the fact that the beliefs of the cult can be quite bizarre (or, at least, seem so to outsiders), yet still command the complete commitment of the members. Founded in 1974 by Marshall Applewhite and Bonnie Nettles, the cult developed a set of beliefs that drew eclectically on Christian asceticism, gnostic beliefs and eastern mysticism, combined with a more modern millenarian belief in extraterrestrials who would come and rescue (or wipe out) the Earth. Interleaved with this was a personality cult based on its two founders who believed they were the messengers alluded to in the New Testament's Book of Revelations (although, in time-honoured fashion, Applewhite did upgrade himself later to being Jesus). It was the kind of mix that appealed to the 'spiritual hippies' of the 1960 and 1970s. In 1997, the surviving members committed group suicide at Applewhite's behest in the expectation that they would be able to join an extraterrestrial force then supposed to be on its way to the Earth in a spaceship tailing the approaching Hale-Bopp comet.

The question hovering in the wings is what motivates people to believe in a charismatic sect leader to the extent that they are willing to die for them. Economists have developed a number of models treating individuals' decisions about joining or leaving a particular religion, or even a specific church, as a problem in optimal shopping: each church offers costs and benefits that we evaluate, choosing the one that involves the largest benefit or the smallest cost of membership. Up to a point, this is of course true: people do transfer allegiance from one church or religion to another precisely because the price of continued membership becomes too high or the benefits too low. Conversions once occurred because missionaries demanded membership as a price for access to the mission hospital, or because a new church or religion provides more engaging services. In Japan, where everyone is both Buddhist and Shinto, people generally get married by Shinto rites (because Shinto weddings are more spectacular than the rather dull Buddhist ones) and buried by Buddhist rites (because these provide an altogether richer ceremonial of departure). Nonetheless, however well these models predict people's choices, they don't really capture the reasons people become religious in the first place. In fact, they assume that people are religious. Nor do they explain the emotional experience that prompts many people to join, and subsequently stay with, a particular religion or church.

Although religious people typically (but not always) score higher on Agreeableness and Conscientiousness of the Big Five personality dimensions,[17] many people adhere to the religion they belong to simply because they were born into it and grew up within its confines. They are content enough with the sense of belonging engendered not to question its value. In some cases, they may simply be prepared to go along with it because they do not wish to fall out with someone whose opinion and friendship they value. In many cases, being banished from a cult or the death of the cult leader generates feelings of loss and disorientation similar to those experienced after divorce or the death of a romantic partner. In such cases, suicide may seem preferable. Many who grew up in 1970s hippy communes describe the sense of camaraderie and belonging they had as teenagers and young adults in these communities as the best time of their lives. It was characterized by the familiarity and protectiveness of intimacy.[18]

However, people also join a religion through a process of conversion. The process of conversion is often presented as an intellectual ordeal, and so it may be in some cases. But most of the time it is actually an emotional journey, and becomes an ordeal as often as not because the new commitment requires something of the old life to be given up, whether this be old habits and pleasures or the forsaking of old friends and family. To the extent that conversion can be traumatic and involve psychological distress, it seems likely that the processes involved trigger the endorphin system and the psychological processes of intense belonging. Joining a new religion or sect may well appeal to those whose lives have descended into crisis, as much for the psychological support it provides as anything. But the pleasurable, calming effects of having your endorphin system activated by rituals must surely also play a significant role by creating a sense of being enfolded into caring arms.

Why followers often imbue their leaders, both secular and religious, with superhuman powers has never really been satisfactorily explained, but it may form part of the natural psychology of community bonding in that the community leader functions as a focus for belonging. In a great many cases, this gives rise to a very human desire to obtain power from the leader through touch. We see this in the widespread tendency to kiss or touch the relics, or even a statue or icon, of a saint. We find it in the concept of the 'Royal Touch' – the belief, common well into the eighteenth century, that the English and French monarchs (of both sexes) could cure diseases like scrofula (a form of tuberculosis) simply by the laying on of hands (or even just by casual contact with their clothing).

In South Asian Hindu charismatic cults, the guru is often sacralized and credited with 'special gifts', such that devotees (women, in particular) have an overwhelming desire 'to touch the guru, to be close to the guru, to eat the guru's leftover food, to wear what the guru has worn, to sleep where the guru has slept'.[19] This has been referred to as *proxemic desire*[20] and is reminiscent of the fact that women (but almost never men) often borrow items of their romantic partner's clothing to wear. In many guru cults there is an implicit, sometimes explicit, hierarchy of physical proximity to the guru that confers status within the community. My guess is that this derives directly from the natural physicality of our closest relationships and the extent to which touch is involved in these.[21] There is clearly also an element of the parent–child relationship – perhaps not too surprising given the unusual length of human childhood with its extension into the teenage years during which parents act as the providers of food and comfort as well as guidance.

We underestimate how important touch is in our social relationships. In his influential 'Triangular Theory of Love', the psychologist Robert Sternberg characterized romantic relationships in terms of the intersection of three key dimensions:

intimacy, commitment and passion. Intimacy reflects a desire to remain in the physical presence of the beloved, while commitment can be characterized in terms of feelings of closeness, connectedness and bondedness.[22] This was later generalized by Arthur and Elaine Aron to suit all kinds of relationships by reducing them to two key dimensions: 'feeling close' and 'behaving close'.[23] That sense of being close is very visceral, and it surely harks back to our primate ancestry in which social grooming played such an important role. Its importance, of course, lies in the way touch triggers the endorphin system via the CT neuron system, creating a sense of physical warmth and intimacy (as described in Chapter 5).

There are striking sex differences in this respect: not only are women much more 'touchy-feely' than men but they are also better at social cognitive abilities like mentalizing (the cognitive mechanism underlying the intuitive management of relationships).[24] This suggests a possible explanation for the single most consistent finding in the psychology of religion, namely that women are more religious than men and, as a result, are more likely to become followers of cults. A 2014 Pew Research Center Report, for example, noted that 60 per cent of American women rated religion as being very important in their lives compared to only 47 per cent of men. Around 64 per cent of women said they prayed daily (compared to 47 per cent of men), and 40 per cent said they attended religious services at least once a week (compared to 30 per cent of men). A later report yielded similar, but somewhat smaller, differences in a wider range of world religions.[25] Women featured prominently among the followers of Tanchelm of Antwerp and the Free Spirit sects in medieval Europe. In the staid social environment of mid-Victorian England, the Rev. Henry Prince attracted large crowds of adoring female disciples, until the remonstrations of his Bishop led him to set up his own religious community of some sixty followers – mostly women, whom he christened, with singular lack of irony, the 'Brides of the Lord'.[26]

Given the relationship between physical touch, the intensity of emotional feelings and sex in the secular context, it is perhaps hardly surprising that the desire to be in direct physical contact with the cult leader readily spills over into sex, even in those cases where it is not actively sought. This may well be an expectation that male cult leaders come to exploit. Joseph Smith, the founder of the Church of Jesus Christ of the Latter Day Saints (the Mormons), famously had a convenient revelation from God instructing him that men should marry polygamously when he needed to overcome his longsuffering wife's objections to his bringing a second, younger wife into her household. Thereafter, Smith took his God-given duties very seriously, allegedly marrying thirty women ranging in age from fourteen to forty. Clerical immorality has, of course, been a mainstay of reformers' complaints throughout history in all the doctrinal religions.

In the early decades of the twentieth century, a string of obscure, now-forgotten cult leaders including Joshua the Second (of the 1900s Holy Rollers cult), Brother Twelfth (of the 1920s Aquarian Foundation on Vancouver Island) and Krishna Ventra (of the 1950s Californian Fountain of the World cult) were all accused of sexual misconduct and the condoning of free love. Rock Thériault fathered twenty children with nine of the women of his Ant Hill Kids cult. David Koresh claimed to have fathered at least twenty-one children in his Branch Davidian community, mostly by claiming the right to sleep with every woman in the community whether or not they were married to another member of the congregation. The Bhagwan Shree Rajneesh was not dubbed 'the sex guru' for nothing: it is said that, in his younger more charismatic days, many of his women followers fell deeply in love with him simply on hearing him speak. As with Koresh, many of the women he slept with were the wives of community members. Sleeping with the guru is to be given the sacred touch, the gateway to salvation and happiness. Nor is the attractiveness of religious power peculiar to the doctrinal religions and their cults: the anthropologist Richard Katz quotes the !Kung shaman Toma Zho as remarking that women really liked healers. 'Whenever I see one who is getting *num* [healing energy during a trance dance],' Toma commented to him one day, 'I say, "Think of the sex the guy's going to get".' There would seem to be a parallel here with the phenomenon of female groupies that surrounded rock bands during the 1960s and 1970s.

In many cases, cult leaders have prevailed on their followers to adopt promiscuous sex as part of the cult ethos. In sixteenth-century Germany, Klaus Ludwig's Chriesterung community in Mulhausen and Jan Brockelson's Münster Anabaptists both advocated free love. During the Cromwellian Commonwealth of 1650s England, the Ranters had a widespread reputation for promiscuity that was not entirely propaganda by their opponents. In Tsarist Russia, the rituals of the Russian Khlysty sect involved celebrants dancing themselves into a frenzy round a fire or a tub of water chanting hymns until, in a state of ecstasy, they were said to couple freely.[27]

John Humphrey Noyes – in many ways, one the most enlight-
ened of all cult leaders, besides being the best connected (his
cousin Rutherford Hayes was the nineteenth President of the
United States), advocated promiscuous coupling within the
Oneida Community that he founded in upstate New York in
1848.[28] In the later twentieth century, both Moses David (formerly David Berg and founder of the Children of God sect,
now the Family International) and Charlie Manson (founder
of the ill-fated Manson Family) advocated complete promiscuity not just as a way of enticing people to join (so-called 'flirty
fishing') but as an essential means of breaking down individual egos so as to enhance members' commitment to the community. I suspect that, intentionally or otherwise, one of the
reasons so many of the nineteenth-century American millenarian communes forbade sex was to avoid the divisiveness and
conflict created between a couple's commitment to each other
(or, worse still, to their children) and their commitment to
the community. The former will always trump the latter, and
especially so for women, leading inevitably to conflict within
the community.

The gender asymmetry in religiosity and women's susceptibility to the sexual interest of cult eaders may not be too
surprising, given the striking sex difference in the dynamics of close relationships. Women form much more intense
and intimate relationships both with romantic partners and
with same-sex best friends than men do; men's relationships
tend to be more casual with something of a here-today-gone-
tomorrow quality, especially so with same-sex friends.[29] It
seems likely that these differences in the psychology of relationships make women more vulnerable to sexual exploitation

when they are combined in a heady mix with expectations about access to both status and a higher spiritual power. Conversely, of course, it provides women with an avenue of access to those sources of secular and spiritual power that is largely denied to men.

I have suggested that the dynamics of small communities leads naturally, in the religious context, to their being built around charismatic leaders. Charismatic leadership seems to be especially susceptible to relationships of such intense intimacy that, for better or for worse, they easily spill over into sexual relationships. This may be why monastic orders are always single sex, and no doubt why the Shakers segregated the men and women in their communities into separate dormitory buildings – although this may simply reflect the fact that both sexes find single-sex groups socially more congenial.[30]

Perhaps on reflection we ought not to be too surprised by the fact that sex spills over into religion. We saw, in Chapter 5, how many of the mystics, especially the women mystics, unashamedly described their experience of being immersed in God in terms of romantic love. In Chapter 8, we noted that the priestesses in the temples of the eastern Mediterranean and Middle East often functioned as temple prostitutes (presumably mainly for the benefit of the temple priests). This is perhaps a reminder that religions, and religious institutions, are social phenomena and underpinned by the same psychological processes that make our social world what it is.

We are intensely social as a species, just like all our anthropoid primate cousins. That sociality has not only been the motor of our evolutionary success, it has also been the driving force of all we are and do. Religion is simply part of the mix. This is not to say, of course, that religion is nothing more than a context for sexual opportunity. Most of those who belong to the larger religions do so for conventionally honest motives related to their beliefs about a transcendental world. But underneath that bubbles all the dark passions and motives that make everyday social life what it is. And that bubbling seems especially prone to emerge in the intimate confines of a cult when there is a heady mix of charisma, ritual, the physical exertions associated with singing and dancing, endorphin activation and psychoactive drugs. That will always be a context for sexual exploitation.

Schisms and Divisions

There are two important conclusions we can draw from the previous chapter. One is that attraction to charismatic leaders plays a seminal role in the formation of cults, a relationship that is almost always a very personal one between guru and disciple; the other is that the doctrinal, or revealed, religions all face a constant battle against grassroots fragmentation through the formation of cults. Both seem to have their origins in the fact that our psyche is designed to handle only a very small-scale social world. The top-down mechanisms we use to create larger scale communities do not work sufficiently well to counteract the natural tendency we have to partition the wider world into small, intimate groupings. It is this handful of relationships that have real meaning for us, introducing the sense of trust and obligation, and of commitment that enable social groups to function effectively. We are more comfortable in small groups and get more out of them.

In this final chapter, I want to bring these themes together to offer an explanation for the one major feature of doctrinal religions that we often seem to overlook, namely the fact that beneath the elegant superstructure of their sophisticated theologies lurk the ancestral shamanic religions of our deep history. These older forms play a crucial role in providing the psychological basis for being a believer, because, deep down, religion is largely an emotional, not an intellectual, phenomenon. They offer an explanation as to why the doctrinal religions are plagued by a constant welling up of cults and sects from within their own grassroots.

Why religions fragment

The speed with which religions fragment is particularly well illustrated by new religious movements which lack an organized administrative hierarchy capable of enforcing discipline. We met Nakayama Miki , the founder of the Japanese Tenrikyo sect, in the last chapter. The sect had become formally established by the 1860s. However, Tenrikyo's formal master-disciple instructional arrangements subsequently spawned a whole series of separate cults, many of which achieved significant success in their own right. In the 1920s, Onishi Aijiro, a younger son of another farming family on the edge of bankruptcy, underwent conversion to Tenrikyo following the death of his mother. After thirteen spectacularly unsuccessful years as a missionary for the sect, he locked himself in his house for six months in a fit of depression, at the end of which he became convinced that he was the living embodiment of the sect's *kanrodai* – the pillar set up on the site of Miki's original residence (the sect's religious and administrative focus). When arrested in 1930 for sedition (he claimed to be the true leader of Japan), he was acquitted on grounds of diminished mental capacity. Excommunicated by the Tenrikyo leadership, he then established his own millenarian sect, the Tenri Hon-michi, which continues to be active with a substantial membership today. In 1962, following Aijiro's death, his daughter

Onishi Tama became convinced that she was God's chosen instrument to save the world. Taking the name Miroku (a Japanese term referring to the Maitreya Bodhisattva who will eventually come to save the world), she broke away from the Tenri Honmichi to found the Honbushin sect that combined meditation practices from the Jodo Shinshu Buddhist sect with Honmichi doctrine; it now boasts around a million members and rivals the original Tenrikyo sect in size.[1]

We also met the LeBaron family in the last chapter. Their breakaway Mormon sect was founded 1924 by Alma Dayer LeBaron, a grandson of Benjamin Johnson who had been Joseph Smith's confidential secretary. LeBaron had split off from the mainstream Mormon Church in a dispute over polygamy when the Mormons finally capitulated to federal pressure to abandon the practice. After his death in 1951, his eldest son Joel took on the mantle of leadership, and named the new foundation the Church of the Firstborn in the Fullness of Times; at the same time, his younger brother Wesley established a separate Church of the Firstborn. Meanwhile, Ervil, the second oldest of the six boys in the family and at the time Joel's second in command, began to preach that he, not Joel, was the true leader. In 1972, Ervil established the rival Church of the Firstborn of the Lamb of God and began a campaign against his older brother that eventually resulted in Joel being murdered. A fourth brother, Verlan, succeeded Joel as head of the Fullness of Times branch, but following his death in an car crash, this sect itself spawned a new branch (the Economic Government of God church) led by another son, Alma Jr., while his brother Floren established a separate, leaderless faction. In addition, there have been at least two other secessions led by non-LeBaron family members. All in all, in little more than half a century, this one breakaway Mormon church spawned at least six separate sects, though none has achieved any significant size.

These examples all have the form of a cult built around a charismatic leader, and in this resemble the origins of all large-scale doctrinal religions. They reflect the fact that as they increase in size (whether by recruitment or biological reproduction), all major religions experience internal stresses. These arise from disputes that threaten to undermine the unity of the community. Some of these disputes are no more than personality clashes between the leaders of different factions. Others may involve disagreements about changes in ritual practice or the interpretation of moral injunctions. Occasionally, they are about arcane matters of theology, though in these cases the reasons for the dispute rarely have any direct relevance to the wider membership of the factions: their interests are almost always focused on the views of their charismatic leaders or 'the way we have always done it here'.

A great many of the major schisms that occurred in Christianity as well as in Islam have resulted from attempts to reform contemporary practice – usually due to a perceived laxity of practice or morality, especially among the clergy. Famously, of course, this was the origin of Martin Luther's triggering of the Protestant Reformation in the early decades of the 1500s. Much the same was true of the Wahabi, Salafist and Jaamat-e-Islami movements that successively emerged in Islam over the last three centuries, all of which have advocated a return to a purist form of Islam against a perceived growing laxity – or, in the case of their collective opposition to Shia Islam, a growing attachment to charismatic saints that is viewed as a drift away from the worship of Allah, the One True God, to the worship of local 'gods'.

One classic early example of this in Christianity concerned an intense dispute that arose following the Emperor Decius's edict in 269 AD that obliged all citizens to sacrifice to the Roman Gods. Decius's edict was one of many attempts to undermine the growing popularity of Christianity within the Roman Empire. Many of the Christians who acceded to the Emperor's demand rather than risk the sanctions of slavery or execution argued that they merely went through the motions without making any 'commitment of the heart'. They were vehemently condemned and even excommunicated by those who had refused to sacrifice to the Roman gods. To the latter, the mere fact of obeying the edict was a betrayal of Christian principles. This internal dispute had followed hard on the heels of an earlier schism among Christians in Rome, itself the result of an attempt by the hierarchy to transfer adultery and fornication from the category of mortal sins to the more pardonable category of venial sins. The general view was that this was nothing less than an attempt to cover up the clergy's own immoral misbehaviour, and it led to the election of the presbyter Hippolytus as a rival Bishop of Rome, the first of many antipopes, in the early third century.

The early history of the Christian Church is, in fact, one of constant battles with one group of heretics after another, each reflecting the views of one particular individual who achieved charismatic status in their local region. Between 150 and the Great Schism of 1054 that gave rise to the Orthodox Church, there were twenty-two major schisms in Christianity.

Most have disappeared without trace, but a few (such as the Coptic, Armenian and Maronite Churches) became established as branches of Christianity in their own right.

To a large extent, this tendency to spawn sects was simply a consequence of the sheer size of the Christian community, combined with its geographical spread and the inevitable slowness of communications in the first millennium AD. Such conditions favour the emergence of novel cults with idiosyncratic beliefs and practices influenced by older local religions or ideas introduced from geographically neighbouring religions. Many of the Church Councils that met during the first five centuries AD were called to legislate against one perceived heresy or another.

The first Council of Nicaea in 325, which produced the Nicene Creed as the defining set of Christian beliefs, was concerned with combatting Arianism – the anti-Trinitarian views promulgated by the Alexandrian presbyter Arius. The Council of Ephesus in 431 was convened to combat Nestorianism, which rejected the concept of 'Mother of God' for Mary and also seemed to question Jesus's status as part of the Trinity. In 451, the Council of Chalcedon was called to condemn the monophysite claim that Christ had only one (divine) nature.[2] Most of these councils resulted either in the suppression of heresy or in the departure of whole sections of the nascent Church to establish themselves as separate communities.

Similar processes can be seen at work even on the small scale of individual monastic orders. The Franciscans (or Friars Minor, to give them their official name), established by St Francis of Assisi in 1209 AD, provide an example. Within a decade of Francis's death, internal disputes about the definition of poverty and ownership of property (the Order's defining criteria) reached the point where the Pope had to step in to circumvent a revolt by the north European provinces who objected to being subjected to direct rule by the Order's Italian centre. Notwithstanding papal intervention, these dissensions rumbled on for the next three centuries, resulting in at least half a dozen secessions (some of whom were later suppressed on papal orders). This eventually culminated in the great division of 1517 between the Conventuals and the reformist Observantists (who felt the rest of the Order had become far too lax). Despite repeated papal attempts to encourage reunification, secessions continued, giving rise to the Discalced, Recollects, Riformati, Capuchins and many others over the following century. Even today, after a major effort at unification by Pope Leo XIII at the end of the nineteenth century, there remain three separate and distinct Franciscan Orders: the Order of Friars Minor, the Order of Friars Minor Conventual and the Order of Friars Minor Capuchin (a reference to the distinctive hood on their habit), each with its own traditions and views of exactly what constitutes St Francis's message.

The historical concerns of the central hierarchy in Rome are reflected in the frequency with which individuals, many of whom later achieved iconic status as saints, were hauled up before the Church authorities because they appeared to be promulgating theologically unorthodox views. Many of these were famous mystics in their day, and their prosecution by the Church seems to reflect the generalized fear that central authorities have for uncontrolled mysticism. Among those who fell foul of the authorities were the Dominican theologian and mystic Meister Eckhart (accused by his order's Franciscan rivals, but who became an important influence on later theologians and thinkers), Peter Waldo (a twelfth-century Lyon-based merchant turned lay preacher who gave away his worldly goods and whose views on Church doctrines and practice anticipated those later espoused by Martin Luther), Amalric of Bena (a renowned twelfth-century philosopher at the University of Paris whose pantheist, millenarian, free love views were roundly condemned, and ten of his followers burned at the stake), St Joan of Arc (burned at the stake for heresy, not for her successes against the English), St Ignatius Loyola (founder of the Jesuits), the famous medieval English mystic Margery Kempe, and the seventeenth-century Spanish mystic Miguel de Molinos (founding inspiration of the seventeenth-century Quietists who favoured mystical contemplation over the rituals of prayer), not to mention the iconic St Francis of Assisi.

The Protestant Reformation of the sixteenth century provided the opportunity for a veritable tsunami of cults and sects. Among the better known are the Taborites, Hussites, Anabaptists and Mennonites, all named after their respective founders. In England, the Ranters, Baptists, Methodists and Quakers all began as mystical or semi-mystical cults that attracted wide popularity, and, notwithstanding the well-respected contemporary status of the last three, were regarded by the local Church authorities at the time with deep suspicion because of their suspect practices and rituals. Later in the nineteenth century, Britain and the USA played host to myriad obscure and not so obscure cults. Most, like John Noyes' Oneidan community and the followers of 'Jumpin'

Jesus' Matthews in New York, or the Agapemonites of the Rev. Henry Prince in the more urbane surroundings of Victorian Somerset, eventually faded quietly away. Others, like Joseph Smith's Mormons and the Shaker communities of upstate New York, prospered well beyond their founders' lifetimes.[3]

It is not obvious why some like the Mormons survived and others like the Oneidans went extinct. Two features were perhaps important. One is the fact that the Mormons successfully developed organizational structures that were able to impose a degree of theological discipline; the second is that they were outward-looking and developed active programmes of recruitment. The fate of the Shakers offers some insights. Though initially very successful, with eighteen large communities and numerous smaller ones in the USA by the mid-nineteenth century, failure to recruit has resulted in just one surviving community (Sabbathday Lake Shaker Community in Maine), probably for three reasons. One is that their communities remained semi-independent, with no central authority to impose uniformity. The second, that the communities were largely inward-looking and the sect as a whole lacked a consistent strategy for promoting conversions and establishing new communities. The third is that, like many of the more obscure cults and communities, the Shakers discouraged marriage and obliged the two sexes to live apart.

Recruitment by birth is probably the single most important strategy for the growth of a sect, since children brought up in a religion or cult readily absorb the ethos of the sect and remain influenced by it for life.[4] Indeed, the heritability (or fidelity of copying from one generation to the next) of religious adherence is around 70 per cent thanks to the power of cultural learning – far higher than the heritability of most genetically inherited biological traits (stature has a heritability of just 20 per cent).[5] Fidelity of copying across the generations is thus much higher for most cultural traits like religion than for biological traits. Since many of the smaller cults forbade sexual intercourse (while sometimes excepting the cult leader), natural recruitment was close to zero, and cult survival depended solely on external recruitment. Changing fashions and interests in the wider world then often resulted in a drying-up of recruits, as happened with the Panacea Society (see Chapter 9).

Similar fragmentation has occurred in Islam, beginning within a matter of months of the Prophet Mohammed's death. The initial divide between the Sunni and Shia branches over who should inherit the Prophet's cloak of authority after his death was followed over the next few centuries, at least within Shia Islam, by repeated fragmentation into a series of sects based on divergent views as to the identity of the last true Imam (the spiritual successor to the Prophet). The Twelvers recognize twelve true, divinely ordained successors to Muhammed, culminating in the Mahdi who, it is believed, went into occlusion and will return at the End Times – which will coincide with the Second Coming of Jesus who will assist the Mahdi in the final arrangements. The Fivers (or Zaidis) accept only the first five Imams, while the Ismailis accept the first six. The Ismailis themselves subsequently split into a number of now independent sects, that include, among many others, the Nizaris (under the religious leadership of the Aga Khan), the Bohras, the Druze and the Satpanths (a group of Hindus who converted to Islam in the fourteenth and fifteenth centuries), as well as several now extinct branches that include the Seveners (who recognized seven Imams) and the Hafizis. Similarly, Sunni Islam developed its own schools, though these differ mainly in the strictness and sparseness with which they practice rituals.

Judaism, likewise, spawned its own divisions. In addition to those mentioned in the Old Testament, there had been a long series of prophets and messiahs in the century or so prior to the time of Jesus of Nazareth, and an equally large number after his time – in many cases, perhaps, a response to the political turbulence created by the expanding Roman Empire. Among the most famous of the later messiahs was Simon bar Kochba, who briefly established an independent Jewish state in the second century AD; although he never made any messianic claims for himself, some of the rabbinical schools in Jerusalem certainly viewed him as the returning Messiah. There were many self-proclaimed messiahs in later centuries, including Moses of Crete in the fifth century AD and Sabbatai Zevi (1626–76), widely regarded as the last of the great Jewish mystics. Each attracted a significant following and had influence over much of the eastern Mediterranean at the height of his fame. Although Sabbatai Zevi converted to Islam in 1666 to avoid execution at the hands of the exasperated Turks, his fame long outlived his death in exile and at least one attempt was made to revive a sect in his name during the eighteenth century. These more charismatic figures aside, Judaism has fragmented since the Diaspora into a number of semi-independent branches broadly identified as Orthodox, Conservative and Reform, each with its own further subdivisions.

The 1960s counterculture, which spawned a variety

movements and communes broadly based around the 'Human Potential Movement' that combined eastern meditation practices with western Gestalt humanistic psychology, provides more contemporary insights. Probably the most influential of these movements was associated with the Esalen Institute at Big Sur in California, founded in 1962 by two Stanford graduates, Michael Murphy and Dick Price.[6]

Price had been influenced by hearing Aldous Huxley lecture on his concept of 'human potentialities' following his experiments with psychoactive drugs in California (see Chapter 2), while Murphy had spent some months at an ashram in India.[7] After renting the vacant Big Sur property from Murphy's grandmother, they established a community that used encounter groups to explore human consciousness[8] and offered alternative education focused on the mind–body connection, eastern philosophy and religion, Gestalt psychology and alternative medicine. It saw its major aim as an attempt to lift humans onto a new, higher plane of consciousness. In many ways, Esalen's success was due to the fact that it attracted many leading intellectuals, musicians and even scientists to its seminars and retreats, many of whom enthusiastically promoted its philosophy.[9]

The Institute greatly influenced the counterculture of the 1970s and the development of many of the New Age movement during the 1980s. These later movements were typically theologically eclectic (but usually with an emphasis on occult knowledge and eastern mystical philosophies), often identified spiritual beings of some kind with whom humans could communicate through a variety of channels, had a distinct sense of cultishness, and often a millenarian perspective that anticipated a new 'Age of Aquarius' (hence New Age) when the ills and inequalities that blight modern society would be swept away and replaced by a more egalitarian social model.

This state of earthly nirvana would, it was invariably claimed, arise only when humans developed a new psycho-spiritual potential by achieving a higher plane of consciousness – the path to which was, of course, provided by the novel insights of the sect in question. In many cases, cults claimed to be able to short circuit, often through the use of psychoactive drugs, the hard mental and physical effort required by the older eastern cults to achieve Enlightenment. Many of these cults died out because they were inward-looking, eschewed contact with the wider world outside, and often deliberately took themselves off to remote locations where contact with the secular world could be avoided.

In short, we find many of the same lessons we learned from the discussion of the sizes of natural human communities and church congregations in Chapter 4. The burden of this was to remind us that congregations, churches and religions are all human organizations and are subject to the same demographic and psychological constraints imposed by the social brain just like any other form of human social group. They contain individuals who, left to their own devices, naturally develop idiosyncratic beliefs, and eventually drift apart culturally and intellectually. If the community is below about 150 in size, such disagreements can be dealt with in face-to-face discussions where compromises may be worked out as a result of the mutual obligations that exist between individuals who know each other well. But once community size significantly exceeds this figure, these mechanisms will not work. People do not meet up sufficiently often to maintain cultural coherence. Disagreements, and the stresses they create, will tear apart the fabric of the organization – unless some form of top-down discipline is imposed.

A Tale of Two Religions

I began this book by suggesting that we can distinguish between two broad types of religion – shamanic, or immersive, religions and doctrinal religions. Athough our surprisingly limited mental capacities invariably oblige us to dichotomize the world in order to make it comprehensible, not only are there in reality many shades of grey in between but the switch from one state to another is rarely instantaneous. More importantly, the steps, or phases, are best understood as attempts to cope with a series of demographically imposed grass ceilings. We can, perhaps, identify four such phases.

In the first phase, ancestral religions were informal, immersive and designed to bond very small hunter-gatherer communities of 100–200 individuals living in dispersed camps of 35–50. They did not have formal gods of any kind, though there may well have been spirits associated with natural features and a spirit world that could be entered through trance. These religions have little to do with morality or moral codes as such, and they have everything to do with community bonding. It was the need to bond groups that were increasingly large (at least, by primate standards) that encouraged the adoption of cognitively more sophisticated devices like religion. In part, that may have been a by-product of the fact that our larger brains (needed to cope with the relationship demands of larger groups) made higher levels of mentalizing possible, and this allowed some of the more inquisitive individuals to wonder about the world in which they lived and what lay behind it in a way that other animals cannot. In addition, our high mentalizing capacities may have caused us to see both the wider world and the trance world in terms of spirit beings with minds similar to ours.

The second phase is defined by the appearance of specialist healers and diviners. We are still firmly in the world of shamanistic, or immersive, religions, so there is still no formal theology. Specific spirit beings become associated with illnesses and conditions such as infertility, miscarriages, the birth of twins or deformed babies – circumstances that, in hunter-gatherer societies in particular, are often considered due to bad luck (in a targeted rather than a casual sense) or being bewitched, but which are, in the harsh reality of these kinds of societies, significant future energetic or social drains on the mother in particular. Some shamans are likely to have attracted clientele from far afield, anxious to take advantage of their reputed ability to intervene with the spirit world. They may even have acquired camp followers both as apprentices and as admirers anxious to serve a master.

The shift into permanent settlements that occurred with the onset of the Neolithic around 10,000 years ago marked a sea-change in the stresses that communities had to cope with, especially once community size significantly exceeded 300–400 individuals. The early part of this period, corresponding to the third phase in our sequence, gave rise to more formal religions characterized by local gods, combined with more formalized rituals, ritual specialists (priests) and ritual spaces (temples). Gods are typically many in number, having been adopted from a longstanding tendency to regard landscape features as the homes of spirits encountered during trance travels. These gods are often a combination of the malicious and benign, though their interest in human affairs may be largely limited to punishment for failing to make the requisite sacrifices needed to appease them. Though still of modest size, these religions evolved to provide a form of top-down collective control over communities that were beyond the size at which coordination and control could be exercised by personal face-to-face relationships and peer pressure alone. The issue is not political control in the sense envisioned by Marx, but one of mitigating the stresses and costs of living in close proximity in order to allow the community to act as a collective defence against external threats.

Around 4,000 years ago, we see the start of the fourth phase, associated with a dramatic rise in the size of settlements and the polities within which these are embedded. This phase coincides with the earliest city states and empires, which appear to be the long-term outcome of unusually benign climatic conditions and population growth within the northern subtropical zone in the previous few millenia. This was associated with a shift from sacrificing to largely indifferent deities to greater ritual complexity and proprietory worship of a more specific set of gods, each associated with different tasks and responsibilities.

This demanded professional priests and rituals, as well as formal temples. These forms of religion essentially constitute clubs whose members are bound together by a common worldview comprising formal ritual practices and theological belief systems, a theologically justified moral system, and priestly hierarchies, combined with centralized bureaucracies that regulated both theological rectitude and good behaviour. Membership is not based on personal knowledge of the other members but simply on the fact of membership, on the knowledge of belonging. The addition of Moralizing High Gods to this mix seems to have come later, during the Axial Age in the northern Subtropical Zone, around 2,500 years ago. Because monotheistic religions necessarily have a more standardized form, with a more specific theology, they may also start to become associated with rising antagonism towards alternative religions.

The fact that monotheism with its Moralizing High Gods seems to be especially associated with pastoral economies is intriguing, and helps put a date on the origins of these religions. Domestic stock (cattle) became common in the Nile Valley and adjacent Sahara wetlands around 9,500 BP, with sheep and goats appearing some time after 7,700 BP. This period seems to have been associated with relatively settled communities and subsistence agriculture. Recognizable pastoralist societies do not, however, emerge until after 6,000 BP,[10] putting the emergence of monotheistic religions late in this sequence – possibly closer to 4,500 BP when a rapid period of climate change led to the increasing desertification of the subtropical zone and heightened competition between tribal groups for access to the increasingly limited number of permanent waterholes and grazing areas. At this stage, pastoral societies were still largely confined to the Sahel, the region of dry seasonal grassland bordering the Sahara, and it was not until around 2,000 years ago that these began to extend down through the Nile Valley into eastern Africa in search of new pastures. Because they are theologically more constrained, monotheistic religions seem to be able to bind together very large communities over large geographical spaces, and hence to create defensive alliances many orders of magnitude beyond the limits of the conventional tribe.

Aside from a possible early informal religious phase among the Neanderthals and other archaic humans, all these developments are associated exclusively with our own species, anatomically modern humans (*Homo sapiens*). Since there has been little if any genetic change associated with the brain's *cognitive* functions across the 200,000 or so years of our species' lifetime, they do not represent significant evolutionary changes at the genetic level. This is not, of course, to say that there have been no genetic changes at all within our species during this time: there have been many small such changes as individual populations have adapted to local environmental conditions, including in genes associated with body shape, skin colour, disease susceptibility and even the visual system.[11] None of these changes impact on cognitive abilities, however. Rather, the sequence of changes in religion must be culturally driven, and were a response to demographic conditions, and the stresses that these created.

Like the growth of knowledge over time, the phases of religion are simply a case of humans finding solutions to the social and environmental threats that have bedevilled them at different stages in history. They represent successive solutions to the stresses that arise as population size increased, much as we have managed to develop more and more efficient agricultural practices in response to the need to feed these populations. In contrast to conventional biological evolution (which, as we saw in Chapter 1, is undirected), these phases of religious evolution form a natural sequence through which all societies evolve sequentially *if the conditions require it*. This is because they were community-level solutions to the problems of social cohesion as community sizes became progressively larger over historical time rather than species-level responses to generalized environmental challenges. They represent part of the human species' remarkable capacity for phenotypic (as opposed to genetic) adaptation.

A central claim of this book has been that the evolution of religion is underpinned by the mystical stance, a capacity that depends in part on high-order mentalizing skills that appear to be unique to modern humans and in part on the role of the endorphin system in producing trance states in which we experience feelings of intense immersion in a consciousness beyond our own. This capacity to engage with a transcendental world seems to have been important for two reasons. First, it triggers the neurobiological basis of social bonding, thereby creating a sense of commitment in a way that no abstract ideological belief seems able to do. There seems to be something that is psychologically especially engaging about belief in an unseen, transcendental world and the beings that inhabit it. Who those beings are will simply depend on the beliefs of individual cultures. Second, the religious dimension seems to scale up in a way that few of our other bonding behaviours seem capable of doing. Laughter, conversation, dancing, storytelling and feasting are all limited in scale and are effective at bonding communities only of modest size. Singing performs better, but even this seems to lack the massive scalability of religion. Religion is also one of the Seven Pillars of Friendship, and so functions effectively to bond large numbers of strangers in what amounts to a one-dimensional club.

A second important claim made in this book is that these stages in the evolution of religion do not involve wholesale replacement of one form of religion by another, but rather the accretion of new layers around an older core. The earliest phases of religion remain firmly entrenched within doctrinal religions, and have not gone away. They are still demonstrably there, not only in the beliefs and behaviour of the less sophisticated members, but also in many of the practices and rituals of the doctrinal religions. They provide both the emotional basis for personal belief and commitment and the psychological foundation for a sense of community within the doctrinal religions every bit as much as they did in the precursor shamanic phase. Just as the Japanese happily slip between Shinto and Buddhism without being troubled by the apparent contradictions in religious paradigm, so the rest of us happily slip between shamanic and doctrinal religion – notwithstanding the clerical hierarchy's disapproval of the former. Those immersive forms of religion are what create the emotional attachment to whichever doctrinal religion we happen to favour for its theological justification. Without it, doctrinal religions probably wouldn't exist.

One reason for supposing that the ancestral immersive forms of religion still underpin doctrinal religions is the fact that most of the elements that are used to bond small-scale communities, and which form part of shamanic or immersive forms of religion, are still present in all the doctrinal religions. These include singing, dancing, synchronized behaviours, the telling of emotionally charged stories (for example, the trials and tribulations faced by the founder), ritual fasting and feasting. These are important because they all activate the endorphin system, the principal primate and human bonding mechanism both at the level of dyadic friendships and at the community level.

The endorphin system plays a central role in all this in three separate respects. First, it bonds individuals, creating a sense of community through a 'friends of friends' cascade. Second, because the endorphin system both increases positive affect and fine-tunes the immune system, it increases the individual's resistance to diseases as well as alleviating adverse psychological conditions like depression, enabling us to cope better with the vagaries of circumstance. Third, it kindles a prosocial disposition that enhances the effectiveness with which the community can function as a support network. The latter two benefits are by-products of living in bonded groups, and act as feedback loops to reinforce the central function of community bonding and, hence, community-level benefits.

Putting these elements together perhaps provides an explanation for two striking features of doctrinal religions, namely the fact that congregations have an optimal size that is surprisingly small and the tendency for all the world religions to fragment constantly into cults and sects. That religions seem to schism so easily is especially puzzling if they are intended to create and bind mega-scale communities: fragmentation is the last thing we would expect. Yet fragment is what religions manifestly do. However, if the psychology that underpins religion was adapted to ancestral societies, whose fundamental community was a unit of just 100–200 men, women and children, then this would all make much more sense.

It also suggests that although the doctrinal religions evolved to paper over the cracks that opened up when communities exceeded this size, they have been less than perfect solutions. They work, but only up to a point. The communities they form are weakly bonded (as clubs based around only one of the Seven Pillars). As a result, they are susceptible to the constant bubbling up from below of cults that reflect the natural community sizes that religion originally evolved to bond. These cults invariably have a charismatic quality to them, and often, but not always, either a strongly mystical element or a puritanical streak. The privations and discipline that invariably form the basis of the latter are, of course, as effective at triggering the required endorphin response as the mystical element.

There would seem to be two general conclusions we can draw from this. One is purely organizational. There is an optimal size for congregations that is a trade-off between two conflicting demands – between creating a sense of belonging and being large enough to tolerate turnover in membership without putting the group's viability at risk. The optimal size is actually quite finely specified at around 150 members, and even a modest overshoot in the size of a congregation inexorably results in a loss of coherence. Above about 300 members, a phase shift in the organizational structure is necessary if its size is to be maintained or increased, but at the unavoidable cost of a gradually eroding the sense of belonging.

The second issue is a sociological one. Because religions evolved to integrate small-scale communities, they exploit a natural us-versus-them psychology. That seems to work extremely well at the very small scale since it creates an intense sense of belonging. It preserves community integrity and allows the community to function as an effective alliance. But as population sizes grew exponentially through the Neolithic and beyond, the crowd effects of mass psychology very easily escalated into religious conflict. It is this that has largely been responsible for the appalling history of militant violence that has characterized all the large-scale religions without exception over the last few millennia. However beneficial religion has been at the personal level, its ability to arouse crowd violence against members of other religions has been far beyond any secular philosophy's capacity to do so. The challenge for religion has always been, and still is, how to solve these two problems simultaneously in a world that is becoming increasingly global.

This, perhaps, raises two last questions. Why, if religion has served such a beneficial role in community bonding, should we be witnessing an apparent decline in religiosity, especially in the West? And, this being so, what will be the longer-term consequences?

There are probably two observations to make with respect to the first of these questions. One is that this is far from being the first time in world history when religion has been in retreat. There is some suggestion that interest in religion declines when economic conditions are good and wealth inequality is low. Religion becomes less valuable as a solace when there is less need for dulling the pangs of poverty and oppression. The other point is that religion is not in retreat everywhere. There are still large sectors of the globe where religion is in anything but retreat. Moreover, even where it is in retreat (mainly the developed West), it is only some religions that are in retreat. Mainstream Christianity is certainly in retreat in the West, but more informal breakaway versions like the house church movement and the more charismatic Pentecostal sects are buoyant, while Islam seems to be maintaining a healthy popularity – in both cases, mainly among the less well-off segments of society. Both Christianity and Islam are relatively vibrant in the Americas, Africa and southern Asia, where wealth is more unequally distributed.

History tells us that religions rise and fall over time with the monotony of the ebb and flow of the tide. Some of the historically most successful religions have all but disappeared. Manichaeism, once hugely successful in the Middle East and the eastern Mediterranean, has long been extinct, its rival Mandaeism almost so while their great precursor Zoroastrianism is in much reduced circumstances – in all three cases, largely as a result of being overwhelmed by the crusading rise of Islam. The gods of Ancient Egypt, and the Roman and Norse gods that once ruled southern and northern Europe, respectively, disappeared a thousand or so years ago in the face of the proselytizing zeal of Christianity. Given that most of the doctrinal religions are little more than 2,000 years old, two millennia hence we might well find a very different mix of religions.

But if religion is on the decline, as the nineteenth-century French social theorists hoped, will that have any consequences? Given the evidence that religion creates a sense of bonding and, through that, confers some genuine benefits in terms of psychological and physical health and wellbeing, not to mention community bonding, it may well. Religion also provides a conduit through which to meet potential friends: places of worship provide somewhere to meet like-minded people. There is also a sense that, whether it is believed or not, religion still gives meaning to the national rituals that underpin mega-scale communal bonding – if only through its sense of solemnity. The incorporation of religious symbolism in communal and national rituals adds an ineffable something that is difficult to replicate with purely secular ceremonial. It is not necessary to believe, but the sense of grandeur, magnificence and sumptuousness created by the sense of belief incapsulated in these rituals is difficult to replace. Analogously, the music of religion the world over has a beauty and an emotional yet calming component to it that is rarely achieved by secular genres. Not every composer of these stirring musical scores has been a believer.[12]

Perhaps this leaves us with one unanswered question: is a secular religion – one that has the same uplift yet does not require belief in a transcendental world – possible? The history of the various attempts to create humanistic religions in the nineteenth and twentieth centuries is not encouraging. The failure of the various twentieth-century Communist regimes to eradicate religion and replace it with what amounts to a secular philosophy also speaks against the possibility. There have occasionally been briefly successful secular religions, often in the form of nationalism, but they have not had the staying power of conventional religions even when they have had all the trappings of a pseudo-religion. The Nazis, with their mythical otherworld concept of the *Volk*, their parades, mass singing and harangues, charismatic leaders and visionary sense of a renewed future, perhaps came closest to creating a genuine sense of secular religious zeal.

Some of the New Age movements worked well enough in the heady days of the 1960s counterculture when they offered the prospect of saving humanity and introducing a new kind of consciousness. But, in the end, most of their enthusiasts drifted away and rejoined the conventional world they had rebelled against, in many cases disillusioned by the behaviour of their charismatic leaders and the fact that they were unable to change the world. The environmental movement, and its latest manifestation in Extinction Rebellion, shares some of the same sense of visionary purpose, charismatic figures and collective action. But its secular focus has always left it bereft of support in the wider population. Time will tell whether it has real staying power, or fizzles out like the counterculture of the 1960s. Its claims are not new, and its focus too narrow and divorced from the human social world to carry the weight of a religion. Its lack of a central management organization leaves it vulnerable to imploding under the weight of internal fractiousness.

In short, it is difficult to see any convincing evidence for anything that will replace religion in human affairs. Religion is a deeply human trait. The content of religion will surely change over the longer term, but, for better or for worse, it is likely to remain with us.

Further Reading

In addition to specific references listed in the endnotes, I give a number of more general references for each chapter. These are indicated by an asterisk.

CHAPTER 1: HOW TO STUDY RELIGION

*Atran, Scott & Norenzayan, Ara (2004). 'Religion's evolutionary landscape: counterintuition, commitment, compassion, communion', *Behavioral and Brain Sciences* 27: 713–30.

*Barrett, Justin L. (2004). *Why Would Anyone Believe in God?* Lanham MD: AltaMira Press.

Bering, Jesse (2006). 'The folk psychology of souls', *Behavioral and Brain Sciences* 29: 453–98.

*Bering, Jesse (2013). *The God Instinct*. London: Nicholas Brearley Publishing.

Bird-David, N. (1999). '"Animism" revisited: personhood, environment, and relational epistemology'. *Current Anthropology* 40(S1): S67–S91.

*Boyer, Pascal (2001). *Religion Explained*. New York: Basic Books.

Dunbar, Robin (1995). *The Trouble With Science*. London: Faber.

*Dunbar, Robin (2020). *Evolution: What Everyone Needs To Know*. New York: Oxford University Press.

Dunbar, Robin (2020). 'Religion, the social brain and the mystical stance'. *Archives of the Psychology of Religion* 42: 46–62.

Durkheim, Émile ([1912] 2008). *The Elementary Forms of the Religious Life*. Oxford: Oxford University Press.

Eliade, Mircea (1985). *A History of Religious Ideas*, vols. 1–3. Oxford: Blackwells.

Eliade, Mircea (2004). *Shamanism: Archaic Techniques of Ecstasy*. Princeton, NJ: Princeton University Press.

Evans-Pritchard, E. E. (1965). *Theories of Primitive Religion*. Oxford: Oxford University Press.

Gerrard, C. M., Annis, R., Caffell, A., Graves, C. P., Millard, A., & Beaumont, J. (2018). *Lost Lives, New Voices: Unlocking the Stories of the Scottish Soldiers at the Battle of Dunbar, 1650*. Oxford: Oxbow.

Hamilton, Malcolm (2001). *The Sociology of Religion*. London: Routledge.

Huxley, Aldous (2010). *The Doors of Perception; And Heaven and Hell*. London: Random House.

James, William ([1902] 1985). *The Varieties of Religious Experience*. Cambridge, MA: Harvard University Press.

Jones, James (2020). 'How ritual might create religion: a neuropsychological exploration'. *Archive for the Psychology of Religion* 4: 29–45.

*Kellett, E. E. (1962). *A Short History of Religions*. Harmondsworth: Penguin Books.

Stringer, M. D. (1999). 'Rethinking animism: thoughts from the infancy of our discipline'. *Journal of the Royal Anthropological Institute* (NS) 5: 541–55.

Tinbergen, N. (1963). 'On the aims and methods of ethology'. *Zeitschrift für Tierpsychologie* 20: 410–33.

Trinkaus, Erik, Buzhilova, Alexandra P., Mednikova, Maria B. & Dobrovolskaia, Maria V. (2014). *The People of Sunghir: Burials, Bodies, and Behavior in the Earlier Upper Paleolithic*. New York: Oxford University Press.

Westwood, Jennifer & Kingshill, Sophia (2009). *The Lore of Scotland: A Guide to Scottish Legends*. London: Random House.

CHAPTER 2: THE MYSTICAL STANCE

Bartels, Andreas & Zeki, Samir (2000). 'The neural basis of romantic love'. *NeuroReport* 11: 3829–34.

*Bourguignon, Erika (1976). *Possession*. San Francisco, CA: Chandler & Sharpe.

Doblin, R. (1991). 'Pahnke's "Good Friday experiment": a long-term follow-up and methodological critique'. *Journal of Transpersonal Psychology* 23: 1–28.

Dulin, John (2020). 'Vulnerable minds, bodily thoughts, and sensory spirits: local theory of mind and spiritual experience in Ghana'. *Journal of the Royal Anthropological Institute* (NS), 61–76.

Dunbar, Robin (2020). 'Religion, the social brain and the mystical stance'. *Archive for the Psychology of Religion* 42: 46–62.

*Eliade, Mircea (2004). *Shamanism: Archaic Techniques of Ecstasy*. Princeton, NJ: Princeton University Press.

Frecska, E. & Kulcsar, Z. (1989). 'Social bonding in the modulation of the physiology of ritual trance'. *Ethos* 17: 70–87.

Guerra-Doce, E. (2015). 'Psychoactive substances in prehistoric times: examining the archaeological evidence'. *Time and Mind* 8: 91–112.

Henry, J. L. (1982). 'Possible involvement of endorphins in altered states of consciousness'. *Ethos* 10: 394–408.

Jilek, Wolfgang (1982). 'Altered states of consciousness in North American Indian ceremonials'. *Ethos* 10: 326–43.

Katz, Richard (1982). 'Accepting "Boiling Energy": the experience of !Kia-healing among the !Kung'. *Ethos* 10: 344–68.

*Knox, Ronald (1950). *Enthusiasm: A Chapter in the History of Religion*. Oxford: Oxford University Press.

Noyes, Russell (1980). 'Attitude change following near-death experiences'. *Psychiatry* 43: 234–42.

Oppenheimer, Stephen (1998). *East of Eden: The Drowned Continent of Southeast Asia*. London: Weidenfeld & Nicholson.

Perham, Margery & Simmons, J. (1952). *African Discovery: An Anthology of Exploration*. London: Faber and Faber.

Prince, R. (1982). 'Shamans and endorphins: hypotheses for a synthesis'. *Ethos* 10: 409–23.

Singh, Manvir (2018). 'The cultural evolution of shamanism'. *Behavioral and Brain Sciences* 41: E66.

Thomas, Elizabeth Marshall (2007). *The Old Way: A Story of the First People*. London: Picador.

*Winkelman, Michael (2000). *Shamanism: The Neural Ecology of Consciousness and Healing*. Westport, CT: Greenwood.

Winkelman, Michael (2013). 'Shamanism in cross-cultural perspective'. *International Journal of Transpersonal Studies* 31: 47–62.

CHAPTER 3: WHY BELIEVING CAN BE GOOD FOR YOU

Akiri, M. (2017). 'Magical water versus bullets: the Maji Maji uprising as a religious movement'. *African Journal for Transformational Scholarship* 3: 31–9.

Atkinson, Quentin, & Bourrat, Pierrick (2011). 'Beliefs about God, the afterlife and morality support the role of supernatural policing in human cooperation'. *Evolution and Human Behavior* 32: 41–9.

Atran, Scott & Norenzayan, Ara (2004). 'Religion's evolutionary landscape: counterintuition, commitment, compassion, communion'. *Behavioral and Brain Sciences* 27: 713–30.

Billingsley, Joseph, Gomes, C. M. & McCullough, M. E. (2018). 'Implicit and explicit influences of religious cognition on Dictator Game transfers'. *Royal Society Open Science* 5: 170238.

Boone, James (1988). 'Parental investment, social subordination and population processes among the 15th and 16th Century Portuguese nobility' in L. Betzig, M. Borgerhoff Mulder and P. Turke (eds.) *Human Reproductive Behaviour: A Darwinian Perspective*, pp. 83–96. Cambridge: Cambridge University Press.

Bourrat, Pierrick, Atkinson, Quentin & Dunbar, Robin (2011). 'Supernatural punishment and individual social compliance across cultures'. *Religion, Brain & Behavior* 1: 119–34.

Brown, Dee (1991). *Bury My Heart at Wounded Knee: An Indian History of the American West.* London: Vintage.

Chatters, L. M. (2000). 'Religion and health: public health research and practice'. *Annual Review of Public Health* 21: 335–67.

Crook, John & Osmaston, Henry (eds.) (1994). *Himalayan Buddhist Villages: Environment, Resources, Society and Religious Life in Zangskar, Ladakh.* Delhi: Motilal Banarsidass Publishers.

Curry, Oliver, Roberts, Sam & Dunbar, Robin (2013). 'Altruism in social networks: evidence for a "kinship premium"'. *British Journal of Psychology* 104: 283–95

Dávid-Barrett, Tamás & Dunbar, Robin (2014). 'Social elites emerge naturally in an agent-based framework when interaction patterns are constrained'. *Behavioral Ecology* 25: 58–68.

Deady, Denis, Smith, Miriam Law, Kent, John P. & Dunbar, Robin (2006). 'Is priesthood an adaptive strategy?' *Human Nature* 17: 393–404.

Dunbar, Robin (1995). *The Trouble With Science.* London: Faber.

Dunbar, Robin (2020). *Evolution: What Everyone Needs To Know.* New York: Oxford University Press.

Dunbar, Robin (2021a). 'Homicide rates and the transition to village life'. [to be completed]

Dunbar, Robin (2021b). 'Religiosity and religious attendance as factors in wellbeing and social engagement'. *Religion Brain and Behavior* 11: 17–26.

Dunbar, Robin, Clark, Amanda & Hurst, Nicola (1995). 'Conflict and cooperation among the Vikings: contingent behavioural decisions'. *Ethology and Sociobiology* 16: 233–46.

Dunbar, Robin, and Shultz, Susanne (2021). 'The infertility trap: the fertility costs of group-living in mammalian social evolution'. *Frontiers in Ecology and Evolution* (in press).

Durkheim, Émile ([1912] 2008). *The Elementary Forms of the Religious Life*. Oxford: Oxford University Press.

van Elk, Michiel, Matzke, D., Gronau, Q. F., Guan, M., Vandekerckhove, J. & Wagenmakers, E.-J. (2015). 'Meta-analyses are no substitute for registered replications: a skeptical perspective on religious priming'. *Frontiers in Psychology* 6:1365.

Gureje, O., Nortje, G., Makanjuola, V., Oladeji, B. D., Seedat, S. & Jenkins, R. (2015). 'The role of global traditional and complementary systems of medicine in the treatment of mental health disorders'. *Lancet Psychiatry* 2: 168–77.

Hames, Raymond (1987). 'Garden labour exchange among the Ye'kwana'. *Ethology and Sociobiology* 8: 259–84.

Henrich, Joe, Ensminger, J., McElreath, R., Barr, A., Barrett, C., Bolyanatz, A., Cardenas, J., Gurven, M. et al. (2010). 'Markets, religion, community size, and the evolution of fairness and punishment'. Science 327: 1480–84.

Herrmann, B., Thöni, C. & Gächter, S. (2008). 'Antisocial punishment across societies'. *Science* 319: 1362–7.

Huffman, Michael, Gotoh, S., Turner, L. A., Hamai, M. & Yoshida, K. (1997). 'Seasonal trends in intestinal nematode infection and medicinal plant use among chimpanzees in the Mahale Mountains, Tanzania'. *Primates* 38: 111–25.

Incayawar, Mario (2008). 'Efficacy of Quichua healers as psychiatric diagnosticians'. *The British Journal of Psychiatry* 192: 390–91.

Johnson, Dominic (2005). 'God's punishment and public goods: a test of the supernatural punishment hypothesis in 186 world cultures'. *Human Nature* 16: 410–46.

Johnson, Dominic & Bering, Jesse (2009). 'Hand of God, mind of man', in J. Schloss & M. J. Murray (eds.) *The Believing Primate: Scientific, Philosophical, and Theological Reflections on the Origin of Religion*, pp. 26–44. Oxford: Oxford University Press.

Katz, Richard (1982). 'Accepting "Boiling Energy": the experience of !Kia-healing among the !Kung'. *Ethos* 10: 344–68.

Knauft, Bruce (1987). 'Reconsidering violence in simple human societies: homicide among the Gebusi of New Guinea'. *Current Anthropology* 28: 457–500.

Koenig, Harold G. (2013). 'Religion and mental health' in *Is Religion Good for Your Health?* pp. 63–90. London: Routledge.

Koenig, Harold G. & Cohen, Harvey J. (2001). *The Link between Religion and Health: Psychoneuroimmunology and the Faith Factor*. Oxford: Oxford University Press.

Lang, Martin, Purzycki, B. G., Apicella, C. L., Atkinson, Q. D., et al. (2019). ' 'Moralizing gods, impartiality and religious parochialism across 15 societies. *Proceedings of the Royal Society* 286B: 20190202.

Le Beau, Bryan (2016). *The Story of the Salem Witch Trials*. London: Routledge.

McCullough, Michael, Hoyt, William, Larson, David, Koenig, Harold & Thoresen, Carl. (2000). 'Religious involvement and mortality: a meta- analytic review'. *Health Psychology* 19: 211–22.

Madsen, Elaine, Tunney, R., Fieldman, G., Plotkin, H., Dunbar, Robin, et al. (2007). 'Kinship and altruism: a cross-cultural experimental study'. *British Journal of Psychology* 98: 339–59.

Norenzayan, Ara & Shariff, Azim F. (2008). 'The origin and evolution of religious prosociality'. *Science* 322: 58–62.

Norenzayan, Ara, Shariff, Azim F., Gervais, Will M., Willard, Aiyana K., et al. (2016). 'The cultural evolution of prosocial religions'. *Behavioral and Brain Sciences* 39: 1–65.

Panter-Brick, Catherine (1989). 'Motherhood and subsistence work: the Tamang of rural Nepal'. *Human Ecology* 17: 205–28.

Peires, J. B. (1989). *The Dead Will Arise: Nongqawuse and the Great Xhosa Cattle-Killing Movement of 1856–7*. Bloomington, IN: Indiana University Press.

Preston, J. L. & Ritter, R. S. (2013). 'Different effects of religion and God on prosociality with the ingroup and outgroup'. *Personality and Social Psychology Bulletin* 39: 1471–83.

Purzycki, B. G., Apicella, C., Atkinson, Q. D., Cohen, E., et al. (2016). 'Moralistic gods, supernatural punishment and the expansion of human sociality'. *Nature* 530: 327–30.

Purzycki, B. G., Henrich, J., Apicella, C., Atkinson, Q. D., et al. (2018). 'The evolution of religion and morality: a synthesis of ethnographic and experimental evidence from eight societies'. *Religion, Brain & Behavior* 8: 101–32.

Sosis, Rich & Alcorta, Candace (2003). 'Signaling, solidarity, and the sacred: the evolution of religious behavior'. *Evolutionary Anthropology* 12: 264–74.

Sosis, Rich & Ruffle, Bradley (2003). 'Religious ritual and cooperation: testing for a relationship on Israeli religious and secular kibbutzim'. *Current Anthropology* 44: 713–22.

Tan, Jonathan & Vogel, Claudia (2008). 'Religion and trust: an experimental study'. *Journal of Economic Psychology* 29: 832–48.

Turner, Victor (1995). *The Ritual Process*. Chicago: Aldine de Gruyter.

Voland, E. (1988). 'Differential infant and child mortality in evolutionary perspective: data from 17th to19th century Ostfriesland (Germany)' in L. Betzig, M. Borgerhoff-Mulder & P. W. Turke (eds.) *Human Reproductive Behaviour*, pp. 253–62. Cambridge: Cambridge University Press.

Voland, E., Dunbar, Robin, Engel, C. & Stephan, P. (1997). 'Population increase and sex-biased parental investment in humans: evidence from 18th- and 19th-century Germany'. *Current Anthropology* 38: 129–35.

Watts, Joseph, Sheehan, O., Atkinson, Q. D., Bulbulia, J. & Gray, R. D. (2016). 'Ritual human sacrifice promoted and sustained the evolution of stratified societies'. *Nature* 532: 228–31.

Webber, Emily & Dunbar, Robin (2020). 'The fractal structure of communities of practice: implications for business organization'. *PLoS One* 15: e0232204.

Williams, David & Sternthal, Michelle (2007). 'Spirituality, religion and health: evidence and research directions'. *Medical Journal of Australia* 186: S47–50.

Winkelman, Michael (2013). 'Shamanism in cross-cultural perspective'. *International Journal of Transpersonal Studies* 31: 47–62.

CHAPTER 4: COMMUNITIES AND CONGREGATIONS

Bretherton, Roger & Dunbar, Robin (2020). 'Dunbar's number goes to church: the social brain hypothesis as a third strand in the study of church growth'. *Archive for the Psychology of Religion* 42: 63–76.

Curry, Oliver, Roberts, Sam & Dunbar, Robin (2013). 'Altruism in social networks: evidence for a "kinship premium"'. *British Journal of Psychology* 104: 283–95

Dunbar, Robin (1995). 'On the evolution of language and kinship' in J. Steele & S. Shennan (eds.) *The Archaeology of Human Ancestry: Power, Sex and Tradition*, pp. 380–96. London: Routledge.

Dunbar, Robin (1998). 'The social brain hypothesis'. *Evolutionary Anthropology* 6: 178–90.

Dunbar, Robin (2014a). *Human Evolution*. Harmondsworth: Pelican and New York: Oxford University Press.

Dunbar, Robin (2018). 'The anatomy of friendship'. *Trends in Cognitive Sciences* 22: 32–51.

Dunbar, Robin (2019). 'Feasting and its role in human community formation' in Kimberley Hockings & Robin Dunbar (eds.) *Alcohol and Humans: A Long and Social Affair*, pp.163–77. Oxford: Oxford University Press.

Dunbar, Robin (2020). 'Structure and function in human and primate social networks: implications for diffusion, network stability and health'. *Proceedings of the Royal Society* 476A: 20200446.

*Dunbar, Robin (2021). *Friends: Understanding the Power of Our Most Important Relationships*. London: Little Brown.

Dunbar, Robin & Shultz, Susanne (2017). 'Why are there so many explanations for primate brain evolution?' *Philosophical Transactions of the Royal Society* 244B: 201602244.

Dunbar, Robin & Sosis, Rich (2018). 'Optimising human community sizes'. *Evolution and Human Behavior* 39: 106–11.

Hamilton, Marcus, Milne, B. T., Walker, R. S., Burger, O. & Brown, J. H. (2007). 'The complex structure of hunter-gatherer social networks'. *Proceedings of the Royal Society* 274B, 2195–2202.

Hayden, B. (1987). 'Alliances and ritual ecstasy: human responses to resource stress'. *Journal for the Scientific Study of Religion* 26: 81–91.

Hill, Russell, Bentley, Alex & Dunbar, Robin (2008). 'Network scaling reveals consistent fractal pattern in hierarchical mammalian societies'. *Biology Letters* 4: 748–51.

Kanai, R., Bahrami, B., Roylance, R. & Rees, G. (2012). 'Online social network size is reflected in human brain structure'. *Proceedings of the Royal Society* 279B: 1327–34.

Kwak, S., Joo, W. T., Youm, Y. & Chey, J. (2018). 'Social brain volume is associated with in-degree social network size among older adults'. *Proceedings of the Royal Society* 285B: 20172708.

Lehmann, Julia, Lee, Phyllis, & Dunbar, Robin (2014). 'Unravelling the evolutionary function of communities' in Robin Dunbar, Clive Gamble & John Gowlett (eds.), *Lucy to Language: The Benchmark Papers*, pp. 245–76. Oxford: Oxford University Press.

Lewis, Penny, Birch, Amy, Hall, Alexander, & Dunbar, Robin (2017). 'Higher order intentionality tasks are cognitively more demanding'. *Social, Cognitive and Affectve Neuroscience* 12: 1063–71.

Lohfink, Gerhard (1999). *Does God Need the Church? Toward a Theology of the People of God*. Wilmington, DE: Michael Glazier.

Luhrmann, T. M. (2020). 'Thinking about thinking: the mind's porosity and the presence of the gods'. *Journal of the Royal Anthropological Institute* 26: 148–62.

McClure, Jennifer (2015). 'The cost of being lost in the crowd: how congregational size and social networks shape attenders' involvement in community organizations'. *Review of Religious Research* 57: 269–86.

Mann, Alice (1998). *The In-Between Church: Navigating Size Transitions in Congregations*. Durham, NC: Alban Institute.

Murray, John (1995). 'Human capital in religious communes: literacy and selection of nineteenth century Shakers'. *Explorations in Economic History* 32: 217–35.

Powell, Joanne, Lewis, Penny, Roberts, Neil, García-Fiñana, Marcia, & Dunbar, Robin (2012). 'Orbital prefrontal cortex volume predicts social network size: an imaging study of individual differences in humans'. *Proceedings of the Royal Society* 279B: 2157–62.

Roberts, Sam & Dunbar, Robin (2015). 'Managing relationship decay: network, gender, and contextual effects'. *Human Nature* 26: 426–50.

Rothauge, Arlin J. (1982). *Sizing Up a Congregation for New Member Ministry*. Congregational Development Services.

Snyder, Howard (2017). 'The church and Dunbar's number'. https://www.seedbed.com/the-church-and-dunbarsnumber/

Stonebraker, Robert (1993). 'Optimal church size: the bigger the better?' *Journal for the Scientific Study of Religion* 32: 231–41.

Stroope, Samuel & Baker, Joseph (2014). 'Structural and cultural sources of community in American congregations'. *Social Science Research* 45: 1–17.

Sutcliffe, Alistair, Dunbar, Robin, Binder, Jens & Arrow, Holly (2012). 'Relationships and the social brain: integrating psychological and evolutionary perspectives'. *British Journal of Psychology* 103: 149–68.

Wasdell, David (1974). 'Let my people grow' (Work Paper 1). London: Urban Church Project.

Webber, Emily & Dunbar, Robin (2020). 'The fractal structure of communities of practice: implications for business organization'. *PLoS One* 15: e0232204.

Wicker, Allen W. (1969). 'Size of church membership and members' support of church behavior settings'. *Journal of Personality and Social Psychology* 13: 278–88.

Wicker, Allen W., & Mehler, Anne (1971). 'Assimilation of new members in a large and a small church'. *Journal of Applied Psychology* 55: 151–6.

Zhou, Wei-Xing, Sornette, D., Hill, R. A. & Dunbar, Robin (2005). 'Discrete hierarchical organization of social group sizes'. *Proceedings of the Royal Society* 272B: 439–44.

CHAPTER 5: SOCIAL BRAIN, RELIGIOUS MIND

Azari, Nina & Slors, Marc (2007). 'From brain imaging religious experience to explaining religion: a critique'. *Archive for the Psychology of Religion* 29: 67–85.

Baron-Cohen, Simon (2003). *The Essential Difference: Men, Women and the Extreme Male Brain*. London: Penguin.

Bartels, Andreas & Zeki, Samir (2000). 'The neural basis of romantic love'. *NeuroReport* 11: 3829–34.

Carney, James, Wlodarski, Rafael & Dunbar, Robin (2014). 'Inference or enaction? The influence of genre on the narrative processing of other minds'. *PLoS One* 9: e114172.

Carrington, S. J. & Bailey, A. J. (2009). 'Are there theory of mind regions in the brain? A review of the neuroimaging literature'. *Human Brain Mapping* 30: 2313–35.

Dávid-Barrett, Tamás, Rotkirch, Anna, Carney, James, Behncke Izquierdo, Isabel, et al. (2015). 'Women favour dyadic relationships, but men prefer clubs'. *PLoS One* 10: e0118329.

*Dennett, Daniel (1978). 'Beliefs about beliefs'. *Behavioral and Brain Sciences* 1: 568–70.

Dezecache, Guillaume & Dunbar, Robin (2012). 'Sharing the joke: the size of natural laughter groups'. *Evolution and Human Behaviour* 33: 775–9.

Dunbar, Robin (2012). *The Science of Love and Betrayal.* London: Faber.

Dunbar, Robin (2017). 'Breaking bread: the functions of social eating'. *Adaptive Human Behavior and Physiology* 3: 198–211.

Dunbar, Robin (2018). 'The anatomy of friendship'. *Trends in Cognitive Sciences* 22: 32–51.

Dunbar, Robin (2020). 'Structure and function in human and primate social networks: implications for diffusion, network stability and health'. *Proceedings of the Royal Society* 476A: 20200446.

*Dunbar, Robin (2021). *Friends: Understanding the Power of our Most Important Relationships.* London: Little Brown.

Dunbar, Robin, Baron, Rebecca, Frangou, Anna, Pearce, Eiluned, et al. (2012). 'Social laughter is correlated with an elevated pain threshold'. *Proceedings of the Royal Society* 279B, 1161–7.

Dunbar, Robin, Teasdale, Ben, Thompson, Jackie, Budelmann, Felix, et al. (2016). 'Emotional arousal when watching drama increases pain threshold and social bonding'. *Royal Society Open Science* 3: 160288.

Ferguson, Michael A., Nielsen, Jared A., King, Jace, Dai, Li, et al. (2018). 'Reward, salience, and attentional networks are activated by religious experience in devout Mormons'. *Social Neuroscience* 13: 104–16.

Gursul, D., Goksan, S., Hartley, C., Mellado, G. S., et al. (2018). 'Stroking modulates noxious-evoked brain activity in human infants'. *Current Biology* 28: R1380–81.

Hall, J. A. (2019). 'How many hours does it take to make a friend?' *Journal of Social and Personal Relationships* 36: 1278–96.

Hove, M. J. & Risen, J. L. (2009). 'It's all in the timing: interpersonal synchrony increases affiliation'. *Social Cognition* 27: 949–60.

Keverne, E. B., Martensz, N. & Tuite, B. (1989). 'Beta-endorphin concentrations in cerebrospinal fluid of monkeys are influenced by grooming relationships'. *Psychoneuroendocrinology* 14: 155–61.

Krems, Jaimie, Neuberg, Steven, & Dunbar, Robin (2016). ''Something to talk about: are conversation sizes constrained by mental modeling abilities? *Evolution and Human Behavior* 37: 423–8.

Launay, Jacques & Dunbar, Robin (2015). 'Does implied community size predict likeability of a similar stranger?' *Evolution and Human Behaviour* 36: 32–7.

Launay, Jacques & Dunbar, Robin (2016). 'Playing with strangers: which shared traits attract us most to new people?' *PLoS One* 10: e0129688.

Lehmann, J., Korstjens, A. & Dunbar, Robin (2007). 'Group size, grooming and social cohesion in primates'. *Animal Behaviour* 74: 1617–29.

Lewis, P. A., Rezaie, R., Browne, R., Roberts, N. & Dunbar, Robin (2011). 'Ventromedial prefrontal volume predicts understanding of others and social network size'. *NeuroImage* 57: 1624–9.

Lewis, Penny, Birch, Amy, Hall, Alexander, & Dunbar, Robin (2017). 'Higher order intentionality tasks are cognitively more demanding'. *Social, Cognitive and Affectve Neuroscience* 12: 1063–71.

Machin, Anna & Dunbar, Robin (2011). 'The brain opioid theory of social attachment: a review of the evidence'. *Behaviour* 148: 985–1025.

*McNamara, Patrick (2009). *The Neuroscience of Religious Experience*. Cambridge: Cambridge University Press.

McPherson, M., Smith-Lovin, L. & Cook, J. M. (2001). 'Birds of a feather: homophily in social networks'. *Annual Review of Sociology* 27: 415–44.

Mandler, R. N., Biddison, W. E., Mandler, R. A. Y. A. & Serrate, S. A. (1986). 'ß-endorphin augments the cytolytic activity and interferon production of natural killer cells'. *Journal of Immunology* 136: 934–9.

Manninen, S., Tuominen, L., Dunbar, Robin, Karjalainen, T., et al. (2017). 'Social laughter triggers endogenous opioid release in humans'. *Journal of Neuroscience* 37: 6125–31.

Masters, Alexander (2006). *Stuart: A life backwards*. New York: Delacorte Press.

Mathews, P. M., Froelich, C. J., Sibbitt, W. L. & Bankhurst, A. D. (1983). 'Enhancement of natural cytotoxicity by beta-endorphin'. *Journal of Immunology* 130: 1658–62.

Newberg, Andrew, d'Aquili, Eugene & Rause, Vince (2001). *Why God Won't Go Away*. New York: Ballantine Books.

Norenzayan, Ara, Gervais, Will M. & Trzesniewski, Kali (2012). 'Mentalizing deficits constrain belief in a personal God'. *PloS One* 7: e36880.

Nummenmaa, Lauri, Tuominen, L., Dunbar, Robin, Hirvonen, J., et al. (2016). 'Reinforcing social bonds by touching modulates endogenous μ-opioid system activity in humans'. *NeuroImage* 138: 242–7.

Oesch, Nathan & Dunbar, Robin (2017). 'The emergence of recursion in human language: mentalising predicts recursive syntax task performance'. *Journal of Neurolinguistics* 43: 95–106.

Olausson, H., Wessberg, J., Morrison, I., McGlone, F. & Vallbo, A. (2010). 'The neurophysiology of unmyelinated tactile afferents'. *Neuroscience and Biobehavioral Reviews* 34: 185–91.

van Overwalle, F. (2009). 'Social cognition and the brain: a metaanalysis'. *Human Brain Mapping* 30: 829–58.

Passingham, Richard E., & Wise, Steven P. (2012). *The Neurobiology of the Prefrontal Cortex: Anatomy, Evolution, and the Origin of Insight*. Oxford: Oxford University Press.

Pearce, Eiluned, Launay, Jacques & Dunbar, Robin (2015). 'The ice-breaker effect: singing mediates fast social bonding'. *Royal Society Open Science* 2: 150221.

Pearce, Ellie, Machin, Anna & Dunbar, Robin (2021). 'Sex differences in intimacy levels in best friendships and romantic partnerships'. *Adaptive Humun Behavior and Physiology* 7: 1–16.

Powell, Joanne, Lewis, Penny, Dunbar, Robin, García-Fiñana, Marcia, & Roberts, Neil. (2010). 'Orbital prefrontal cortex volume correlates with social cognitive competence'. *Neuropsychologia* 48: 3554–62.

Powell, Joanne, Lewis, Penny, Roberts, Neil, García-Fiñana, Marcia, & Dunbar, Robin (2012). 'Orbital prefrontal cortex volume predicts social network size: an imaging study of individual differences in humans'. *Proceedings of the Royal Society* 279B: 2157–62.

Roberts, Sam & Dunbar, Robin (2015). 'Managing relationship decay: network, gender, and contextual effects'. *Human Nature* 26: 426–50.

Stiller, James & Dunbar, Robin (2007). 'Perspective-taking and memory capacity predict social network size'. *Social Networks* 29: 93–104.

Sutcliffe, Alistair, Dunbar, Robin, Binder, Jens & Arrow, Holly (2012). 'Relationships and the social brain: integrating psychological and evolutionary perspectives'. *British Journal of Psychology* 103: 149–68.

Suvilehto, Juulia, Glerean, Enrico, Dunbar, Robin, Hari, Riitta & Nummenmaa, Lauri (2015). 'Topography of social touching depends on emotional bonds between humans'. *Proceedings of the National Academy of Sciences*, USA, 112: 13811–16.

Suvilehto, Juulia, Nummenmaa, Lauri, Harada, Tokiko, Dunbar, Robin, et al. (2019). 'Cross-cultural similarity in relationship-specific social touching'. *Proceedings of the Royal Society* 286B: 20190467.

Tarr, Bronwyn, Launay, Jacques & Dunbar, Robin (2014). 'Silent disco: dancing in synchrony leads to elevated pain thresholds and social closeness'. *Evolution and Human Behavior* 37: 343–9.

Tarr, Bronwyn, Launay, Jacques & Dunbar, Robin (2017). 'Naltrexone blocks endorphins released when dancing in synchrony'. *Adaptive Human Behavior and Physiology* 3: 241–54.

Watts, J., Passmore, S., Rzymski, C. & Dunbar, Robin (2020). 'Text analysis shows conceptual overlap as well as domain-specific differences in Christian and secular worldviews'. *Cognition* 201: 104290.

Weinstein, Daniel, Launay, Jacques, Pearce, Eiluned, Dunbar, Robin & Stewart, Lauren (2014). 'Singing and social bonding: changes in connectivity and pain threshold as a function of group size'. *Evolution and Human Behavior* 37: 152–8.

Wlodarski, Rafael & Pearce, Ellie (2016). 'The God allusion: individual variation in agency detection, mentalizing and schizotypy and their association with religious beliefs and behavior'. *Human Nature* 27: 160–72.

CHAPTER 6: RITUAL AND SYNCHRONY

Bachorowski, J.-A. & Owren, M. J. (2001). 'Not all laughs are alike: voiced but not unvoiced laughter readily elicits positive affect'. *Psychological Science* 12, 252–7.

Bannan, Nicholas, Bamford, Joshua & Dunbar, Robin (2021). 'The evolution of gender dimorphism in the human voice: the role of octave equivalence'. *Current Anthropology* (in press).

Bastian, Brock, Jetten, Jolanda & Fasoli, Fabio (2011). 'Cleansing the soul by hurting the flesh: the guilt-reducing effect of pain'. *Psychological Science* 22: 334–5.

*Bellah, Robert (2011). *Religion in Human Evolution*. Cambridge, MA: Harvard University Press.

Burton, Chad & King, Laura (2004). 'The health benefits of writing about intensely positive experiences'. *Journal of Research in Personality* 38: 150–63.

Charles, Sarah, Farias, Miguel, van Mulukom, Valerie, Saraswati, Ambikananda, et al. (2020a). 'Blocking mu-opioid receptors inhibits social bonding in rituals'. *Biology Letters* 16: 20200485.

Charles, Sarah, van Mulukom, Valerie, Brown, Jennifer, Watts, Fraser, et al. (2020b). 'United on Sunday: the effects of secular rituals on social bonding and affect'. *PLoS One* 16(1): e0242546.

Charles, Sarah, van Mulukom, Valerie, Saraswati, Ambikananda, Watts, Fraser, Dunbar, Robin & Farias, Miguel. (2021). 'Bending and bonding: a 5-week study exploring social bonding during spiritual and secular yoga'. [forthcoming].

Cohen, Emma, Ejsmond-Frey, Robin, Knight, Nicola, & Dunbar, Robin (2010). 'Rowers' high: behavioural synchrony is correlated with elevated pain thresholds'. *Biology Letters* 6: 106–8.

Dávid-Barrett, Tamás, Rotkirch, Anna, Carney, James, Behncke Izquierdo, Isabel, et al. (2015). 'Women favour dyadic relationships, but men prefer clubs'. *PLoS One* 10: e0118329.

Dunbar, Robin (2021). *Friends: Understanding the Power of our Most Important Relationships*. London: Little Brown.

Dunbar, Robin, Kaskatis, K., MacDonald, I. & Barra, V. (2012). 'Performance of music elevates pain threshold and positive affect'. *Evolutionary Psychology* 10: 688–702.

Fischer, Ronald, Callander, Rohan, Reddish, Paul & Bulbulia, Joseph (2013). 'How do rituals affect cooperation? An experimental field study comparing nine ritual types'. *Human Nature* 24: 115–25.

Fischer, Ronald & Xygalatas, D. (2014). 'Extreme rituals as social technologies'. *Journal of Cognition and Culture* 14: 345–55.

Hobson, N. M., Schroeder, J., Risen, J. L., Xygalatas, D. & Inzlicht, M. (2018). 'The psychology of rituals: an integrative review and process-based framework'. *Personality and Social Psychology Review* 22: 260–84.

Hove, M. J. & Risen, J. L. (2009). 'It's all in the timing: interpersonal synchrony increases affiliation'. *Social Cognition* 27: 949–60.

Jackson, Joshua, Jong, J., Bilkey, D., Whitehouse, H., et al. (2018). 'Synchrony and physiological arousal increase cohesion and cooperation in large naturalistic groups'. *Scientific Reports* 8: 1–8.

Jilek, Wolfgang (1982). 'Altered states of consciousness in North American Indian ceremonials'. *Ethos* 10: 326–43.

Karl, J. A. & Fischer, R. (2018). 'Rituals, repetitiveness and cognitive load'. *Human Nature* 29: 418–41.

Lang, Martin, Bahna, V., Shaver, J. H., Reddish, P. & Xygalatas, D. (2017). 'Sync to link: Endorphin-mediated synchrony effects on cooperation'. *Biological Psychology* 127: 191–7.

Lawrie, Louisa, Jackson, M. C., & Phillips, L. H. (2019). 'Effects of induced sad mood on facial emotion perception in young and older adults'. *Aging, Neuropsychology, and Cognition* 26: 319–35.

Lewis, Z. & Sullivan, P. J. (2018). 'The effect of group size and synchrony on pain threshold changes'. *Small Group Research* 49: 723–38.

Mogan, R., Fischer, R. & Bulbulia, J. A. (2017). 'To be in synchrony or not? A meta-analysis of synchrony's effects on behavior, perception, cognition and affect'. *Journal of Experimental Social Psychology* 72: 13–20.

Neher, Andrew (1962). 'A physiological explanation of unusual behavior in ceremonies involving drums'. *Human Biology* 34: 151–60.

Price, Michael, & Launay, Jacques (2018). 'Increased wellbeing from social interaction in a secular congregation'. *Secularism and Nonreligion* 7: 1–9.

Reddish, Paul, Fischer, Ronald & Bulbulia, Joseph (2013). 'Let's dance together: synchrony, shared intentionality and cooperation'. *PloS One* 8: e71182.

Sosis, Rich & Alcorta, Candace (2003). 'Signaling, solidarity, and the sacred: the evolution of religious behavior'. *Evolutionary Anthropology* 12: 264–74.

Tarr, Bronwyn, Launay, Jacques, Cohen, Emma, Dunbar, Robin (2015). 'Synchrony and exertion during dance independently raise pain threshold and encourage social bonding'. *Biology Letters* 11: 20150767.

Tarr, Bronwyn, Launay, Jacques & Dunbar, Robin (2016). 'Silent disco: dancing in synchrony leads to elevated pain thresholds and social closeness'. *Evolution and Human Behavior* 37: 343–9.

Walter, V. J. & Grey Walter, W. (1949). 'The central effects of rhythmic sensory stimulation'. *EEG and Clinical Neurophysiology* 1:57–86.

Wyczesany, Miroslaw, Ligęza, T., Tymorek, A. & Adamczyk, A. (2018). 'The influence of mood on visual perception of neutral material'. *Acta Neurobiologiae Experimentalis* 78(2): 163–72.

von Zimmermann, Jorina & Richardson, Daniel C. (2016). 'Verbal synchrony and action dynamics in large groups'. *Frontiers in Psychology* 7: 2034.

CHAPTER 7: RELIGION IN PREHISTORY

Carney, James, Wlodarski, Rafael & Dunbar, Robin (2014).
'Inference or enaction? The influence of genre on the narrative
processing of other minds'. *PLoS One* 9: e114172.

Conde-Valverde, M., Martínez, I., Quam, R. M., Bonmatí, A., et
al. (2019). 'The cochlea of the Sima de los Huesos hominins
(Sierra de Atapuerca, Spain): new insights into cochlear
evolution in the genus Homo'. *Journal of Human Evolution*
136: 102641.

Devaine, Marie, San-Galli, A., Trapanese, C., Bardino, G., et al.
(2017). 'Reading wild minds: a computational assay of Theory
of Mind sophistication across seven primate species'. *PLoS
Computational Biology* 13: e1005833.

Dietrich, Oliver, Heun, M., Notroff, J., Schmidt, K. & Zarnkow,
M. (2012). 'The role of cult and feasting in the emergence of
Neolithic communities. New evidence from Göbekli Tepe,
south-eastern Turkey'. *Antiquity* 86: 674–95.

Dietrich, Oliver & Dietrich, Laura (2019). 'Rituals and feasting as
incentives for cooperative action at early Neolithic Göbekli
Tepe' in Kimberley Hockings & Robin Dunbar (eds.) *Alcohol
and Humans: A Long and Social Affair*, pp. 93–114. Oxford:
Oxford University Press.

Dunbar, Robin (2009). 'Why only humans have language' in
Rudolph Botha & Chris Knight (eds.) *The Prehistory of
Language*, pp. 12–35. Oxford: Oxford University Press..

*Dunbar, Robin (2014a). *Human Evolution*. Harmondsworth:
Pelican and New York: Oxford University Press.

Dunbar, Robin (2014b). 'Mind the gap: or why humans aren't just
great apes' in Robin Dunbar, Clive Gamble & J. A. J. Gowlett
(eds.) *Lucy to Language: The Benchmark Papers*, pp. 3–18.
Oxford: Oxford University Press.

Dunbar, Robin (2021). 'Homicide rates and the transition to village
life'. [forthcoming].

Guerra-Doce, E. (2015). 'Psychoactive substances in prehistoric times: examining the archaeological evidence'. Time and Mind 8: 91–112.

Hockings, Kimberley & Dunbar, Robin (eds.) (2019). *Alcohol and Humans: A Long and Social Affair*. Oxford: Oxford University Press.

Huffman, Michael, Gotoh, S., Turner, L. A., Hamai, M. & Yoshida, K. (1997). 'Seasonal trends in intestinal nematode infection and medicinal plant use among chimpanzees in the Mahale Mountains, Tanzania'. *Primates* 38: 111–25.

Knauft, Bruce (1987). 'Reconsidering violence in simple human societies: homicide among the Gebusi of New Guinea'. *Current Anthropology* 28: 457–500.

*Lewis-Williams, David (2002). *A Cosmos in Stone: Interpreting Religion and Society Through Rock Art*. Rowman Altamira.

McGovern, Patrick (2019). 'Uncorking the past: alcoholic fermentation as humankind's first biotechnology' in Kimberley Hockings & Robin Dunbar (eds.) *Alcohol and Humans: A Long and Social Affair*, pp. 81–92. Oxford: Oxford University Press.

*Mithen, Stephen (2005). *The Singing Neanderthals: The Origins of Music, Language, Mind and Body*. Cambridge, MA: Harvard University Press.

Moggi-Cecchi, J. & Collard, M. (2002). 'A fossil stapes from Sterkfontein, South Africa, and the hearing capabilities of early hominids'. *Journal of Human Evolution* 42: 259–65.

Oesch, Nathan & Dunbar, Robin (2017). 'The emergence of recursion in human language: mentalising predicts recursive syntax task performance'. *Journal of Neurolinguistics* 43: 95–106.

Pearce, E. & Bridge, H. (2013). 'Is orbital volume associated with eyeball and visual cortex volume in humans?' *Annuals of Human Biology* 40: 531–40.

Pearce, E., Stringer, C. & Dunbar, R. (2013). 'New insights into differences in brain organisation between Neanderthals and anatomically modern humans'. *Proceedings of the Royal Society* 280B: 1471–81.

Pearce, E., Shuttleworth, A., Grove, M. J. & Layton, R. H. (2014). 'The costs of being a high-latitude hominin' in Robin Dunbar, Clive Gamble & J. A. J. Gowlett (eds.) *Lucy to Language: The Benchmark Papers*, pp. 356–79. Oxford: Oxford University Press.

Peoples, Hervey & Marlowe, Frank (2012). 'Subsistence and the evolution of religion'. *Human Nature* 23: 253–69.

Peoples, Hervey, Duda, Pavel & Marlowe, Frank (2016). 'Hunter-gatherers and the origins of religion'. *Human Nature* 27: 261–82.

*Pettitt, Paul (2013). *The Palaeolithic Origins of Human Burial*. London: Routledge.

Pomeroy, E., Bennett, P., Hunt, C. O., Reynolds, T., et al. (2020). 'New Neanderthal remains associated with the "flower burial" at Shanidar Cave'. *Antiquity* 94: 11–26.

Randolph-Quinney, P. S. (2015). 'A new star rising: biology and mortuary behaviour of Homo naledi'. *South African Journal of Science* 111: 1–4.

Rusch, Neil (2020). 'Controlled fermentation, honey, bees and alcohol: archaeological and ethnohistorical evidence from southern Africa'. *South African Humanities* 33: 1–31.

Turner, S. E., Fedigan, L. M., Matthews, H. D. & Nakamichi, M. (2014). 'Social consequences of disability in a nonhuman primate'. *Journal of Human Evolution* 68: 47–57.

CHAPTER 8: A CRISIS IN THE NEOLITHIC

Adler, M. A., & Wilshusen, R. H. (1990). 'Large-scale integrative facilities in tribal societies: cross-cultural and southwestern US examples'. *World Archaeology* 22: 133–46.

Alt, K. W., Rodríguez, C. T., Nicklisch, N., Roth, D., et al. (2020). 'A massacre of early Neolithic farmers in the high Pyrenees at Els Trocs, Spain'. *Scientific Reports* 10: 1–10.

Atkinson, Quentin, Gray, Russell, & Drummond, Alexei (2009). 'Bayesian coalescent inference of major human mitochondrial DNA haplogroup expansions in Africa'. *Proceedings of the Royal Society* 276B: 367–73.

Bandy, Matthew (2004). 'Fissioning, scalar stress, and social evolution in early village societies'. *American Anthropologist* 106: 322–33.

Baumard, Nicholas, Hyafil, A., Morris, I. & Boyer, P. (2015). 'Increased affluence explains the emergence of ascetic wisdoms and moralizing religions'. *Current Biology* 25: 10–15.

Bonds, M. H., Dobson, A. P. and Keenan, D. C. (2012). 'Disease ecology, biodiversity, and the latitudinal gradient in income'. *PLoS Biol* 10(12): e1001456.

Bowles, Sam (2009). 'Did warfare among ancestral hunter-gatherers affect the evolution of human social behaviors?' *Science* 324: 1293–8.

Bowles, Sam (2011). 'Cultivation of cereals by the first farmers was not more productive than foraging'. *Proceedings of the National Academy of Sciences*, USA, 108: 4760–65.

Bradley, Kenneth (1943). *The Diary of a District Officer*. London: Harrap.

Chagnon, Napoleon & Bugos, Paul (1979). 'Kin selection and conflict: an analysis of a Yanomamö ax fight' in Napoleon Chagnon & William Irons (eds.) *Evolutionary Biology and Human Social Behavior*, pp. 213–38. London: Duxbury.

Daly, Martin & Wilson, Margo (1983). *Sex, Evolution, and Behavior*, 1st edition. Boston: Willard Grant Press.

Dietrich, Oliver & Dietrich, Laura (2019). 'Rituals and feasting as incentives for cooperative action at early Neolithic Göbekli Tepe' in Kimberley Hockings & Robin Dunbar (eds.) *Alcohol *and Humans: A Long and Social Affair*, pp. 93–114. Oxford: Oxford University Press.

Dietrich, Oliver, Heun, M., Notroff, J., Schmidt, K. & Zarnkow, M. (2012). 'The role of cult and feasting in the emergence of Neolithic communities. New evidence from Göbekli Tepe, south-eastern Turkey'. *Antiquity* 86: 674–95.

Dunbar, Robin (2019). 'Fertility as a constraint on group size in African great apes'. *Biological Journal of the Linnaean Society* 129: 1–13.

Dunbar, Robin (2020). 'Structure and function in human and primate social networks: implications for diffusion, network stability and health'. *Proceedings of the Royal Society* 476A: 20200446.

Dunbar, Robin (2021). 'Homicide rates and the transition to village life'. [forthcoming]

Dunbar, Robin & MacCarron, P. (2019). 'Group size as a trade-off between fertility and predation risk: implications for social evolution'. *Journal of Zoology* 308: 9–15.

Dunbar, Robin & Shultz, S. (2021). 'The infertility trap: the costs of group-living and mammalian social evolution'. *Fronters of Evolution and Ecology* (in press).

Dunbar, Robin, MacCarron, P. & Robertson, C. (2018). 'Tradeoff between fertility and predation risk drives a geometric sequence in the pattern of group sizes in baboons'. *Biological Letters* 14: 20170700.

Dunbar, Robin, MacCarron, P. & Shultz, S. (2018). 'Primate social group sizes exhibit a regular scaling pattern with natural attractors'. *Biology Letters* 14: 20170490.

Fausto, Carlos (2012). *Warfare and Shamanism in Amazonia*. Cambridge: Cambridge University Press.

Fincher, Corrie & Thornhill, Randy (2008). 'Assortative sociality, limited dispersal, infectious disease and the genesis of the global pattern of religion diversity'. *Proceedings of the Royal Society* 27B: 2587–94.

Fincher, Corrie & Thornhill, Randy (2012). 'Parasite-stress promotes in-group assortative sociality: the cases of strong family ties and heightened religiosity'. *Behavioral and Brain Sciences* 35: 61–79.

Fincher, Corrie, Thornhill, Randy, Murray, D. R. & Schaller, M. (2008). 'Pathogen prevalence predicts human cross-cultural variability in individualism/collectivism'. *Proceedings of the Royal Society* 275B: 1279–85.

Håkanson, L. & Boulion, V. V. (2001). 'A practical approach to predict the duration of the growing season for European lakes'. *Ecological Modelling* 140: 235–45.

*Johnson, Allen & Earle, Timothy (2001). *The Evolution of Human Societies: From Foraging Group to Agrarian State.* 2nd edition. Palo Alto, CA: Stanford University Press.

Johnson, Dominic (2005). 'God's punishment and public goods: a test of the supernatural punishment hypothesis in 186 world cultures'. *Human Nature* 16: 410–46.

Katz, Richard (1982). 'Accepting "Boiling Energy": the experience of !Kia-healing among the !Kung'. *Ethos* 10: 344–68.

Knauft, Bruce (1987). 'Reconsidering violence in simple human societies: homicide among the Gebusi of New Guinea'. *Current Anthropology* 28: 457–500.

Lehmann, J., Lee, P. & Dunbar, Robin (2014). 'Unravelling the evolutionary function of communities' in Robin Dunbar, Clive Gamble & J. A. J. Gowlett (eds.) *Lucy to Language: The Benchmark Papers*, pp. 245–76. Oxford: Oxford University Press.

Liebmann, Matthew, Ferguson, T. & Preucel, Robert (2005). 'Pueblo settlement, architecture, and social change in the Pueblo Revolt era, AD 1680 to 1696'. *Journal of Field Archaeology* 30: 45–60.

MacEachern, Scott (2011). 'Enslavement and everyday life: living with slave raiding in the north-eastern Mandara Mountains of Cameroon' in Paul Lane & Kevin C. MacDonald (eds.), *Slavery in Africa: Archaeology and Memory*, pp. 109–24. London: Taylor and Francis.

Meador, Betty De Shong (2000). *Inanna, Lady of Largest Heart: Poems of the Sumerian High Priestess Enheduanna*. Austin TX: University of Texas Press.

Meyer, C., Lohr, C., Gronenborn, D. & Alt, K. W. (2015). 'The massacre mass grave of Schöneck-Kilianstädten reveals new insights into collective violence in Early Neolithic Central Europe'. *Proceedings of the National Academy of Sciences*, USA, 112: 11217–22.

van Neer, W., Alhaique, F., Wouters, W., Dierickx, K., et al. (2020). 'Aquatic fauna from the Takarkori rock shelter reveals the Holocene central Saharan climate and palaeohydrography'. *Plos one* 15(2): e0228588.

Nelson, Margaret & Schachner, Gregson (2002). 'Understanding abandonments in the North American southwest'. *Journal of Archaeological Research* 10: 167–206.

Nettle, Daniel (1998). Explaining global patterns of language diversity. *Journal of Anthropological Archaeology* 17: 354–74.

Neuberg, Steven, Warner, C. M., Mistler, S. A., Berlin, A., et al. (2014). 'Religion and intergroup conflict: findings from the global group relations project'. *Psychological Science* 25: 198–206.

Oliver, Douglas L. (1955). *Solomon Island Society: Kinship and Leadership among the Siuai of Bougainville*. Cambridge, MA: Harvard University Press.

Roser, Max (2013). 'Ethnographic and archaeological evidence on violent deaths'. https://ourworldindata.org/ethnographic-and-archaeological-evidence-on-violent-deaths#share-of-violent-deaths-in-prehistoric-archeological-state-and-non-state-societies

Thomas, Elizabeth Marshall (2007). *The Old Way: A Story of the First People*. London: Picador.

Thomas, Mark, Stumpf, M. P. & Härke, H. (2006). 'Evidence for an apartheid-like social structure in early Anglo-Saxon England'. *Proceedings of the Royal Society* 273B: 2651–7.

Wade, James (2019). 'Ego-centred networks, community size
and cohesion: Dunbar's Number and a Mandara Mountains
conundrum' in David Shankland (ed.), *Dunbar's Number*,
pp. 105–24. Royal Anthropological Institute Occasional Papers
No. 45. Canon Pyon: Kingston Press.

Walker, R. S. & Bailey, D. H. (2013). 'Body counts in lowland
South American violence'. *Evolution and Human Behavior*
34: 29–34.

Watts, Joseph, Greenhill, S. J., Atkinson, Q. D., Currie, T. E.,
et al. (2015). 'Broad supernatural punishment but not
moralizing high gods precede the evolution of political
complexity in Austronesia'. *Proceedings of the Royal Society*
282B: 20142556.

Watts, Joseph, Sheehan, O., Atkinson, Q. D., Bulbulia, J. &
Gray, R. D. (2016). 'Ritual human sacrifice promoted and
sustained the evolution of stratified societies'. *Nature*
532: 228–31.

Wahl, J., & Trautmann, I. (2012). 'The Neolithic massacre
at Talheim: a pivotal find in conflict archaeology' in Rick
J. Schulting & Linda Fibiger (eds.) *Sticks, Stones, and Broken
Bones: Neolithic Violence in a European Perspective*, pp. 77–100.
Oxford: Oxford University Press.

Whitehouse, Harvey, Francois, P., Savage, P. E., Currie, T. E.,
et al. (2019). 'Complex societies precede moralizing gods
throughout world history'. *Nature* 568: 226–9.

Wiessner, Polly (2005). 'Norm enforcement among the Ju/ 'hoansi
Bushmen'. *Human Nature* 16: 115–45.

Willey, P. (2016). *Prehistoric Warfare on the Great Plains:
Skeletal Analysis of the Crow Creek Massacre Victims*. London:
Routledge.

Wrangham, Richard, Wilson, M. L. & Muller, M. N. (2006).
'Comparative rates of violence in chimpanzees and humans'.
Primates 47(1): 14-26.

Zerjal, T., Xue, Y., Bertorelle, G., Wells, R. S., et al. (2003). 'The genetic legacy of the Mongols'. *American Journal of Human Genetics* 72: 717–21.

CHAPTER 9: CULTS, SECTS AND CHARISMATICS

Aron, Arthur, Aron, Elaine N. & Smollan, Danny (1992). 'Inclusion of Other in the Self Scale and the structure of interpersonal closeness'. *Journal of Personality and Social Psychology* 63: 596–612.

Bryant, J. M. (2009). 'Persecution and schismogenesis: how a penitential crisis over mass apostasy facilitated the triumph of Catholic Christianity in the Roman Empire' in James R. Lewis & Sarah M. Lewis (eds.) *Sacred Schisms: How Religions Divide*, pp. 147–68. Cambridge: Cambridge University Press.

Chidester, David (1991). *Salvation and Suicide: Jim Jones, the Peoples Temple, and Jonestown*. Bloomington, IN: Indiana University Press.

*Cohn, Norman (1970). *The Pursuit of the Millennium: Revolutionary Millenarians and Mystical Anarchists of the Middle Ages*. Oxford: Oxford University Press.

Dávid-Barrett, Tamás & Dunbar, Robin (2014). 'Social elites emerge naturally in an agent-based framework when interaction patterns are constrained'. *Behavioral Ecology* 25: 58–68.

Dávid-Barrett, Tamás, Rotkirch, A., Carney, J., Behncke Izquierdo, I., et al. (2015). 'Women favour dyadic relationships, but men prefer clubs'. *PLoS-One* 10: e0118329.

Davis, W. (2000). 'Heaven's Gate: A study of religious obedience'. *Nova Religio* 3: 241–67.

Dawson, Lorne L. (ed.) (2006). *Cults and New Religious Movements*. Oxford: Blackwell.

Dien, Simon (2019). 'Schizophrenia, evolution and self-transcendence' in David Shankland (ed.) *Dunbar's Number*, pp. 137–54. Royal Anthropological Institute Occasional Papers No. 45. Canon Pyon: Kingston Press.

Dunbar, Robin (1991). 'Sociobiological theory and the Cheyenne case'. *Current Anthropology* 32: 169–73.

Dunbar, Robin (2012). *The Science of Love and Betrayal*. London: Faber.

Dunbar, Robin (2018). 'The anatomy of friendship'. *Trends in Cognitive Sciences* 22: 32–51.

Dunbar, Robin (2020). 'Structure and function in human and primate social networks: implications for diffusion, network stability and health'. *Proceedings of the Royal Society* 476A: 20200446.

Dunbar, Robin (2021). *Friends: Understanding the Power of Our Most Important Relationships*. London: Little Brown.

Katz, Richard (1982). 'Accepting "Boiling Energy": the experience of !Kia-healing among the !Kung'. *Ethos* 10: 344–68.

Kisala, Robert (2009). 'Schisms in Japanese new religious movements' in James R. Lewis & Sarah M. Lewis (eds.) *Sacred Schisms: How Religions Divide*, pp. 83–105. Cambridge: Cambridge University Press.

Lockhart, Alastair (2019). *Personal Religion and Spiritual Healing: The Panacea Society in the Twentieth Century*. Albany, NY: State University of New York Press

Lockhart, Alastair (2020). 'New religious movements and quasi-religion: cognitive science of religion at the margins'. *Archive for the Psychology of Religion* 42: 101–22.

Lucia, Amanda (2018). 'Guru sex: charisma, proxemic desire, and the haptic logics of the guru-disciple relationship'. *Journal of the American Academy of Religion* 86: 953–88.

McNamara, Patrick (2009). *The Neuroscience of Religious Experience*. Cambridge: Cambridge University Press.

Miller, Timothy (ed.). (1991). *When Prophets Die: The Postcharismatic Fate of New Religious Movements*. Albany, NY: State University of New York Press.

Newport, Kenneth G. C. (2006). *The Branch Davidians of Waco: The History and Beliefs of an Apocalyptic Sect*. Oxford: Oxford University Press.

Palchykov, V., Kaski, K., Kertész, J., Barabási, A.-L. & Dunbar, Robin (2012). 'Sex differences in intimate relationships'. *Scientific Reports* 2: 320.

Panacea Charitable Trust and Museum (2021). 'From Mabel Barltrop to Ocavia'. https://web.archive.org/web/20170130010424/http:// panaceatrust.org/history-of-the-panacea-society/octavia/

Partridge, Christopher (2009). 'Schism in Babylon: colonialism, Afro- Christianity and Rastafari' in James R. Lewis & Sarah M. Lewis (eds.) Sacred Schisms: How Religions Divide, pp. 306–31. Cambridge: Cambridge University Press.

Peters, Emmanuelle, Day, S., McKenna, J. & Orbach, G. (1999). 'Delusional ideation in religious and psychotic populations'. *British Journal of Clinical Psychology* 38: 83–96.

Pew Research Centre (2013). 'The gender gap in religion around the world'. https://www.pewforum.org/2016/03/22/ the-gender-gap-in-religion-around-the-world/

Prince, R. (1982). 'Shamans and endorphins: hypotheses for a synthesis'. *Ethos* 10: 409–23.

Saroglou, Vassilis (2002). 'Religion and the five-factors of personality: a meta-analytic review'. *Personality and Individual Differences* 32: 15–25.

Shaw, Jane (2011). *Octavia, Daughter of God: The Story of a Female Messiah and her Followers*. London: Jonathan Cape.

Singh, Manvir (2018). 'The cultural evolution of shamanism'. *Behavioral and Brain Sciences* 41: E66.

Srinivas, Tulasi (2010). *Winged Faith: Rethinking Globalization and Religious Pluralism Through the Sathya Sai Movement*. New York: Columbia University Press.

Sternberg, Robert J. (1986). 'A triangular theory of love'. *Psychological Review* 93: 119–35.

Sumption, Jonathan (2011). *The Albigensian Crusade*. London: Faber

Suvilehto, Juulia, Glerean, E., Dunbar, Robin, Hari, R. & Nummenmaa, L. (2015). 'Topography of social touching depends on emotional bonds between humans'. *Proceedings of the National Academy of Sciences*, USA, 112: 13811–16.

Suvilehto, Juulia, Nummenmaa, L., Harada, T., Dunbar, Robin, et al. (2019). 'Cross-cultural similarity in relationship-specific social touching'. *Proceedings of the Royal Society* 286B: 20190467.

Turner, Guinevere (2019). 'My childhood in a cult'. *New Yorker*, 6 May 2019. https://www.newyorker.com/magazine/2019/05/06/my-childhood-in-a-cult

CHAPTER 10: SCHISMS AND DIVISIONS

Cavalli-Sforza, Luca & Feldman, Marcus. (1981) *Cultural Transmission and Evolution: A Quantitative Approach*. Princeton NJ: Princeton University Press.

Dunbar, Robin (2020). *Evolution: What Everyone Needs To Know*. New York: Oxford University Press.

Kisala, Robert (2009). 'Schisms in Japanese new religious movements' in James R. Lewis & Sarah M. Lewis (eds.) *Sacred Schisms: How Religions Divide*, pp. 83–105. Cambridge: Cambridge University Press.

Lewis, James R. & Lewis, Sarah M. (eds.) (2009). *Sacred Schisms: How Religions Divide*. Cambridge: Cambridge University Press.

Pearce, E. & Bridge, H. (2013). 'Is orbital volume associated with eyeball and visual cortex volume in humans?' *Annuals of Human Biology* 40: 531–40.

Pearce, E. & Dunbar, Robin (2012). 'Latitudinal variation in light levels drives human visual system size'. *Biology Letters* 8: 90–93.

Pearce, E., Stringer, C. & Dunbar, Robin (2013). 'New insights into differences in brain organisation between Neanderthals and anatomically modern humans'. *Proceedings of the Royal Society* 280B: 1471–81.

Smith, Andrew (1992). 'Origins and spread of pastoralism in Africa'. *Annual Review of Anthropology* 21: 125–41.

Notes

INTRODUCTION

1   The collective term for Judaism, Christianity and Islam, reflecting their common descent from the Old Testament patriarch Abraham.

2   Besides the Abrahamic religions, other monotheistic religions include Sikhism, Zoroasterianism, the religions of the Yazidis and the Druze, Mandaeanism, the Bahá'í Faith, Rastafarianism, the ancient Chinese *Shangdi* religion, and the tribal religions of, among others, the Namibian Himba, the Igbo of Nigeria and the Cushitic tribes of northeast Africa.

3   In Mahāyāna Buddhism (one of the two main schools of Buddhism), a bodhisattva is someone who has reached the final state of enlightenment to achieve Buddhahood, but voluntarily decides to postpone that final transition in order to assist other sentient beings, human or otherwise, in their personal struggles towards enlightenment.

4   Their services often involved dancing naked around a fire – a ritual resurrected by nineteenth-century witches' covens. The Adamites survived for almost two centuries from the second century AD until the fourth century. A number of later sects in medieval Europe adopted the same practice. In the fifteenth century, the Bohemian Taborites and the Dutch Brethren of the Free Spirit advocated complete nakedness even in public on the grounds that salvation lay in a return to the original state of sinlessness of Adam and Eve before the Fall.

5   The sect survived from the 1740s until as late as the 1940s, though the practice of mutilation seems to have died out around 1900.

6   Though elements of dualism appear in earlier philosophies, the concept is usually associated with the seventeenth-century French philosopher René Descartes – hence its common designation as 'Cartesian dualism'.

7   The philosophical claim that nothing exists outside my own mind.

NOTES

CHAPTER 1: HOW TO STUDY RELIGION

1   John Dulin (2020).

2   Richard Munslow, who died in 1906 at the age of seventy-three, was reputed to have been the last sin-eater in England. His grave (which was restored by public subscription in 2010) can be found in the churchyard of St Margaret's Church in the Shropshire village of Ratlinghope.[12]

3   During the 2018 excavations of the nineteenth-century Park Street cemetery in central Birmingham (to make room for the new Curzon St HS2 railway station), a dozen of these plates turned up in burials. Initially, the archaeologists were perplexed, until someone remembered the sin-eaters of the nearby Welsh Marches.

4   For more on this, see my 1995 book *The Trouble With Science*.

5   The date was not fixed to 25 December until AD 336, although the theologian Clement of Alexandria had suggested it over a century earlier. The main reason for choosing that date was that the theologians had already settled on the spring equinox (which at that time occurred on 25 March due to the precession of the equinoxes) for the Feast of the Annunciation (the putative date for Jesus' conception), making the winter solstice a convenient nine months later.

6   See, among others, Pascal Boyer (2001), Justin Barrett (2004), Scott Atran & Ara Norenzayan (2004), Jesse Bering (2006, 2013).

7   The seventeenth-century French mathematician Blaise Pascal argued that even if you didn't believe in God, it made rational sense to do so since the cost of being wrong (and you could only ever ascertain that when it is too late to regret your decision) is *much* greater than what you lose by making the few sacrifices in this life that believing in God entails.

8   James Jones (2020).

9   For more on the theory of evolution, see my recent book *Evolution: What Everyone Needs To Know*.

10 Richard Dawkins coined the term *meme* for these. Memes are the cultural equivalent of a biological trait: like biological traits, they are inherited from other individuals, except that in this case they are inherited by cultural transmission (via social learning or copying).

11 I should be clear that I do not intend to imply that viruses, or indeed cultures, have motivations or intentions. Evolutionary biologists use this form of wording as a convenient shorthand because natural selection operates in a way that *looks* like intentional actions. We could phrase everything in terms of 'selection acting to maximize

fitness', but doing so repeatedly becomes tedious and unnecessarily longwinded.

12 In many ways, it all sounds very Buddhist with its successive reincarnations eventually ending in Enlightenment and immersion in the 'universal principle'. The only difference is that, in the Buddhist version, there are snakes as well as ladders, so that individuals can slip down to lower rungs if they behave badly in any given life. It is not beyond the bounds of possibility that Aristotle knew about Buddhist philosophy. Alexander the Great encountered Buddhism during his conquest of western India during Aristotle's lifetime. Indeed, the philosopher Pyrrho of Elis, who accompanied Alexander's army, was directly influenced by Buddhist thinking.

13 In fact, it is currently thought that there may have been two separate origins to life. One gave rise to the group of single-celled organisms known as the Archaeobacteria, the anaerobic bacteria that lack a nucleus; the other gave rise to all the other forms of life on earth, from conventional bacteria to humans. This is evidenced by the fact that all the viruses, bacteria, plants and animals that make up the second group have the same genetic code, with life sustained by the same chemical processes; the Archaeobacteria use a slightly different set of chemical processes.

14 See Justin Barrett (2004)

CHAPTER 2: THE MYSTICAL STANCE

1 In evolutionary biology, an exaptation is a trait that has evolved for, or as part of the response to, one function but later turns out to provide the basis for an adaptation to an entirely different selection pressure. One classic example is the three tiny bones that form the ossicles – the bones that allow us to hear by connecting the ear drum in the outer ear to the base of the cochlea in the inner ear. They were adapted from the back three of the five bones that formed the lower jaw of our reptile ancestors. All reptiles 'hear' ground vibrations through their lower jaw. The other two bones remained to form the mammalian jaw, one forming the upright component and the other the horizontal part, now fused together to provide stability while chewing.

2 The anonymous writer of these tracts referred to himself as Dionysius the Areopagite, an early Athenian convert of St Paul who is mentioned in the

Acts of the Apostles. However, the tracts were written much later, hence the addition of the 'Pseudo-' prefix.

3 Ronald Knox provides a very readable account of these early movements in the western Christian tradition from the fourth through to the eighteenth centuries in his book *Enthusiasm: A Chapter in the History of Religion.*

4 The title given to someone on the first step (beatification) towards canonization as a saint of the Catholic Church. Controversial in his own lifetime, Jan van Ruusbroec was not beatified until 1908, 630 years after his death.

5 A title given by the Catholic Church to thirty-six saints deemed to have made special contributions to theology through their writings or study. Four of these are women, including Hildegard of Bingen.

6 The stigmata represent the wounds left by the nails driven through the hands and feet used to pin Jesus to the cross, and, according to the Gospels, the spear thrust through his side that was given by a Roman soldier to put an end to his suffering. In some cases, stigmata have the form of simple red marks on the skin, in other cases open wounds that weep blood. Padre Pio often wore woollen mittens to absorb and hide the blood seeping from his hands. Stigmata on the hands usually appear in the centre of the palms (as depicted in many paintings of medieval saints). However, the victims of crucifixion were never pinned through the palms of the hands: had they been, their struggles to breath would have caused the nails to be torn out. To prevent this, the nails (when used in crucifixions) were in fact usually placed through the wrist. Crucifixion usually results in death by suffocation because the weight of the body hanging on the arms eventually restricts the ability to breath out. In order to breathe, victims have to pull themselves up using their arms until they are too exhausted to do this; to hasten death, their shins were often broken. The Catholic Church authorities have always been rather ambivalent about stigmata: Padre Pio was investigated by medical doctors on several occasions at the behest of the authorities to try to determine whether his wounds were self-inflicted or not.

7 The three cages still hang in their original position high on the tower of St Lambert's church.

8 Erika Bourguignon (1976).

9 Andreas Bartels & Samir Zeki (2000).

10 Russell Noyes (1980).

11 Raymond Prince (1982).

12 Mircea Eliade (2004).

13 The cosmic tree (also known as the tree of life or tree of knowledge) links the physical world with both heaven and the underworld. It is a motif that appears in many early religions throughout the world. Stephen Oppenheimer (1998) has suggested it had its origins in the densely forested islands of modern Indonesia and became dispersed throughout Asia and Europe during the mass population movements that took place after sea levels rose abruptly around 12,000 years ago at the end of the Younger Dryas climatic event.

14 Manvir Singh (2018).

15 Michael Winkelman (2000, 2013).

16 By warfare, I refer mainly to the provision of medicine or charms related to taking part in warfare, much as priests in medieval times blessed the assembled troops at the start of a battle, or to the casting of omens to determine when to go to war; it does not mean making political decisions about whether to go to war.

17 Originally, the oracle was always a young virgin. But after some scoundrel kidnapped and violated one of the oracles, it was an older woman.

18 The experiment (also known as the Good Friday Experiment) was run by Walter Panhke, then a graduate student at Harvard University, as part of the Harvard Psilocybin Project supervised by Timothy Leary, the father of LSD. The Marsh Chapel itself was the official place of worship of nearby Boston University.

19 In the Rabbinical tradition of Judaism, the burning of incense during synagogue services died out during the Middle Ages, although it continues to this day among the Jewish communities of Samaria.

20 Contrary to popular myth, it was not the British East India Company that was responsible for introducing opium to China and encouraging its widespread use.

CHAPTER 3: WHY BELIEVING MIGHT BE GOOD FOR YOU

1 See my book *Evolution: What Everyone Needs To Know*.

2 Dee Brown (1991).

3 M. Akiri (2017).

4 J. B. Peires (1989).

5 Michael Huffman et al. (1997).

6 Mario Incayawar (2008).

7   Michael Winkelman (2013).

8   David Williams & Michelle Sternthal (2007).

9   Michael McCullough et al. (2000).

10 Elainie Madsen et al. (2007); Oliver Curry, Sam Roberts & Robin Dunbar (2013).

11 Raymond Hames (1987); Catherine Panter-Brick (1989); Robin Dunbar, Amanda Clark & Nicola Hurst (1995).

12 This is also known as the Common Pool Resource Problem or the Freerider Problem.

13 The term was proposed by Dominic Johnson & Jesse Bering (2009).

14 Dominic Johnson (2005).

15 Jonathan Tan & Claudia Vogel (2008).

16 Rich Sosis & Bradley Ruffle (2003). Neither participant knew who the other person was, other than that they were from the same kibbutz.

17 Joe Henrich et al. (2010).

18 Ara Norenzayan et al. (2016); see also Michiel van Elke et al. (2015).

19 Michiel van Elk et al. (2015); Joseph Billingsley et al. (2018).

20 Quentin Atkinson & Pierrick Bourrat (2011).

21 Pierrick Bourrat, Quentin Atkinson & Robin Dunbar (2011).

22 Bryan Le Beau (2016). Although posthumous pardons were issued on behalf of a number of the victims in 1711 and 1712, the last of them was not exonerated until 2001.

23 Bruce Knauft (1987).

24 Joseph Watts et al. (2016).

25 The losers in this system were the spare daughters, since only one in each family was ever likely to marry. The rest remained with their natal families to live a rather miserable life as domestic drudges for their brothers.

26 John Crook & Henry Osmaston (1994)

27 Denis Deady et al. (2006).

28 Such manipulative strategies by parents are far from uncommon in agricultural economies where land is a fixed commodity and its equal partition among all children over successive generations will very quickly result in a substantial estate being reduced to a set of peasant smallholdings. Other strategies employed in historical times in Europe included the introduction of primogeniture (eldest son inherits everything) in the late medieval period and, in northern (Protestant) Germany, after the Reformation removed the monastic option, the 'heir-and-a-spare' strategy that was still in use as late as the end of the nineteenth century by peasant farmers. The heir-and-spare strategy involved ensuring that you

only had two sons – one to inherit and one as a back-up in case he died. This was achieved by reducing investment in all boys after the second-born son, such that their chances of surviving their first year of life were reduced to below 50 per cent; girls, in contrast, were not discriminated against because they could be married off, if necessary down the social scale (Voland 1988). Just how sensitive these strategies can be to the exigencies of circumstance is indicated by the fact that willingness to apply this strategy varied over time within the population depending on when new farmland became available that could be used to provide opportunities for the additional sons (Voland et al. 1997).

29 James Boone (1988).

30 Rich Sosis & Candace Alcorta (2003).

31 Robin Dunbar & Susanne Shultz (2021). The infertility trap: the fertility costs of group-living in mammalian social evolution. *Frontiers in Ecology and Evolution* (in press).

32 Tamás Dávid-Barrett & Robin Dunbar (2014); Emily Webber & Robin Dunbar (2020); Robin Dunbar (2021a).

CHAPTER 4: COMMUNITIES AND CONGREGATIONS

1 Allen Wicker (1969).

2 Allen Wicker & Anne Mehler (1971).

3 Robert Stonebraker (1993).

4 Dunbar (1998); Dunbar & Shultz (2017).

5 Dunbar (2020).

6 Dunbar (2018).

7 Dunbar (2018, 2020).

8 Russell Hill, Alex Bentley & Robin Dunbar (2008).

9 Reproduced with permission from Dunbar (2020).

10 Oliver Curry, Sam Roberts & Robin Dunbar (2013).

11 Alistair Sutcliffe et al. (2012).

12 More detail on this can be found in my book *Friends: Understanding the Power of Our Most Important Relationships* (2021).

13 Sam Roberts & Robin Dunbar (2015).

14 Dunbar (1995).

15 Wei-Xing Zhou et al. (2005); Marcus Hamilton et al. (2007).

16 Lehmann, Lee & Dunbar (2014).

17 David Wasdell (1974).

18 Roger Bretherton & Robin Dunbar (2020).

19 Otherwise known as the 'miracle of the five loaves and two fishes' when Jesus is said to have produced enough food for a very large group who had come to hear him preach using only the meagre offering of one small boy. It is the only miracle referred to by all four gospels in the New Testament.

20 Gerhard Lohfink (1999).

21 Howard Snyder (2017).

22 Robin Dunbar & Rich Sosis (2018).

23 Robert Owen (1771–1858) was a Welsh textile manufacturer, philanthropist and early socialist who campaigned for a form of utopian socialism based around the idea of worker cooperatives. After helping to develop and manage the innovative mill complex at New Lanark in southern Scotland (now a World Heritage site), he became frustrated by the bureaucracy of early nineteenth-century Britain, and took his ideas to the more politically casual USA. There, in 1825, he established the New Harmony community in Indiana. Although the community folded after just a couple of years, it had a major influence on the development of social amenities throughout the Midwest in subsequent decades. It instituted the first free public library, first civic drama club and the first school for both sexes in the USA, and its members were later responsible for the establishment of the Smithsonian Institution in Washington DC as the country's national museum.

24 Robin Dunbar & Richard Sosis (2018).

25 Jennifer McClure (2015).

26 John Murray (1995).

27 Shaker communities rarely rejected membership requests, believing that it was better for individuals to make their own decisions after experiencing community life. Equally, members were very rarely expelled from a Shaker community. Most leavers were sent on their way with a gift of cash and tools to help them resettle in the outside world.

28 John Murray (1995).

29 Jennifer McClure (2015).

30 Roger Bretherton & Beth Warman (unpublished study).

31 Alice Mann (1998).

32 Communities of Practice are informal gatherings of people with similar interests in the workplace: a work team of computer programmers on a temporary project, a group of accountants or administrators from different organizations that meet from time to time to discuss matters of common interest and good practice, or national professional associations.

33 Emily Webber & Robin Dunbar (2020).

34 At a conference on theology and Darwinism at the Vatican's Pontifical
Gregorian University some years ago, the parish priests of a Catholic
church in the English Midlands (all scientists by background) remarked
to me that their parish numbered around 500 in total, but was divided
into three separate Sunday masses (each, therefore, of about 150) whose
members hardly ever interacted with each other.

CHAPTER 5: SOCIAL BRAIN, RELIGIOUS MIND

1   The name is, in fact, a contraction of 'endogenous morphine' (meaning
the 'brain's own morphine') and refers to the fact that endorphins are
chemically very similar to morphine. Despite being thirty times more
powerful as analgesics than morphine, a very slight difference in their
molecular structure means that we do not get destructively addicted to
endorphins in the way we do to morphine and other 'unnatural' opiates.
We find their release very rewarding, and that entices us to keep coming
back for more, but we do not get physiologically addicted.

2   Juulia Suvilehto et al. (2015, 2019).

3   Lauri Nummennmaa et al. (2016). PET, or Positron Emission
Tomography, uses the brain's uptake of radioactively labelled tracers
injected into the bloodstream to measure blood flow in the brain, thus
allowing us to determine which parts of the brain are working on a task
(and hence require extra oxygen). As it requires two doses of radioactively
labelled tracers to be given, and these can only be given several hours
apart, it is rather a demanding procedure for those who volunteer to take
part in an experiment. It is now used mainly for certain kinds of medical
imaging.

4   For more detail, see my recent book *Friends: Understanding the Power of
our Most Important Relationships*.

5   *Stuart: A Life Backwards* is a made-for-TV film starring Benedict
Cumberbatch and Tom Hardy, based on a book of the same name by
Alexander Masters. It describes Masters' friendship with Stuart Shorter,
a disabled down-and-out misfit, childhood abuse survivor, drug addict
and sometime petty criminal. The film ends with Stuart, unable to cope
any longer with his circumstances, committing suicide – an ending which
becomes increasingly inevitable as the story progresses.

6   Guillaume Dezecache & Robin Dunbar (2012).

7   Daniel Weinstein et al. (2014).

8   For a more extended discussion of this, see my two books *The Science of Love and Betrayal* and *Friends: Understanding the Power of Our Most Important Relationships.*

9   All five of the sisters became nuns; four joined the Carmelite nunnery in Lisieux, the fifth joining the Visitandine (or Salesian) Order in nearby Caen. In 2015, their parents, Zélie and Louis Martin, shared the distinction of being the only married couple ever to be canonized together as saints of the Catholic Church.

10 Tamás Dávid-Barrett et al. (2015); Ellie Pearce, Anna Machin & Robin Dunbar (2021).

11 This can give rise to de Clérambault's syndrome, an extreme delusional form of romantic stalking where even attempts by the target to avoid the stalker are interpreted as evidence that the target really is deeply in love with the stalker and is simply trying to test the strength of the stalker's commitment. De Clérambault's syndrome exhibits a marked gender bias, being much more common in women.

12 Andreas Bartels & Samir Zeki (2000).

13 For more on this see Robin Dunbar (2018) or my book *Friends: Understanding the Power of Our Most Important Relationships* (2021).

14 Jacques Launay & Robin Dunbar (2015, 2016)

15 Joanne Powell et al. (2012); James Carney et al. (2014); Nathan Oesch & Robin Dunbar (2017).

16 Joanne Powell et al. (2012).

17 Penny Lewis et al. (2017).

18 Nathan Oesch & Robin Dunbar (2017)

19 Rafael Wlodarski & Ellie Pearce (2016).

20 Ara Norenzayan et al. (2012).

21 The psychologist Simon Baron-Cohen has argued that autism is essentially a form of extreme male brain: Baron-Cohen (2003).

22 A standard deviation is a measure of the range of variation in the distribution of a data set. In the standard bell curve of a normal distribution, the first standard deviation either side of the mean accounts for 68 per cent of the datapoints, two standard deviations account for 95 per cent and three standard deviations for virtually everything else.

23 Andrew Newberg et al. (2001).

24 Nina Azari & Marc Slors (2007).

25 Michael Ferguson et al. (2018).

26 Patrick McNamara (2009).

27 Ibid.

CHAPTER 6: RITUAL AND SYNCHRONY

1 Robert Bellah (2011).

2 Louisa Lawrie et al. (2019).

3 Chad Burton & Laura King (2004)

4 Miroslaw Wyczesany et al. (2018).

5 Between 1986 and 2019, the sign painter Ruben Enaje is said to have been crucified thirty-three times in thanks for having survived a fall from a three-storey billboard in 1986.

6 The scourge has one cord for each of the seven deadly sins. Though largely confined to Catholic monastic orders, it also occurs in some lay religious organizations like Opus Dei and in the Anglican and Lutheran churches. In her *Story of a Soul*, St Thérèse of Lisieux describes hearing, as a young novice, the nuns in the adjacent cells flagellating themselves while engaged in private prayer just before bedtime; she did not at first understand what was going on.

7 Throat singing creates remarkable harmonics so that the singer appears to be singing in several registers at the same time. It is thought to have originated as a style of folk song in Mongolia and spread from there to neighbouring regions of southern Siberia and into Tibet.

8 Wolfgang Jilek (1982).

9 V. J. Walter & William Grey Walter (1949).

10 Andrew Neher (1962).

11 During the 1980s the British and French governments were accused of committing this error as a result of their huge investment in *Concorde*, still the only supersonic aircraft to have flown commercially. While known as the *Concorde* fallacy in evolutionary biology, it is also known in economics as the sunk-cost fallacy.

12 The test here would be to see whether, post service, people are more generous to anyone no matter who they are (the prosocial hypothesis) or only to beggars who are obviously members of their own community (the bonding hypothesis). So far as I know, this has never been tested. Willingness to make donations to a communion plate or charity box would not test this, since the recipients of any such charity are necessarily

anonymous. It needs to be tested by alms given in person to specific individuals.

13   Brock Bastian et al. (2011).

14   Sarah Charles et al. (2020a); see also Dunbar et al. (2012).

15   Sarah Charles et al. (2021).

16   The placebo is usually a sugar pill that has no active pharmacological effect. The important thing is that the subject in the experiment does not know which they have taken, otherwise they might bias their behaviour.

17   Redrawn from Charles et al. (2020b).

18   Ibid.

19   Michael Price & Jacques Launay (2018).

20   Tamás Dávid-Barrett et al. (2015); Robin Dunbar (2021).

21   Emma Cohen et al. (2010).

22   Bronwyn Tarr et al. (2015, 2016).

23   Martin Lang et al. (2017).

24   Joshua Jackson et al. (2018).

25   Jorina von Zimmermann & Daniel Richardson (2016).

26   Paul Reddish, Ronald Fischer & Joseph Bulbulia (2013).

27   Ronald Fischer et al. (2013).

28   A popular form of Brazilian martial arts that incorporates dance, acrobatics and music.

29   Nicholas Bannan, Joshua Bamford & Robin Dunbar (2021).

CHAPTER 7: RELIGION IN PREHISTORY

1   Unfortunately, exaggerated claims of this kind are not uncommon in attempts to make fossil species appear more like modern humans. In fact, both monkeys and chimpanzees have survived with equally disabling conditions (for example, missing hands or limbs) in the wild without need of the altruism of fellow group members. Though not ostracized by their companions, these disabled animals are less often engaged in exchanges of social grooming, and are socially somewhat peripheral. Yet they adapt to the constraints of their condition and survive well enough. See S. E. Turner et al. (2014).

2   David Lewis-Williams (2002).

3   E. Guerra-Doce (2015).

4   Patrick McGovern (2019).

5   Oliver Dietrich et al. (2012); Oliver Dietrich & Laura Dietrich (2019).

6   Neil Rusch (2020).

7   As long ago as the end of the eighteenth century, it was realized that Sanskrit (and its derivatives such as Hindi and Bengali from northern India) shares many words in common with Ancient Greek and Latin, and hence with most of the languages of Europe – forming the Indo-European language family, one of 142 major families (although only about fourteen of these families are of any size). Historical linguists have spent the last two centuries working out the likely descent patterns among the world's 7,000 or so languages by grouping together those that share words in common. What this gives us is a family tree that allows us to determine how closely related any two languages are, and hence how likely they are to have inherited a given trait from a common ancestor.

8   Hervey Peoples & Frank Marlowe (2012); Hervey Peoples et al. (2016).

9   Marie Devaine et al. (2017).

10 James Carney, Rafael Wlodarski & Robin Dunbar (2014).

11 Nathan Oesch & Robin Dunbar (2017).

12 We know that great apes can achieve second-order intentionality (albeit only just) and that monkeys fail these tasks, while we know that modern humans can achieve fifth-order. These values represent the anchor points for the distribution. The only thing we have to decide is the pattern that links these. Since intentionality is directly linked to frontal lobe volume, both across primates and within humans, the best way to do this is to estimate intentional competence for each species based on its brain size (as represented by its cranial volume). For each fossil for which there is an estimate of cranial volume size, I estimated first brain volume and then frontal lobe volume from the equations relating these variables for primates as a whole; finally, I used the equation relating mentalizing competences (achievable level of intentionality) to frontal lobe volume for primates to estimate the achievable order of intentionality. From these values, I calculated the mean value for each species. The value for Neanderthals is based on their observed brain size adjusted downwards for their unusually large visual system (see Pearce et al. 2013, 2014; Pearce & Bridge 2013). The values for monkeys (represented by macaques) and great apes (orangutan, gorilla and chimpanzee) are based on Devaine et al. (2017) and sources cited in Dunbar (2009, 2014a, b).

13 Based on Dunbar (2014a), Figure 7.4.

14 At this point, some scholars might argue that it is *relative* brain volume (brain volume divided by body weight) that is the issue, and indeed many

comparative analyses would automatically include body mass in the calculations for this reason. Unfortunately, from a neurological point of view, this is complete nonsense. Cognitive capacities always correlate with absolute brain (or brain region) volume, not with relative brain volume. In any case, *Homo naledi*'s brain *and* body size is the same as those of the australopithecines, so it is most unlikely to have a relative brain size of modern human proportions. An obvious case in point are the pygmies of central Africa: if body size was an issue, they should have much smaller brains than the other occupants of Africa, but they don't. They just have smaller bodies. Conversely, the fact that pygmies have larger brains relative to body size than most other humans does not mean they are super-intelligent. Absolute brain size is everything.

15 Other examples include *Homo erectus* who survived in China until around 60,000 years ago (the date at which modern humans arrived in Australia!), and the dwarf *Homo floriensis* (also known as the 'Hobbit') that survived on the small Indonesian island of Flores until around 60,000 years ago.

CHAPTER 8: A CRISIS IN THE NEOLITHIC

1 Sam Bowles (2011).

2 Allen Johnson & Timothy Earle (2001).

3 Quentin Atkinson, Russell Gray & Alexei Drummond (2009).

4 Margaret Nelson & Gregson Schachner (2002).

5 Matthew Liebmann, T. Ferguson & Robert Preucel (2005).

6 Scott MacEachern (2011); James Wade (2019).

7 P. Willey (2016).

8 Wahl & Trautmann (2012); Meyer et al. (2015); Alt et al. (2020).

9 Carlos Fausto (2012).

10 Zerjal, T. (2003). The historical records tell us that every time they captured a major city, the Mongols pursued the simple strategy of killing all the males and taking the women into their harems. It is remarkable that, eight centuries later, we can still see the genetic signature of this in the populations they conquered.

11 Mark Thomas et al. (2006). Mitochondria provide the energy for every cell: the genes for mitochondria are inherited only from the mother, and hence identify unbroken female lineages in the same way that the Y-chromosomes

identify unbroken male lineages because these are inherited only from the father.

12 The Anglo-Saxons referred to the natives as *wealasc* (meaning foreigners or slaves), which survives in the modern name Welsh for the descendants of those who managed to survive the Anglo-Saxon depredations in the mountains in the west of the island.

13 They are commonly referred to in the Icelandic family sagas.

14 Ironically, this only attempted to prevent slaving by the Irish. It did not ban the Church itself from holding slaves. The Irish practised slavery from pre-Roman times right through to the end of the twelfth century, with the enslavement of defeated Irish enemies and captives from slave raids on the British mainland being the main component of this. Between the nineth and the twelfth centuries, Dublin functioned as the main port for the export of British slaves into the Viking slave trade to the Arab and Turkish empires of the Near East via Russia.

15 Elizabeth Marshall Thomas (2007).

16 Robin Dunbar & Susanne Shultz (2021).

17 Polly Wiessner (2005).

18 Bruce Knauft (1987).

19 Statistics for the regression equation: $r^2 = 0.857$, $N = 9$, $p = 0.003$. Source: Sam Bowles (2011).

20 Richard Wrangham et al. (2006).

21 Napoleon Chagnon & Paul Bugos (1979).

22 Martin Daly & Margo Wilson (1983).

23 Robin Dunbar (2021).

24 Matthew Bandy (2004).

25 Dominic Johnson (2005).

26 Harvey Whitehouse et al. (2019).

27 Joseph Watts et al. (2015).

28 Nicholas Baumard et al. (2015).

29 In the words of the famous nineteenth-century couplet referring to West Africa:

> Beware, beware the Bight of Benin;
> Few come out where many go in.

30 Corrie Fincher & Randy Thornhill (2008, 2012); Fincher et al. (2008).

31 Redrawn after Corrie Fincher & Randy Thornhill (2008).

32 Redrawn after Corrie Fincher et al. (2008).

33 Redrawn after Daniel Nettle (1998).

34 Growing season from Håkonson & Boulion (2001); disease prevalence from Bonds et al. (2012).

35 Steven Neuberg et al. (2014).

CHAPTER 9: CULTS, SECTS AND CHARISMATICS

1   Jonathan Sumption (2011).

2   Most of these views seem to have derived from the seventh-century Paulicians of Armenia (named after a third-century Bishop of Antioch): they apparently rejected the Trinity, the Old Testament, the Cross, the sacraments as practised in the mainstream Church, the entire hierarchy of the Church and the veneration of the Virgin Mary. These ideas reached France via the Bogomils sect (otherwise known as the 'Friends of God') that emerged in Bulgaria in the tenth century, and then spread into southern Europe. They may well have been influenced by ideas filtering through from the Persian Manichaeans, who were active in the Mediterranean region between the fourth and tenth centuries (and who were in turn heavily influenced by Persian Zoroastrianism), and perhaps even by Jain and Buddhist views filtering through from further east.

3   I should, perhaps, clarify my terminology here. I use the term 'cult' in the knowledge that it has attracted some opprobrium in recent decades from those who study new religious movements, mainly because of a sense that the word 'cult' has acquired a derogatory connotation. Their preferred term is 'new religious movement'. As with most neologisms, this seems to be unnecessarily cumbersome and fails to make what I think is a crucial distinction between a cult (as a small community centred around a single charismatic leader) and a sect (a cult that has grown sufficiently to have a number of communities, perhaps even many, and has shifted its allegiance from an individual to a doctrine). The distinction is largely demographic.

4   We are also fortunate in that the history of the Society has been very thoroughly researched by a number of scholars of new religious movements, including Jane Shaw and Alastair Lockhart.

5   Almost all personal social networks, from the age of five to eighty-five, exhibit strong gender bias: 70 per cent of women's social networks consist of women, and 70 per cent of men's social networks consist of men (see Dunbar 2018, 2021).

6   Contrast this with the success of the Rev. Moon's Unification Church based on its active programme of proselytizing, or that of the Franciscans whose growth was largely attributable to the widespread public status, both as saint and as miracle-worker, of its founder even within his own lifetime.

7   He was eventually hacked to death on the orders of Aurelius, bishop of Puy (see Norman Cohn, 1970).

8   Unfortunately, the Lady was apparently otherwise engaged that day, but was nonetheless kind enough to send a statue of herself as substitute.

9   Christopher Partridge (2009).

10 Tamás Dávid-Barrett & Robin Dunbar (2014).

11 He died in prison of natural causes.

12 After he was imprisoned, he fathered four children with the women of the cult during conjugal visits.

13 Psychiatrists define delusional ideation as bizarre beliefs that are so intense the individual cannot be persuaded to change their mind by evidence to the contrary. These can include, for example, the belief that the person is actually dead or that some of their organs have been replaced without leaving a scar; other beliefs may be that the person is controlled by God or aliens (who usually give the person instructions), that someone else is deeply in love with them (when they are not, or have never even met the person in question), that others are scheming against them or intend to kill them, or that they have extreme delusions of grandeur.

14 Emmanuelle Peters et al. (1999).

15 Patrick McNamara (2009).

16 Robin Dunbar (1991).

17 Vassilis Saroglou, 2002).

18 Guinevere Turner (2019).

19 Amanda Lucia (2018).

20 Tulasi Srinivas (2010).

21 Juulia Suvilehto et al. (2015, 2019).

22 Robert Sternberg (1986).

23 Arthur Aron et al. (1992).

24 Juulia Suvilehto et al. (2015); Robin Dunbar (2018).

25 The one striking exception to this pattern was a substantially higher frequency of male attendance at religious services in Islam compared to females, despite the fact that slightly higher numbers of women than men reported that Islam was important in their daily life. This may have something to do with the fact that men's worship is very public in Islam, whereas women are often concealed behind a curtain or screen. Men sign

up to the community of the mosque by being *seen* at prayer. It is a form of club. In contrast, women's religiosity may be more personalized, just as their friendships are.

26 It is alleged that he took this so far as to have public sex with one of them on the altar table of their chapel during a service, causing several members to leave the community.

27 One of the cult's former adherents, the 'Mad Monk' Rasputin, acquired a reputation for both his capacities as a healer and his influence over women, not least the ladies of the Romanov court. There were rumours of sexual innuendo.

28 Despite his advocacy of a form of male contraception by preventing ejaculation through self-control, he fathered at least eight children after the age of fifty-eight.

29 Tamás Dávid-Barrett et al. (2015); Robin Dunbar (2012, 2021).

30 I noted earlier that 70 per cent of personal social networks are gender-biased. See also Robin Dunbar (2021).

CHAPTER 10: SCHISMS AND DIVISIONS

1 Robert Kisala (2009).

2 This dispute gave rise to the the Coptic Churches of North Africa, the Near East and Ethiopia, who adopted the view that Christ had only one divine nature (monophysitism). The rest of Christendom (that in due course became the Roman and Eastern Orthodox Churches) adhered to the original doctrine of the Council of Nicea, upheld by the Council of Chalcydon, that Christ had two distinct natures, one divine and one human, united in one person (dyophysitism). The distinction continues to the present day. This seemingly trivial distinction continued to dominate theological disputes for much of the following millennium.

3 The Shakers were known officially as the United Society of Believers in Christ's Second Coming, founded as an offshoot of the Quakers by Mother Jane Wardley in England in the 1750s. In 1774 an early convert, Mother Ann Lee, emigrated to America together with a small band of followers to establish the Shakers as we now know them. The name 'Shakers' stems from the ecstasy that they experienced in these early decades rather than the slow, mesmerizing dance routines that formed so central a part of their services in the second half of the nineteenth century.

4 'Give me the child for the first seven years and I will give you the man [i.e. a Catholic for life]': attributed to St Ignatius Loyola, but originally stated (without the religious implication) by Aristotle.

5 Luca Cavalli-Sforza & Marcus Feldman (1981). Heritability is the technical term in genetics for the relative contribution of genes versus environmental effects to the variation in a trait within a population. It is *not* what determines a trait, but rather what determines the observed *variability* in a trait.

6 The name derives from the Esselen, a small Native American tribe that lived in the area historically. In its early years, Price was largely responsible both for running the Institute and developing its objectives and programmes. It was thrown into crisis when he was killed in a hiking accident in 1985. However, the board was able to institute changes that introduced a more formal administrative structure with a more coherent business plan that saved the Institute and allowed it to continue as a viable organization – though now as a business rather than the informal-commune-on-the-edge-of-society that had originally been the secret of its success.

7 An ashram is an informal Hindu monastery, often centred around a charismatic teacher.

8 In encounter groups participants were challenged to learn about themselves through a combination of role play and introspection in dyadic encounters in which each person articulated their emotional responses to the other's thoughts and actions. This became extremely fashionable during the 1960s and 1970s in both military and industrial contexts, where it was used as an early form of team-building. However, the method achieved some notoriety in counterculture contexts because it could have disturbing effects when people were forced to confront their inner demons too closely.

9 Notably the English writers Aldous and Laura Huxley and Gerry Heard, and anthropologist Gregory Bateson, all of whom were then living in California. Additional formative influences were the humanistic psychologist Abraham Maslow and the German psychiatrist Fritz Perls (who took up residency teaching Gestalt psychotherapy at the Institute for a number of years).

10 Andrew Smith (1992).

11 These include the sickle cell and thalassaemia genes (that protect against malaria in West Africa and the eastern Mediterranean, respectively), pale skin colour and lactose tolerance in Caucasoid populations (to allow enhanced vitamin D synthesis and calcium absorption), and larger eyeballs

and visual system in high latitude populations (to maintain visual acuity under low ambient light conditions). I discuss these at greater length in my book *Evolution: What Everyone Needs To Know.*

12 Well known recent examples include Vaughan Williams (the prolific composer of sacred music for the Anglican Church who described himself as a 'cheerful agnostic'), Berlioz (*L'enfance du Christ*), Brahms (*Ein Deutsches Requiem*), Verdi (*Requiem*) and Rimsky-Korsakov (who wrote much music for the Romanov Imperial Court Chapel Choir).